ESSENTIALS OF POLITICAL SCIENCE

Essentials of Political Science

By
Durgesh Pande

CYBER TECH PUBLICATIONS
4264/3, Ansari Road, Daryaganj, New Delhi-110002 (India)
Ph.: 011-23244078, 011-43559448 Fax: 011-23280028
E-Mail: cyberpublicationsdelhi@yahoo.com
Website: www.cybertechpublications.com

Essentials of Political Science
Durgesh Pande

First Edition 2011

Asian Offset Printers

Published by
G.S. Rawat for Cyber Tech Publications
4264/3, Ansari Road, Daryaganj, New Delhi-110002 (India)
Ph.: 011-23244078, 011-43559448 Fax: 011-23280028
E-Mail: cyberpublicationsdelhi@yahoo.com
cyberpublications@gmail.com
Website: www.cybertechpublications.com

Contents

Preface

As we all know, political science is a social science concerned with the theory and practice of politics and the description and analysis of political systems and political behavior. It is often described as the pragmatic application of the art and science of politics defined as "who gets what, when and how", leaving out of the picture most of the "why". Political science has several subfields, including: political theory, public policy, national politics, international relations, and comparative politics. Political science is methodologically diverse, to the discipline include classical political philosophy, positivism, interpretivism, structuralism, post-structuralism, behavioralism, realism, pluralism, and institutionalism.

As the title of the book suggests, this work is devised to reinterpret political science, its main elements, theories, practices, main fields and subfields, philosophy etc. exhaustively.

The vital information is gathered under the following chapters—Introduction; Political Science and the Other Social Sciences; Political History; Political Economy; Major Elements; Political Behaviour; Old and New Concepts; International Relations and Bibliography etc.

Certainly, students, teachers, researchers, political scientists and administrators will find this of utmost use.

With the sole aim of furnishing authentic information, I have consulted piles of literature available in printed or digital forms. I have cited or reproduced vital information from these sources. I am deeply beholden to the authors of these and this publishers as well as copyright holders. Here it is apt to mention the assistance and guidance I received from my seniors, colleagues and family members.

Last but not the least I appreciate the enthusiasm of my publishers to bring out this work within shortest possible time. I will feel amply rewarded if this endeavour could benefit all those for whom it is meant.

—Author

1

Introduction

Political science is a social science concerned with the theory and practice of politics and the description and analysis of political systems and political behavior. It is often described as the pragmatic application of the art and science of politics defined as "who gets what, when and how", leaving out of the picture most of the "why". Political science has several subfields, including: political theory, public policy, national politics, international relations, and comparative politics.

Political science is methodologically diverse, to the discipline include classical political philosophy, positivism, interpretivism, structuralism, post-structuralism, behavioralism, realism, pluralism, and institutionalism. Political science, as one of the social sciences, uses methods and techniques that relate to the kinds of inquiries sought: primary sources such as historical documents and official records, secondary sources such as scholarly journal articles, survey research, statistical analysis, case studies and model building.

"As a discipline" political science, possibly like the social sciences as a whole, "lives on the fault line between the 'two cultures' in the academy, the sciences and the humanities." Thus, in some American colleges where there is no separate School or College of Arts and Sciences per se, political science may be a separate department housed as part of a division or school of Humanities or Liberal Arts.

Political scientists study anything about and related to the allocation and transfer of power in decision making, the roles and systems of governance including governments and international organizations, political behavior and public policies. They measure the success of governance and specific policies by examining many factors, including stability, justice, material wealth, and peace. Some political scientists seek to advance positive (attempt to describe how things are, as opposed to how they should be) theses by analyzing politics. Others advance normative theses, by making specific policy recommendations.

Political scientists provide the frameworks from which journalists, special interest groups, politicians, and the electorate analyze issues. According to Chaturvedy, "...Political scientists may serve as advisers to specific politicians, or even run for office as politicians themselves. Political scientists can be found working in governments, in political parties or as civil servants. They may be involved with non-governmental organizations (NGOs) or political movements. In a variety of capacities, people educated and trained in political science can add value and expertise to corporations. Private enterprises such as think tanks, research institutes, polling and public relations firms often employ political scientists." In the United States, political scientists known as "Americanists" look at a variety of data including elections, public opinion and public policy such as Social Security reform, foreign policy, US Congressional committees, and the US Supreme Court —

to name only a few issues – but in a period of seventy five years, only two American political scientists, J. Allen Smith and Charles A. Beard, have dealt intensively with the economics of politics.

Most United States colleges and universities offer B.A. programs in political science. M.A. or M.A.T. and Ph.D or Ed.D. programs are common at larger universities. The term *political science* is more popular in North America than elsewhere; other institutions, especially those outside the United States, see political science as part of a broader discipline of *political studies, politics,* or *government.* While *political science* implies use of the scientific method, *political studies* implies a broader approach, although the naming of degree courses does not necessarily reflect their content. Separate degree granting programs in international relations and public policy are not uncommon at both the undergraduate and graduate levels. Master's level programs in political science are common while political scientists engage in public administration.

The national honour society for college and university students of government and politics in the United States is Pi Sigma Alpha.

Political science is a late arrival in terms of social sciences. However, the discipline has a clear set of antecedents such as moral philosophy, political philosophy, political economy, political theology, history, and other fields concerned with normative determinations of what ought to be and with deducing the characteristics and functions of the ideal state. In each historic period and in almost every geographic area, we can find someone studying politics and increasing political understanding.

The antecedents of Western politics can trace their

roots back to Plato (427–347 BC) and Aristotle (384–322 BC), particularly in the works of Homer, Hesiod, Thucydides, Xenophon, and Euripides. Later, Plato analyzed political systems, abstracted their analysis from more literary- and history- oriented studies and applied an approach we would understand as closer to philosophy. Similarly, Aristotle built upon Plato's analysis to include historical empirical evidence in his analysis. Plato wrote *The Republic* and Aristotle wrote the *Politics*.

The Rise and Fall of the Roman Empire

During the height of the Roman Empire, famous historians such as Polybius, Livy and Plutarch documented the rise of the Roman Republic, and the organization and histories of other nations, while statesmen like Julius Caesar, Cicero and others provided us with examples of the politics of the republic and Rome's empire and wars. The study of politics during this age was oriented toward understanding history, understanding methods of governing, and describing the operation of governments. Nearly a thousand years elapsed, from the foundation of the city of Rome in 753 BC to the fall of the Roman empire or the beginning of the Middle Ages. In the interim, there is a manifest translation of Hellenic culture into the Roman sphere. The Greek gods become Romans and Greek philosophy in one way or another turns into Roman law e.g. Stoicism. The Stoic was committed to maintaining the *status quo* no matter how oppressive it might become. Among the best known Roman Stoics were philosopher Seneca and the emperor Marcus Aurelius. Seneca accepted an Eastern cult that worshiped the emperor as a god; it was adopted by the Roman emperor Caligula. *The Meditations of Marcus Aurelius* are not really the reflections of a philosopher king bent on seeking political and social reform but rather the notes written down while he was not engaged in his multiple military campaigns; notes that betray a preoccupation for his own soul but show no sign that he was a Roman emperor. According to Polybius, Roman institutions were the backbone of the empire but Roman law is the medulla.

The Middle Ages

With the fall of the Western Roman Empire, there arose a more diffuse arena for political studies. The rise of monotheism and, particularly for the Western tradition, Christianity, brought to light a new space for politics and political action. Works such as Augustine of Hippo's *The City of God* synthesized current philosophies and political traditions with those of Christianity, redefining the borders between what was religious and what was political. During the Middle Ages, the study of politics was widespread in the churches and courts. Most of the political questions surrounding the relationship between church and state were clarified and contested in this period. The Arabs lost sight of Aristotle's political science but continued to study Plato's *Republic* which became the basic text of Judeo-Islamic political philosophy as in the works of Alfarabi and Averroes; this did not happen in the Christian world, where Aristotle's *Politics* was translated in the 13th century and became the basic text as in the works of Saint Thomas Aquinas.

The Orient

In ancient India, the antecedents of politics can be traced back to the *Rig-Veda*, *Samhitas*, *Brahmanas*, the Mahabharata and Buddhist *Pali Canon*. Chanakya (c. 350-275 BC) was a political thinker in Takshashila. Chanakya wrote the *Arthashastra*, a treatise on political thought, economics and social order, which can be considered a precursor to Machiavelli's *The Prince*. It discusses monetary and fiscal policies, welfare, international relations, and war strategies in detail, among other topics. The Manusmriti, dated to about two centuries after the time of Chanakya is another important political treatise of ancient India.

Ancient China was home to several competing schools of political thought, most of which arose in the Spring and Autumn Period. These included Mohism (a utilitarian philosophy), Taoism, Legalism (a school of thought based on the supremacy of the state), and Confucianism, which became the dominant political philosophy in China during the Imperial Period. Confucian political ideas also deeply influenced and were expounded upon by scholars in Korea and Japan.

In Persia, works such as the Rubaiyat of Omar Khayyam and Epic of Kings by Ferdowsi provided evidence of political analysis, while the Middle Eastern Aristotelians such as Avicenna and later Maimonides and Averroes, continued Aristotle's tradition of analysis and empiricism, writing commentaries on Aristotle's works. Averroe did not have at hand a text of Aristotle's *Politics*, so he wrote a commentary on Plato's *Republic* instead.

The Renaissance

During the Italian Renaissance, Machiavelli established the emphasis of modern political science on direct empirical observation of political institutions and actors. For Machiavelli, nothing seems to be too good nor too evil if it helps to attain and preserve political power. Machiavelli shatters political illusions, reveals the harsh reality of politics and could be considered the father of the politics model. Later, the expansion of the scientific paradigm during the Enlightenment further pushed the study of politics beyond normative determinations.

Like Machiavelli, Thomas Hobbes, well-known for his theory of the social contract, believed that a strong central power, such as a monarchy, was necessary to rule the innate selfishness of the individual but neither of them believed in the divine right of kings. John Locke, on the other hand, who gave us Two Treatises of Government and who did not believe in the divine right of kings either, sided with Aquinas and stood against both Machiavelli and Hobbes by accepting Aristotle's dictum that man seeks to be happy in a state of social harmony as a social animal. Unlike Aquinas' preponderant view on the salvation of the soul from original sin, Locke believed man comes into this world with a mind that is basically tabula rasa. According to Locke, an absolute ruler as proposed by Hobbes is unnecessary, for natural law is based on reason and equality, seeking peace and survival for man.

The Enlightenment

Religion would no longer play a dominant role in politics. There would be separation of church and state. Principles similar to those that dominated the material sciences could be applied to society as a whole, originating the social sciences. Politics could be studied in a laboratory as it were, the social milieu. In 1787, Alexander Hamilton wrote: "...The science of politics like most other sciences has received great improvement." (*The Federalist Papers* Number 9 and 51). Both the marquis d'Argenson and the abbé de Saint-Pierre described politics as a science; d'Argenson was a philosopher and de Saint-Pierre an allied reformer of the enlightenment.

Other important figures in American politics who participated in the Enlightenment were Benjamin Franklin and Thomas Jefferson.

It is pertinent to note that political science, as a discipline, has become increasingly mature and professionalised. As an important pre-liminary to that discussion, we must address, necessarily briefly, a few threshold questions. What is it for political science to constitute a discipline? What is politics? In what sense can the study of politics aspire to the status of a science?

Inured as we are to speaking of the subdivisions of academic learning as "disciplines," it pays to reflect upon the broader implications of that phrase. According to the *Concise Oxford English Dictionary* a discipline is variously defined as: "a branch of instruction; mental and moral training, adversity as effecting this; military training, drill . . .; order maintained among schoolboys, soldiers, prisoners, etc.; system of rules for conduct; control exercised over members of church; chastisement; (Ecclesiastical) mortification by penance." The last dictionary definition would seem to have only marginal application to academic disciplines, but most of the others have clear counterparts. An academic "discipline" may enjoy minimal scope to "punish," at least in the most literal senses (Foucault 1977).

Still, the community of scholars which collectively constitutes a discipline does exercise a strict supervisory function—both over those working within it and, most especially, over those aspiring to do so. The "order maintained" is not quite the same as that over soldiers or schoolboys, nor is the training strictly akin to military drill. Nonetheless, there is a strong sense (shifting over time) of what is and what is not "good" work within the discipline, and there is a certain amount of almost rote learning involved in "mastering" a discipline.

Branches of academic learning are "professions" as

well as disciplines. "Professional" connotes, first of all, a relatively high-status occupational grade; and the organisation of national and international "professional associations" doubtless has to do, in no small part, with securing the status and indeed salaries of academics thus organised. But the term "professional" also, and more importantly, indicates a certain attitude toward one's work. A profession is a self-organising community, oriented toward certain well-defined tasks or functions.

A professional community is characterised by, and to a large extent denned in terms of, certain self-imposed standards and norms. Incoming members of the profession are socialised into those standards and norms, ongoing members are evaluated in terms of them. These professional standards and norms not only form the basis for evaluation of professionals by one another; they are "internalised," with professionals themselves taking a "critical reflective attitude" toward their own performances in light of them.

The specific standards and norms vary from profession to profession, of course. But across all professions there is a sense of "minimal professional competence," captured by the ritual of "qualifying examinations" for intending political scientists in North American post-graduate training programs. And across all professions there is a notion of particular "role responsibilities" attaching to membership in a profession. The professional ethics of academics do not touch on issues of life and death in quite the same way as those of doctors or lawyers, perhaps. But virtually all academic professions have increasingly formal codes of ethics, touching largely on matters to do with integrity in the conduct and promulgation of research; and all professionals are expected to adhere to them faithfully (APSA 1991). One of our themes in this chapter is the increasing "professionalism" within political science as a whole.

By this we mean, firstly, that there is increasing agreement to a "common core" which can be taken to define "minimal professional competence" within the profession. Secondly, there is an increasing tendency to judge work, one's own even more than others', in terms of increasingly high standards of professional excellence.

While the minimal standards are largely shared ones, the higher aspirations are many and varied. But as in medicine so too in political science, each sub-speciality within the larger profession has its own internal standards of excellence, by which each member of that fraction of the profession is properly judged. And in political science just as in medicine, there is some broad sense across the profession as a whole as to how all the sub-specialities sit together to form a coherent larger whole.

What is Politics?

The foregoing discussion, by and large, pertains to academic disciplines quite generally. Disciplines are differentiated one from another in many ways, principally among them by their substantive concerns and by the methodologies that they have made their own. Although there are, as we shall argue, a number of useful "tricks" in political science's tool-kit which are shared by most members of most of its subdisciplines, Alker is undeniably correct in saying that political science does not have—much less define itself in terms of—a single big methodological device all its own, the way that many disciplines do. Rather, political science as a discipline is defined by its substantive concerns, by its fixation on "politics" in all its myriad forms.

"Politics" might best be characterised as the *constrained use of social power.* Following on from that, the study of politics—whether by academics or practical politicians might be characterised, in turn, as the study of the *nature and source of those constraints* and the *techniques for the use of social power within* those constraints. When defining politics in terms of power, we follow many before us. "Power" is, by now, well known to be a fraught conceptual field. Respectful though we are of its complexities, we decline to let ourselves get bogged down in them. Dahl's (1957) old neo-Weberian definition still serves well enough. In those terms, X has power over *Y* insofar as: (i) X is able, in one way or another, to get *Y to do* something (ii) that is more to *X*'s liking, and (iii) which *Y* would not otherwise have done. Where our analysis departs from tradition is in defining politics in terms of the *constrained* use of power. To our way of thinking, unconstrained power is force, pure and simple. It is not a political power play at all, except perhaps in some degenerate, limiting-case sense. Pure force, literally speaking, is more the province of physics (or its social analogues: military science and the martial arts) than of politics. It is the constraints under which political actors operate, and strategic maneuvering that they occasion and that occurs within them, that seems to us to constitute the essence of politics.

It is the analysis of those constraints—where they come from, how they operate, how political agents might operate within them—that seems to us to lie at the heart of the study of politics. We talk, broadly, about the *use* of social power (rather than, more narrowly, about its "exercise") as a gesture toward the multitude of ways in which political agents might maneuver within such constraints.

We mean the term to cover intentional acts as well as unintended consequences of purposeful action (Merton 1936). We mean it to cover covert manipulatory politics as well as overt power plays (Schattschneider 1960; Goodin 1980; Riker 1986). We mean it to cover passive as well as active workings of power, internalised norms as well as external threats (Bachrach and Baratz 1963; Lukes 1974). The infamous "law of anticipated reactions," non-decisions and the hegemonic shaping of people's preferences (Laclau and Mouffe 1985) must all be accommodated in any decently expansive sense of the political.

Important though it undeniably is that our understanding of politics should be attuned to distributive struggles, then, it is equally important that it not be committed in advance to analysing all else exclusively in terms of them. One further comment on concepts. In denning politics (and the study of it) as we do, we explicitly depart from the purely *distributional* tradition of Lasswell's (1950) classic formulation of "politics" as "who gets what, when and how." Perhaps it is true that all political acts ultimately have distributional consequences; and perhaps it is even true that therein lies most of our interest in the phenomenon. But in terms of the meaning of the act to the actor, many political acts are at least in the first instance distinctly non-distributional. And even in the final analysis, much of the social significance—objective as well as subjective—of certain political interactions might never be reducible to crass questions of dividing up the social pie.

Distributive, regulative, redistributive (Lowi 1964) and identity (Sandel 1982) politics may all have their own distinctive styles. Distributional struggles are characterised, in welfare economists' terms, as squabbles over where we sit on the Paretian frontier; but getting to the Paretian frontier is itself a tricky problem, involving a lot of politicking of quite a different sort which is often distinctively non-distributional, at least in the first instance.

Much has been written over the question of whether, or in what sense, the study of politics is or is not truly a science. The answer largely depends upon how much one tries to load into the term "science." We prefer a minimalist definition of science as being just "systematic enquiry, building toward an ever more highly-differentiated set of ordered propositions about the empirical world." In those deliberately spartan terms, there is little reason to think that the study of politics cannot aspire to be scientific. Many, of course, mean much more than that by the term. A logical positivist might cast the aspirations of science in terms of finding some set of "covering laws" so strong that even a single counter-example would suffice to falsify them.

Clearly, that sets the aspirations of science much too high ever to be attained in the study of politics. The truths of political science, systematic though they may be, are and seem inevitably destined to remain essentially probabilistic in form. The "always" and "never" of the logical positivist's covering laws find no purchase in the political world, where things are only ever "more or less likely" to happen. The reason is not merely that our explanatory model is incomplete, not merely that there are other factors in play which we have not yet managed to factor in. That will inevitably be true, too, of course. But the deeper source of such errors in the positivist model of political science lies in a misconstrual of the nature of its subject.

A covering law model may work well enough for billiard balls subject to the sorts of forces presupposed by models of Newtonian mechanics: there all actions can be said to be caused, and the causes can be exhaustively traced to forces acting externally upon the "actors." But human beings, while they are undeniably subject to certain causal forces as well, are also in part intentional actors, capable of cognition and of acting on the basis of it. "Belief," "purpose," "intention," "meaning" are all potentially crucial elements in explaining the actions of humans, in a way that they are not in explaining the "actions" of a billiard ball. The subjects of study in politics, as in all the social sciences, have an ontological status importantly different from that of billiard balls; and that, in turn, makes the logical positivist's covering law model deeply inappropriate for them, in a way it would not be for billiard balls themselves."

To say that scientific understanding in politics must crucially include a component relating to the meaning of the act to the actor is not, however, necessarily to deny political science appropriate access to all the accoutrements of science. Mathematical modelling and statistical testing remain as useful as ever. The interpretation of the results is all that has to change.

What we are picking up with those tools are seen, now, not as inexorable workings of external forces on passive actors, but rather as common or conventional responses of similar people in similar plights. Conventions can change, and circumstances all the more, so the truths thereby uncovered are less "universal" perhaps than those of Newtonian physics. But since we can, in like fashion, aspire to model (more or less completely) changes in conventions and circumstances themselves, we might eventually aspire to closure even in this more amorphous branch of science.

A Matured Profession

Whether or not "progress" has been made, after the optimistic fashion of Gabriel Almond (below: chap. 2), is perhaps another matter. But maturity, understood in ordinary developmental terms of a growing capacity to see things from the other's point of view, does indeed seem to have been substantially achieved across most quarters of the discipline.

It was not always so. The "behavioral revolution," in its heyday, was from many perspectives a thoroughly Jacobin affair; and it would hardly be pressing the analogy too far to say that the reaction was decidedly Thermidorian to boot. Early behavioral revolutionaries, for their part, were devoted to dismissing the formalisms of politics—institutions, organisational charts, constitutional myths and legal fictions—as pure sham. Those whom the behavioral revolution left behind, just as those who would later try to leave it behind in turn, heaped Olympian scorn upon the scientific pretensions of the new discipline, calling down the wisdom of sages and of the ages. A generation later, the scenario replayed itself with "rational choice" revolutionaries imposing formal order and mathematical rigor upon loose logic borrowed by behavioralists from psychology.

Once again, the struggle assumed a Manichean Good-versus-Evil form. No halfway houses were to be tolerated. In the name of theoretical integrity and parsimony, rational choice modellers strove (at least initially) to reduce all politics to the interplay of narrow material self-interest—squeezing out, in the process, people's values and principles and personal attachments as well as a people's history and institutions. In the rational choice just as in the behavioral revolution, many famous victories were scored (Popkin *et al.* 1976).

But while much was gained, much was also lost. In contrast to both those revolutionary moments, we now seem to be solidly in a period of rapprochement. The single most significant contribution toward that rapprochement, running across a great many of the following chapters, is the rise of the "new institutionalism."

Political scientists no longer think in the either/or terms of agency or structure, interests or institutions as the driving forces: now, virtually all serious students of the discipline would say it is a matter of a judicious blend of both Political scientists no longer think in the either/or terms of behavioral propensities or organisation charts: again, virtually all serious students would now say it is a matter of analysing behavior within the parameters set by institutional facts and opportunity structures. Political scientists no longer think in the either/or terms of rationality or habituation: virtually all serious rational choice modellers now appreciate the constraints under which real people take political actions, and incorporate within their own models many of the sorts of cognitive shortcuts that political psychologists have long been studying.

Political scientists no longer think in the either/or terms of realism or idealism, interests or ideas as driving forces in history: virtually all serious students of the subject carve out a substantial role for both Political scientists no longer think in either/or terms of science or story-telling, wide-ranging cross-national comparisons or carefully crafted case studies unique unto themselves: virtually all serious students of the subject now see the merit in attending to local detail and appreciate the possibilities of systematic, statistically compelling study even in small-N situations. Political scientists no longer think in either/or terms of history or science, mono-causality or hopeless complexity: even hard-bitten econometricians have now been forced to admit the virtues of estimation procedures which are sensitive to "path" effects and simplistic early models of politico-economic interactions have now been greatly enriched.

Remarkably, point is not just that rapprochement has been achieved on all these fronts. What is more important is the way in which that has been achieved and the spirit pervading the discipline in its newly configured form. Although each scholar and faction would place the emphasis differently on the elements being combined, the point remains that the concessions have been made gladly rather than grudgingly.

They have been made, not out of a "live and let live" pluralism, still less out of postmodern nihilism. Rather, concessions have been made and compromises struck in full knowledge of what is at stake, what alternatives are on offer and what combinations make sense. The upshot is undoubtedly eclectic, but it is an ordered eclecticism rather than pure pastiche. Political scientists of the present generation come, individually and collectively, equipped with a richer tool-kit than their predecessors. Few of those trained at any of the major institutions from the 1970s forward will be unduly intimidated (or unduly impressed, either) by theories or techniques from behavioral psychology, empirical sociology or mathematical economics.

Naturally, each will have his or her own predilections among them. But nowadays most will be perfectly conversant across all those methodological traditions, willing and able to borrow and steal, refute and repel, as the occasion requires. There are many ways of telling and retelling these disciplinary histories, with correspondingly many lessons for how to avoid the worst and achieve the best in the future. One way to tell the tale would be in terms of the rise and decline of the "guru." Unproductive periods in the prehistory of modern political science, just as in mid-century political philosophy, were characterised by gurus and their camp followers, the former engaging with one another minimally, the latter hardly at all.

These dialogues of the deaf are transformed into productive, collaborative engagements only once factional feuds have been displaced by some sense of a common enterprise and of some shared disciplinary concerns. Another lesson to draw from that tale concerns the bases upon which a sufficiently overlapping consensus is most likely for founding such a common enterprise.

As in liberal politics itself (Rawls 1993), so too in the liberal arts more generally: a *modus vivendi* sufficient for productive collaboration is likely to emerge within an academic discipline only at lower levels of analysis and abstraction. It is sheer folly to seek to bully or cajole a diverse and dispersed community of scholars into an inevitably false and fragile consensus on foundational issues—whether cast in terms of the one true philosophy of science (logical positivism or its many alternatives) or in terms of the one true theory of society (structural-functionalism, systems theory, rational choice or whatever). Endless disputation over foundations is as unnecessary as it is unproductive, however. The simple sharing of "nuts and bolts"—the building-blocks of science—goes a long way toward consolidating a shared sense of the discipline (Elster 1989).

Tricks and tools and theories which were initially developed in one connection can, as often as not, be transposed into other settings—*mutatis mutandis*. Much mutation, adaptation and reinter-pretation is, indeed, often required to render borrowed tools appropriate to their new uses. But the borrowing, cross-fertilisation and hybridisation, and the conceptual stretching which it imposes on both sides of the borrowing and lending relationship is what scientific progress today seems principally to be about.

Whether it is a "science," strictly speaking, which has been achieved is an open question—and one best left as open, pending the ultimate resolution of interminable disputes among philosophers of science themselves over the "true" nature of science. But by the standards of the spartan definition of science we proposed in Section IC above—"systematic enquiry, building toward an ever more highly-differentiated set of ordered propositions about the empirical world"—our discipline has indeed become more scientific.

Certainly it is now more highly differentiated, both in its own internal structure and in its propositions about the world. It is yet another open question, however, whether the growth of science thus understood is a help or a hindrance to genuine scientific understanding. It is an open question whether we know more, or less, now that we have carved the world up into increasingly smaller pieces. More is not necessarily better.

Metaphysicians cast their aspirations in terms of "carving reality at its joints." Scientists, in their theory-building, are always in danger not only of carving at the wrong places but also, simply, of taking too many cuts. Niche theorising and boutique marketing could well prove a serious hindrance to genuine understanding in political science, as in so many of the other social and natural sciences. It is the job of the integrators of the profession's subdisciplines to overcome these effects, to pull all the disparate bits of knowledge back together.

Professional Criteria

The increasing professionalisation of the profession is manifest in many ways. Perhaps the most important are the extent to which practitioners, whatever their particular specialities, share at least a minimal grounding in broadly the same methodological techniques and in broadly the same core literature. These have been acquired in myriad ways—in postgraduate training, at Michigan or Essex summer schools, or on the job, teaching and researching.

The depth and details of these common cores vary slightly, depending on country and subfield. But virtually all political scientists nowadays can make tolerably good sense of regression equations, and virtually everyone is at least loosely familiar with broadly the same corpus of classics in the field.

Political science, like virtually all the other natural and social sciences, is increasingly becoming an article-based discipline. But while some classic journal articles never grow into a book, and some whole debates have been conducted on the pages of journals alone, the most lasting contributions still come predominantly in book form. Olson's *Logic of Collective Action* (1965): all these are the common currency of the profession, the *lingua franca* of our shared discipline and the touchstones for further contributions to it.

One of the denning manifestations of the new professionalism within political science is the phenomenon of the "instant classic " These are books which, almost immediately upon publication, come to be incorporated into the canon—books which everyone is talking about and presumed to know, at least in passing. Whether these instant classics will have the same staying power as those older pillars of the profession is, perhaps, an open question. Cynics may say that is a reflection of pure faddishness. Others may say, more sympathetically, that it is an inevitable reflection of the way in which the next building-block inevitably fits on the last in any cumulative discipline. Whatever the source of the phenomenon, it is transparently true that several books which were much discussed, at some particular period, have now been substantially superseded in professional discourse. Still, for conveying a quick impression of substantive developments within the discipline over the past quarter-century, we could hardly do better than simply list "great books" produced over that period which have initiated a professional feeding frenzy of just that sort. The list is long, inevitably incomplete and disputable at the margins. Like the larger profession, it is also strongly Anglophone and largely U.S.-oriented. But by almost any account, these contemporary classics would probably have to include:

- Graham Allison's *Essence of Decision* (1971);
- Robert Axelrod's *Evolution of Co-operation* (1984);
- Samuel Barnes, Max Kaase *et al's Political Action* (1979);
- Morris Fiorina's *Retrospective Voting in American National Elections* (1981);
- Ronald Inglehart's *Silent Revolution* (1977);
- James March and Johan Olsen's *Rediscovering Institutions* (1989);
- Elinor Ostrom's *Governing the Commons* (1990);
- Theda Skocpol's *States and Social Revolution* (1979);
- Sidney Verba and Norman Nie's *Participation in America* (1972);

At the outset, we defined politics as the constrained use of social power. As we noted there, any novelty that that definition might claim lies in its emphasis upon *constraint* as a key to politics. But that novelty is not ours alone. Politics as (and the politics of) constraints has, in one way or another, been a recurring theme of political science over the past quarter-century. Running across virtually all the following chapters is, as has already been remarked upon, a renewed recognition of the importance of institutional factors in political life.

With the rise of this "new institutionalism" comes a renewed appreciation of history and happenstance, rules and regimes as constraining forces in political life. Of course, it has long been a commonplace in some corners of the discipline that "history matters": for those who cut their professional teeth on Upset and Rokkan's (1967) notions of "frozen cleavages" or Moore's (1966) developmental models of communism, fascism or parliamentary democracy or Burnham's (1970) theories of "critical realignment;.," there is little novelty in the thought that the coalition structure at crucial moments in the past might have shaped political life for years to come. But these new institutionalist themes are now central to the discipline as a whole, across its several subfields.

The legacy of history, then, is one of the constraints to which new institutionalism points us. Another is the nested and embedded nature of social rules and regimes, practices and possibilities. In this Russian-doll model of social life, ordinary machinations occur relatively near the surface. But, to take just the most straightforward legalistic example, the rules we invoke in enacting ordinary legislation are embedded higher-order principles, rules of a constitutional sort. And, as many have recently discovered, even constitution-writers do not enjoy a completely free hand: even those "highest" laws are embedded in some other even higher-order principles, rules and procedures, albeit of an extra-legal sort.

The same is true of all the other practices and procedures and rules and regimes that collectively frame social life. None is free-standing: all are embedded in, denned in terms of, and work on and in relation to, a plethora of other similar practices and procedures and rules and regimes. None is ultimate: each is nested within an ever-ascending hierarchy of yet-more-fundamental, yet-more-authoritative rules and regimes and practices and procedures.

Standing behind all those nested rules and regimes, practices and procedures are, of course, socio-economic constraints of a more standard sort. Perhaps the more deeply nested aspects of social organisation are as robust as they are only because they are sociologically familiar and materially productive: therein, in the final analysis, may well lie the ultimate source of their strength as constraints on the use of social power.

Most of the time, however, those most deeply nested aspects of the social order exercise their influence unobtrusively, passing unnoticed and unquestioned. The ultimate sources of their strength as constraints are therefore virtually never on display (Granovetter 1985). At other times, the use of social power is shaped and constrained by socio-economic forces that work right at the surface of social life. This may seem to be a tired old theme, reworked endlessly from the days of Marx (1852/1972&; 1871/1972a) and Beard (1913) forward.

However, these themes have been powerfully formalised

and elaborated in contemporary classics such as Lindblom's *Politics and Markets* (1977) and Tufte's *Political Control of the Economy* (1978). And surprisingly much remains to be said on these themes, judging from recent works such as Przeworski and Sprague's *Paper Stones* (1986), on the socio-economic logic limiting the prospects of electoral socialism, and Rogowski's *Commerce and Coalitions* (1989), grounding the structure of domestic coalitions in the terms of international trade. The use of social power is also constrained in yet another way which has recently come to the fore across several subfields of political science.

The constraints here in view are of a cognitive sort, constraints on the exercise of pure (and, more especially, practical) reason. Political sociologists and psychologists have long been sensitive to the irrational and arational aspects of political life: the workings of socialisation and ideology within mass belief systems (Jennings and Niemi 1981; Converse 1964). But even rational choice modellers are now coming to appreciate the analytic possibilities that open up when relaxing heroic assumptions of complete information and perfect rationality. Of course, what political economists see as informational shortcuts others construe as psychological imprints, and for all sorts of purposes that difference clearly still matters. But it is the convergence that has been achieved rather than the differences that remain which, from the present perspective, seems the more remarkable. Political scientists of virtually every ilk are once again according a central role to people's beliefs and what lies behind them.

What people believe to be true and important, what they believe to be good and valuable, not only guides but also constrains their social actions. Those beliefs, in turn, are framed around past teachings and past experiences.

Shaping those teachings and experiences can shape people's beliefs and values and thereby their political choices (Neustadt and May 1986; Edelman 1988). The manipulation of these constraints, like the manipulation of people within those constraints, is a deeply political act meriting—and, increasingly, receiving—as much analytic attention as any other. Among notable recent contributions are Allison's (1971) work on "conceptual maps," March's (1972) on "model bias," Axelrod's (1976) schema theory, Jervis's (1976) on the role of perceptions in international relations, and much work in political communications (Nimmo and Sanders 1981; Swanson and Nimmo 1990; Graber 1993).

Finally, there has been a virtual meltdown of the fact vs. value distinction, that old bugbear of the behavioral revolution in its most insistently positivist phase. There are meta-theoretical reasons aplenty for resisting the distinction; and insofar as the distinction can be defensibly drawn at all, there are ethical reasons for insisting upon the primacy of values, for insisting upon a "political science with a point" (Goodin 1980; 1982).

But what eventually proved compelling was the simple recognition that political agents themselves are ethical actors, too (Taylor 1967; 1985). They internalise values and act upon them; and occasionally they find themselves persuaded (occasionally, perhaps, even by academic political philosophers)' to internalise other, better values.

If we want to understand such people's behavior, we must incorporate values into our analysis—both the values that they actually have, and the ones that they might come to have. Thus, James Scott's *Moral Economy of the Peasant* (1976) explains peasant rebellions in Southeast Asia to perplexed policy-makers in simple terms of people's reactions against policies they perceive to be unjust, according to conventional local understandings of what justice requires; and Barrington Moore's *Injustice* (1978) aspires to generalise the proposition. The spread of the democratic ideal across southern Europe, then Latin America, then eastern Europe might similarly be seen as political action inspired by a vision of what was good, combined with a vision of what was possible. Trying to disentangle facts and values in the mental processes and political dynamics underlying these developments would be pure folly. Similarly, political scientists find themselves increasingly wanting to employ complex research designs systematically relating structures, processes and outcomes. To do so, they need a theoretical framework which can straddle and integrate all these levels of analysis.

Therein arguably lies the great power of rational choice analysis and new institutionalism; and that, in turn, may go some way toward explaining the predominance of those intellectual agendas across contemporary political science as a whole (see Section IV below). At the same time, however, those complex research designs also aspire to the *normative* evaluation of structures, processes and outcomes, and in so doing they integrate normative political philosophy into their designs in ways that would have been an anathema to previous generations.

Therein arguably lies the explanation for the prevalence of Rawls's works on justice (1971; 1993), among the most commonly referenced books, and for the presence of normative theorists like Barry, Dahl and Rawls among the most the most frequently referenced and important integrators of the discipline.

Since we have learned, from feminists, deconstructionists and postmodernists more generally, to be attentive to "silences"—to what is left out and what goes unsaid. When surveying a whole discipline, trying to think what is not there but should be is always a daunting task. Certainly it is true enough that whole subfields wax and wane. Of late, there has been rather less public law and rather less public administration finding its way into mainstream political science than once was the case. Commentators on public policy in general nowadays find far fewer occasions than once they would have done to reflect upon urban politics (Banfield and Wilson 1963; Banfield 1970; Katznelson 1981); commentators on international relations say less nowadays than they would have done, only a few years ago, about strategic studies (Schelling 1960; Freedman 1981); writers on institutions say rather little nowadays about the once-thriving field of representation (Eulau and Wahlke 1978; Fenno 1978); and writers on behavior say rather less than once they would have done about political influence (Banfield 1961), political communication and political participation more generally. Finally, there has always been too little attention paid, within the Anglo-centric political science mainstream, to Marxian theories and foreign-language sources—although, again, there is evidence that that, too, is now changing.

Among the most notable new voices clearly represented in political science today, compared to a quarter-century ago, are those of postmodernists and of feminists themselves. Not only is there now a large literature on the distinctive roles played by women in politics (Nelson and Chowdhury 1994); there is now a distinctively feminine voice to be heard, particularly in political theory (Pateman 1988; Shanley and Pateman 1991; Young below: chap. 20), international relations.

Postmodernism more generally has made rather more modest inroads, in part because its central precepts are cast on such a high theoretical plane (White 1991). Political theorists, however, have certainly shown an interest (Young below: chap. 20; von Beyme below: chap. 22). Moreover, such theories prove to be a rich source of inspiration and insights for those studying the so-called "new political movements" fracturing of the old international order. Wherever once there were clearly defined structures, and now there are none (or many disconnected ones), the post-structural theoretical arsenal may well offer insights into how that happened and why. Whether fully postmodern, contemporary political science is decidedly substantially post-positivist, in that it certainly has taken lessons of the hermeneutic critique substantially on board. Subjective aspects of political life, the internal mental life of political actors, meanings and beliefs and intentions and values—all these are now central to political analysis across the board (Edelman 1964; 1988; Scott 1976; Riker 1986; Popkin 1991; Kaase, Newton and Scarbrough 1995). Political methodology, more generally, seems to be entering something of a postmodern phase. Perhaps few methodologists would embrace that self-description quite so enthusiastically as Alker (below: chap. 35). Many now do, however, emphasise the need for contextualised and path-dependent explanations. That, in turn, represents something of a retreat away from generality and toward particularity, away from universality and toward situatedness, in the explanatory accounts we offer for political phenomena. In that sense, these recent developments in political methodology might be seen as a "postmodern turn."

Indeed, treating the history of the discipline as a whole as our "text," postmodern techniques might help us see many possible narratives in our collective past—and correspondingly many possible paths open for future development (Dryzek, Farr and Leonard 1995). Those fixated on a "big science" vision of linear progress might be disappointed by that prospect of development along disparate trajectories. But on Dogan's account of progress within the discipline, this proliferation of "new breeds" among political scientists is to be greatly welcomed for the fruitful possibilities for hybridisation that it creates.

The Shape of the Profession

Perhaps the best way to substantiate these broader claims about the nature of the discipline, as revealed in the New *Handbook,* is through a closer bibliometric analysis of the references contained herein. The conventional style of bibliometric analysis counts how frequently works or, more commonly, works by particular authors are cited. Albeit inevitably flawed in various respects, these are nonetheless useful measures for all sorts of purposes: for gauging the reputation and standing of individuals and departments within the profession, for assessing the intensity of use of any particular piece or type of work or of works by any particular individual, and so on.

What is of more interest in the present context, however, is the penetration of works by members of one subdiscipline into other subdisciplines, and the resulting integration across the discipline provided by those authors and works. For those purposes, we have preferred to concentrate, not on counts of the number of times authors or pieces of work are cited in the body of the text, but rather on the number of times authors or pieces of work are cited in the reference lists of the other chapters of the New *Handbook.* This approach, while not without its distortions, seems to be the most appropriate to our task. Various things emerge relatively clearly from the resulting bibliometric counts. The first is that the vast majority of political scientists are specialists contributing primarily to their own subdisciplines.

A great majority of the authors and works mentioned at all are found in the reference lists of only one subdisciplinary section of the New *Handbook.* Indeed almost two-thirds of authors are mentioned only once, in a single chapter's reference list.

At the other extreme, a handful of scholars reappear frequently in New *Handbook* chapters' reference lists. Some thirty-five authors. No particular importance should be attached to anyone's precise standing in the resulting league of honor: we are dealing with a small sample, here, in looking across only thirty-four chapters' reference lists. While exact rankings within this list may therefore be imprecise, and the membership of the list itself somewhat unreliable at the margins, in broad outline this list seems to have both surface plausibility and broad reliability as an indicator of whose work is of broad interest across several subfields of the discipline. Inspection of the names on that list—and of the most frequently referenced books, more especially—reveals with remarkable clarity the intellectual agendas currently dominating the political science community as a whole.

We see quite strikingly the residues of the "two revolutions," first the behavioral revolution and then the rational choice one, on the contemporary profession. Looking at the list of most widely referenced books, the old classics of the behavioral revolution—Campbell, Converse, Miller and Stokes's *American Voter;* Almond and Verba's *Civic-Culture;* Lipset and Rokkan's *Party Systems and Voter Alignments*—are still there, albeit in the lower tiers. But sweeping all three top tiers are the classics of the subsequent rational choice revolution: Downs's *Economic Theory of Democracy* and Olson's *Logic of Collective Action,* joined recently by Ostrom's *Governing the Commons.*

The rational choice putsch has been remarkably successful, not so much in pushing out the old behavioral orthodoxy, as in carving out a predominant role for itself alongside it. That the residue of the older revolution is still so strongly in evidence is in itself an impressive fact about the discipline. Cynics say that scientific revolutions are simply the product of fad and fashion. If so, we would expect one fad to disappear completely when another takes over. However, that clearly has not happened. Whether knowledge is strictly cumulative is, perhaps, another issue. But at least the older insights have not been lost as new ones are added, in successive revolutions within political science.

The next step in our bibliometric profile of the profession is to search among those frequently-referenced members of the discipline for "integrators" of the discipline as a whole. We define as an "integrator" anyone who appears at least once in the reference lists in more than half (that is, five or more) of the eight subdisciplinary parts of the *New Handbook*. Of the 1630 authors represented in the *New Handbook's* references, only seventy-two (4.4 percent) appear in five or more chapters. Of those, only twenty-one constitute "integrators" of the discipline as a whole—in the sense that their influence spreads across more than half the subdisciplinary parts of the New *Handbook*. Using much the same techniques, we see how well each subdiscipline itself is integrated into the larger discipline. Here we focus on each subdiscipline's first three tiers of most frequently referenced authors. To see how well the subdiscipline is integrated into the larger discipline, we then ask two questions. To what extent are that subdiscipline's most frequently referenced authors also the most frequently referenced in the discipline as a whole (defined as being among its first ten tiers of most frequently referenced)? And to what extent are that subdiscipline's most frequently referenced authors among the integrators of the discipline as a whole?

Two subdisciplines (Comparative Politics and Political Economy) are, on both measures, particularly well-integrated into the profession as a whole. There are other subdisciplines (Public Policy and Administration and Political Theory) whose own most referenced authors serve as integrators for the discipline as a whole, while there are others (notably. Political Institutions) which largely lack integrators but whose own most frequently referenced authors are among the most frequently referenced within the discipline as a whole.

There is one other subdiscipline (Political Methodology) whose own most frequently referenced authors figure neither among the larger discipline's integrators nor among its most-frequently-referenced. This latter subdiscipline seems to stand substantially outside and to develop relatively independently of the larger discipline. A good composite view of the shape of the discipline emerges from combining all these criteria: who are the "integrators" of the profession, who are "most frequently referenced in the discipline as a whole," and who are "most frequently referenced within their own subdisciplines." There are some ten key scholars—"powerhouses" of the discipline, we call them—who score highly on all three criteria. These ten individuals are among the "most frequently referenced" authors, both within the discipline as a whole and within their respective subdisciplines; and, at the same time, they are integrators of the discipline as a whole. Another twenty-eight scholars play one or the other of those discipline-wide roles, with yet another thirty-nine playing similarly key roles within subdisciplines alone.

The general pattern is clear enough: there are highly differentiated sub-disciplinary communities making great advances. But there is also a small band of scholars at the peak of the profession who genuinely do straddle many (in a few cases, most) of those subdisciplinary communities and integrate them into one coherent disciplinary whole.

The old aspiration of a Unified Science might still remain a chimera (Neurath, Carnap and Morris 1955). But at the turn of the century, ours looks to be at least a potentially unifiable science. The intellectual energy, curiosity and openness that has been required to carry us even that far is, in itself, surely something to celebrate.

The British have always been a bit uneasy about using the term 'political science'. The London School of Economics (LSE) was opened in London in 1895 as a school of economics and political science. However, British universities throughout the twentieth century have veered away from this nomenclature, preferring to use titles such as government, politics, political theory and institutions, or politics and international relations. The UK has a Political *Studies* Association rather in contrast to the American Political *Science* Association. The coyness about using the term 'science' undoubtedly reflects the special status claimed by natural scientists for their discipline and the disdain for the social *sciences* occasionally expressed by leading politicians. The most infamous illustration of the low esteem that some politicians have for the social sciences is the late Sir Keith Joseph's insistence that the United Kingdom's Social Science Research Council, the leading official hinder of research, be renamed the Economic and Social Research Council (ESRC).

It expresses a commitment to recapturing the term 'science' to describe all organised academic disciplines.

The word 'science' is 'derived from the Latin *scientia* meaning simply knowledge acquired by study' (Potter *et al.,* 1981, p. 7). Following Mackenzie (1967, p. 17) we refer to political science to indicate 'simply that there exists an academic tradition of the study of politics, a discipline communicated from teacher to pupil, by speech and writing'. The discipline does not copy the method of the natural sciences because they would not be appropriate. It offer; 'organised knowledge' and demands of its practitioners certain intellectual disciplines in debate.

Above all, the discipline of political science rests its claim on the tenet that all knowledge is public and subject to challenge. There are no hidden truths and no purveyors of truth that can never be wrong. Political science demands from its practitioners that they produce arguments and evidence that will-convince-others.

> Emotional attachments, personal hunches and intuitive understanding do not adequately justify knowledge claims . . . Logical coherence and adequate evidence are the most widely accepted criteria by which we judge claims to knowledge (Zuckerman, 1991, p. 3).

Political science demands logical coherence. This implies precise and clear definitions of key concepts and justified derivations. Arguments should be constructed in a way that avoids inconsistencies and vagueness. Political science also demands a commitment to assessing whether the evidence assembled to support a proposition is adequate to the task. As will become clear, different approaches within political science emphasise different types of evidence, but none denies the *need* for evidence. Even in the case of political theory, arguments are often grounded in textual analysis, or normative principles are illustrated in practice.

Having provided a claim to the title 'science', the reader

might think that task of this section is almost complete. Unfortunately this is not the case. If 'science' is a loaded word, then so too is 'political*. As Heywood (1994, p. 16) comments:

> Most academic study starts with a discussion of what the subject itself is about, usually provoked by asking a question such as 'What is Physics?', "What is History?' or 'What is Economics?'. Such discussions have the virtue of letting students know what they are in for: what they are about to study and what issues and topics are going to be raised. Unfortunately for the student of politics, however, the question 'What is Politics?' is more likely to generate confusion than bring comfort or reassurance. The problem with politics is that debate, controversy and disagreement lie at its very heart, and the definition of 'the political' is no exception.

The expansion of political science has been accompanied by demands to widen the scope of its study. The chapters reviewing approaches to the study of political science in Part 1 of this book offer progressively wider definitions of what is 'political'. In Britain, traditional institutional studies which directed attention towards parliament and the Civil Service were challenged from the 1950s' onwards to widen their scope in order to analyse elections, the mass public political parties and pressure groups. Political scientists adopting a behavioural approach can claim much of the credit for this expansion in the coverage of political science. As Gamble (1990, p. 412) comments:

> What behavioural methods have . . . done . . . is to advance the study of mass political behaviour and widen the definition of things political. The breach in the wall made by behaviouralism has been followed by other broader methodological approaches.

The 1970s and 1980s saw pressure to widen the definition of political still further. Dearlove and Saunders

(1984) argue for a political science that pays attention to the non-democratic aspects of politics and places politics within the context of the social and economic environment. The demand was for a political science that took into account a wider range of institutions and related the analysis of politics to the concerns of other disciplines, especially economics and sociology.

Feminist writers took the argument a further step forward. Politics cannot be confined to a narrowly-defined range of public issues such as the economy or foreign affairs. Writing from a feminist perspective. Jenny Chapman argues in Chapter 5 that 'Politics is about *all* decisions that shape our lives, not only those made in a restricted arena conventionally defined as "politics".' Private matters can become public matters. A letter (1991, pp. 340-1) argues, 'The "political" becomes actually political if men and women so desire that it should be discussed, contested, decided in the public domain . . . No-one and nothing is excluded in principle.' In most Western democracies, for example, the negative experiences of some women in relation to male violence in the home is no longer seen as a private issue but rather as a matter for political discussion and action in the public arena.

Political science in the 1990s sees the political in a much broader way. As Gamble puts it:

> The political has come to be defined . . . to embrace other areas of social life such as gender, race and class. Politics has come to be understood as an aspect of all social relations, rather than an activity centred on the institutions of government. (Gamble, 1990, p. 412)

Leftwich (1984) argues that to confirm the drift away from a focus on the institutions of government the academic discipline of politics should adopt a process definition of politics. Politics, he argues, should be defined not in terms of an arena or set of institutions in which certain activities take place, but rather in terms of a generalised process within human societies.

> Politics is not a separate realm of public life and activity. On the contrary, politics comprises all the activities of co-operation and conflict, within and between societies, whereby the human species goes about organising the use, production and distribution of human, natural and other resources in the course of the production and reproduction of its biological and social life. (Lefrwich, 1984, pp. 64-5)

Politics occurs throughout society: from family groups to the state, and from the voluntary association to the multinational corporation. Politics involves conflict and co-operation and reflects and indeed influences the structure of society.

Politics is a collective activity. As Anderson (1977, p. vii) comments:

> In essence, we act politically whenever we make decisions on behalf of other people and not for ourselves alone. Politics means planning and organising common projects, setting rules and standards that define the relationships of people to one another, and allocating resources among rival human needs and purposes.

It is easy to accept the claim that political activity of this form might be observed in the family, voluntary organisation and multinational corporations as well as in political parties and government.

Leftwich (1984, pp. 83-4) concludes that broadening the definition of politics demands a shift away from the identification of political science with the study of government and public affairs, to a focus on 'the politics of 'everyday life'. Students should be encouraged to study more systematically 'all groups and institutions they may be familiar with or interested in, whether it be in their families, clubs, departments, colleges, offices and factories'. By seeking 'to expand the study and understanding of politics in human societies' Leftwich's aim is to 'help prevent the discipline of Politics from withering, stagnating or becoming irrelevant'.

There is much of value in Leftwich's argument, but it would be a mistake for political science to go down the route he proposes towards an undifferentiated 'study of the politics of everyday life'. Politics is an aspect of all social relations, but as political scientists we should recognise that its practice in some arenas is more relevant and challenging. In particular politics has a special character in the arena of public affairs and government in relation to the making and determination of allocations or decisions through institutions which claim a legitimate authority. It is a collective, binding and justified activity whose special character makes a strong claim to be at the core of political science.

In more abstract terms, we need a combination of both an arena and a process definition of the subject matter of political science. As a process of conflict and co-operation over the resources necessary to the production and reproduction of our lives, politics is an ubiquitous activity. Yet the discipline of politics should give special consideration to how that process is resolved in the act of government - in particular how issues reach and leave the governmental agenda and how, within that arena, issues are discussed, contested and decided.

The special character of government becomes clearer once it is seen as part of the modern state. Governments seek to provide orderly rule and they do so in a variety of different ways and institutional forms in the context of the powerful and extensive entity of the modern state. As Heywood (1994, p. 37) comments:

> The state is best thought of not just as a set of institutions but as a particular kind of political association, specifically one that establishes sovereign jurisdiction within denned territorial boundaries .. . The state commands supreme power in that it stands above all other associations and groups in society; its laws demand the compliance of all those who live within the territory.

The state, in the abstract, stands apart from civil society, but through the processes of politics and the practice of government the state and civil society have a complex, controversial and disputed relationship. It is precisely because of the centrality of the state to political science that in the final part of this book we examine a number of rival theories of the state.

Much political activity is managed at the interface of state and society. Not all politics, however, results in compromise and consensus. Sometimes the conflict is so sharp that violence, civil war and revolution become political instruments. In these circumstances the relatively orderly pursuit of politics gives way to more chaotic and more brutal forms. All forms of politics should be within the scope of political science. When studying constitutional, humdrum politics its latent potential to take more violent and dramatic forms should not be forgotten.

To summarise the view of political science that informs this book: by science we mean the organised production of knowledge that demands of its practitioners certain intellectual disciplines, in particular, logical coherence and adequate evidence.

Politics is a wide spread activity which occurs in all arenas where human beings are engaged in the production and reproduction of their lives. It can involve conflict and co-operation, leading to the raising and resolution of issues through collective decision-making.

Political science is an academic discipline which seeks systematically to describe, analyse and explain collective decision-making and the values and perspectives that underlie it. However, political science should pay particular attention to the collective arena constituted by the operation of government in the modern state because of the particular form of extensive and compulsory authority embodied within its activities. It should also recognise that if 'normal' politics breaks down, political activity can take a variety of more violent and brutal forms.

Diversity of Approaches to Political Science

From what has been argued so far, it should be clear that political science is not 'a hard and fast area of study whose character and scope we have to take for granted, or assume to be unchanging or permanent'. The discipline of political science, to put it bluntly, is defined by those who do it. It should not come as a surprise to any reader that if there is some dispute and disagreement among practitioners about what political science is there is also a dispute about how to do it. Zuckennan refers to the 'cacophonous sound of political science'. He goes on to note that political scientists 'display deep conflicts over appropriate assumptions, foci and methods of analysis, and they offer hypotheses and theories that directly contradict one another. They frequently describe the same phenomenon but offer very different analyses of it. They may even observe the world in different ways'. Political science is characterised by a diversity of approaches.

'Approaches' is our choice because the term 'schools' creates an exaggerated sense of cohesion and order within the various sub-divisions of political science. The approaches that we identify do, however, guide practitioners towards different ways of doing political science. They answer questions about the core subject matter to be addressed; the mode by which evidence should be obtained; the nature of the theoretical enterprise that should be undertaken; and offer diverse underlying assumptions about the nature and dynamics of politics. Some of the key characteristics of our six approaches to political science are presented.

The choice of six approaches can be explained in terms of the evolution of the discipline. Normative theory and institutional studies are the 'twin pillars' of traditional political science (Held and Leftwich, 1984, p. 147) and despite 'reports of their death' remain central to the discipline. The first approach - normative theory - has an extremely long lineage within the study of politics. It is widely perceived to have suffered a decline in the 1950s and 1960s but to have bounced back since the 1970s. Writing in 1990, Miller concludes: 'There has been an upsurge of interest in the subject and confidence in its practitioners. Its standing within the political studies community as a whole seems also to have increased.

Normative political theory is concerned with the discovery and application of moral notions in the sphere of political relations and practice. As Daryl Glaser shows doubts about this branch of the discipline devoted to the examination of what 'ought to be' have been expressed in several quarters. In broad terms, some have questioned the value of such debate and seen it as a pointless exercise producing tautological propositions that are true by definition but not in any wider sense. Others have questioned whether human agents are capable of moral choices. Yet political scientists have responded to these challenges to reestablish the claim strongly that normative theory can offer a rigorous and developed way of addressing the options open to human beings.

The study of political institutions is concerned with the rules, procedures and formal organisations of the political system and their impact on political practice. Historically, the strength of the institutional approach in political science reflects the influence of law, philosophy and historical studies in its development as an autonomous field of study. Much of the work of traditional institutional studies has rightly been subject to criticism for the weakness of its methods, the anti-theoretical, descriptive nature of its product, and an underlying prescriptive perspective based on an idealised conception of the virtues of liberal democratic government. Yet, as R.A.W. Rhodes argues, the institutional approach has not disappeared as a result of these criticisms, but rather its substantive focus on the core institutions of the state and its reformulation in a variety of ways has ensured its continued centrality to the discipline of political science.

Behavioural and rational choice theory constitute more recent but well-established approaches within the discipline of political science. Indeed, in the USA the behavioural approach is dominant within the discipline. Its impact in Britain and continental Europe has been substantial but it remains one of many approaches. Behaviouralism concentrates on explaining political behaviour at the individual and aggregate level. In the 1950s and 1960s, behaviouralists were often highly critical of the traditional twin pillars of political science. Institutional studies were seen as being descriptive and lacking in rigour, and their focus on institutions less relevant than a focus on behaviour. The rules and regulations of institutions tell us what people should do, but as political scientists we should be interested in the way they in fact behave, in practice. Behaviouralists also made great play of the need to separate facts from values.

Normative political theory was seen as being concerned with values and as such considered to be a rather pointless activity, an expression of various opinions but an approach incapable of providing evidence to resolve matters of dispute. The behaviouralists of the 1950s and 1960s expressed a preference for theory derived from 'the facts' and therefore beyond dispute. Their claim was to offer a new 'scientific' approach to the study of politics through the production of a series of laws or generalisations.

Under criticism and challenge behaviouralism has backed away from some of the claims of its early advocates. In particular, the simplistic understanding of the facts/values distinction has been abandoned. Behaviouralists now acknowledge that facts do not speak for themselves but only make sense in the context of a framework of investigation. Ideas about what is important and the way things work structure all observations. Theory and fact are not independent of one another. Further claims to value-free analysis have been played down. The pluralist assumptions behind much earlier behaviouralist work is recognised. The claim to be able to derive 'scientific' laws and generalisations has also been watered down. Modern behaviouralism is more sophisticated in its approach and modest in its claims. Yet behaviouralism remains a strong force within political science. It distinctive character is provided by its focus on individual behaviour and a concern to generate causal and falsifiable theory. As Sanders suggests the pivotal behavioural question is: How would you know if your analysis was incorrect?

Rational choice theory has also established a strong following since the mid-1950s. The underlying assumption is that political behaviour can be understood as the result of choices made by self-interested individuals. Rational choice studies have sought to illuminate issues throughout the field of political science, from electoral competition to bureaucratic behaviour. A variety of rational choice, literatures have been established, including game theory, social choice theory and public choice theory. The latter particularly has a strong, normative, anti-state. New Right thrust to many of its arguments. As Hugh Ward demonstrates the rational choice approach has been subject to a number of criticisms. He proposes that, if the approach is to develop, it needs to be both more modest in its claims, and more adventurous. The nature of human beings -their psychological complexity and frequent irrationality - suggests there are limits to the approach. Yet because individuals do make efforts at rational decision-making relative to their goals, considerable scope for the approach exists. Rational choice theory needs to develop further a capacity to examine choice-making under conditions of limited information and uncertainty. Scope for non-egoistic and moral motivations should be given. It should also be emphasised that the New Right premises associated with the public choice variant are not inherent in the approach. The rational choice approach has drawn (and should continue to draw) on a range of theoretical traditions. Its status is as a useful element in the 'tool kit' of political scientists.

The final pairing in terms of our identification of approaches to political science - feminism and discourse analysis - provide an important challenge to more established approaches. While both approaches can claim antecedents in the evolution of the discipline they have only come to the fore from the 1970s onwards.

The impact of feminism has in some respects been considerable. It has stimulated much rethinking in the more established elements of political science. Orthodox perspectives in normative theory and in the empirical studies of institutionalists and behaviouralists have been challenged and forced into a recognition of previous gender-blindness. Feminism has been instrumental in widening the scope (and understanding the nature) of political science, yet, as Jenny Chapman argues it still remains on the margins of the discipline. This partly reflects the 'dynamic conservatism' of mainstream political science which has displayed a capacity to incorporate elements of the feminist critique while retaining much of its original orientation. It also reflects the failure of some advocates of the feminist perspective to provide a sharp, empirical cutting edge to their work. The potential contribution of feminism to political science, however, remains considerable.

Discourse analysis has had less impact than has feminism. It offers an important link with post-modernism for political science because it sees the structuring of social meaning as the central political act. Discourse studies examine the way systems of meaning or 'discourses' shape the way people understand their position and their political activity. According to this approach, the production, functioning and changing of 'discourses' should be a focus of study because it provides a powerful tool for understanding the dynamics and character of politics in complex societies. Few political scientists would dispute the validity of such claims or deny the importance of language, symbols and the structuring of political debates. What remains unclear, however, is how far discourse analysis, which often operates at a high level of generality and abstraction, can tackle such concerns effectively. David Howarth provides a relatively optimistic assessment of the potential for discourse analysis}—

It is difficult, however, to include Marxism as a distinctive approach within political science because the thrust of its argument is to challenge the existence of political science as a separate discipline. As Callinicos (1984) argues, the historical materialism of Marxism demands a holistic approach cutting across disciplinary boundaries. Marxism disqualifies itself 'from being merely another approach to the study of polities' and 'makes claims that are obviously incompatible with the notion of an autonomous discipline of Polities' (Callinicos, 1984, p. 124). This is not to deny that the work of political scientists has been influenced by Marxist thought, and indeed many would accept the challenge laid down by Marxism to relate developments in politics to developments within the social totality. Marxist analysis of society plainly has implications for the study of politics, but it is inappropriate to include it as a separate approach to the subject.

Methodological Issues and Challenges

The approaches to political science we identify are associated with particular ways of producing knowledge; that is, they have a certain methodological orientation. In the study of political sciencc it is important to be aware of the methodological choices that are available. The challenge involves more than coping with the demands raised by a range of research techniques, although this is a considerable task in itself. The issue of methods brings into focus questions of broader philosophical concern. How can we know the social world? What counts as an adequate explanation of a social phenomenon?

In debating the production of knowledge, political scientists use terms that may not be familiar to all readers; these terms are used as shorthand for describing complex understandings of the social world. An *ontological position* refers to a view about the nature of social existence and social beings. An *epistemology* expresses a view about how we know what we know and in particular about what constitutes an adequate explanation of a political event or process. Different broad ontological and epistemological positions inform different methodological orientations or preferences. The various approaches to political science that we have identified tend to prefer and find valuable different ways of knowing the world.

Several concepts are particularly worth introducing at this stage because they are used in chapters throughout the book; these concepts express different attitudes towards knowing the world. They are distinctive positions within a wide spectrum of opinion. *Positivists* hold that it is possible to know the world through experience and observation; the truth or otherwise of a statement can be determined through systematic empirical observation. Positivist political science would examine the available data and claim to produce general and sustainable propositions about political behaviour.

Critical realists primarily see knowledge as having some universal character. Individuals act in a world that is not of their own choosing and their actions often produce unintended structural effects. Yet the ability of individuals to understand the structure of the social world is seen as being severely limited. The role of the political observer is to explain events with reference to the actions of individuals and organisations in a structural context. The observer of this political world can claim a particularly insightful vantage point from which to offer an explanation. *Relativists,* in contrast, repudiate the idea that objective, universal and timeless knowledge is possible: criteria for judging truth are relative to time, place and culture. For extreme relativists, to understand a political event would require the construction of an overall picture based on each individual conception of the events. A less extreme position suggests that the role of the observer is to tease out the broad patterns of meaning attached to an event by different groups within society.

Another common distinction to be made relates to how the observer forms his or her theories. Tne *deductive method* emphasises the value of drawing conclusions from first principles through a process of conceptual analysis and reflection. The *inductive method, on* the other hand, draws its conclusions by empirical observation and the search for patterns and generalisations.

REFERENCES

Almond, G. A. 1990. *A Discipline Divided.* Newbury Park, Calif.: Sage.

APSA (American Political Science Association). 1991. A *Guide to Professional Ethics in Political Science.* 2nd edn. Washington, D.C.: APSA.

Axelrod, R., 1984. *The Evolution of Cooperation.* New York: Basic Books.

Bachrach, P. and Baratz, M. S. 1963. Decisions and non-decisions: an analytic framework. *American Political Science Review,* 57: 632-42.

Banfield, E. C. 1961. *Political Influence.* Glencoe, Ill.: Free Press.

—— 1970. *The Unheavenly City.* Boston: Little, Brown.

—— and Wilson, J. Q. 1963. *City Politics.* New York: Vintage.

Barnes, S.; Kaase, M.; *et al.* 1979. *Political Action: Mass Participation in Five Western Democracies.* Beverly Hills, Calif.: Sage.

Barry, B. 1974. Review ankle: exit, voice and loyalty. *British Journal of Political Science,* 4: 79-107. Reprinted in Barry 1989: 186-221.

——1978. *Sociologists. Economists and Democracy. 2nd* edn. Chicago: University of Chicago Press; originally published 1970.

—— 1989, *Democracy, Power and Justice.* Oxford: Clarendon Press.

Beard, C. A. 1913. *An Economic Interpretation of the Constitution of the United States.* New York: Macmillan.

Bell, D, E.; Raiffa, H.; and Tversky, A., eds. 1988. *Decision Making.* Cambridge: Cambridge University Press.

Berger, P. L. 1963. *Invitation to Sociology.* New York: Doubleday.

Berlin, 1.1953. *The Hedgehog and the Fox.* London: Weidenfeld and Nicolson.

Braybrooke, D., and Lindblom, C. E. 1963. *A Strategy of Decision.* New York: Free Press.

Burnham, W. D. 1970. *Critical Elections and the Mainsprings of American Politics.* New York: Norton.

Campbell, A.; converse, P. E.; miller, W.; and stokes, D. 1960. *The American Voter.* New York: Wiley.

Chester, N. 1986. *Economics, Politics and Social Studies in Oxford, 1900-85.* London: Macmillan.

Converse, P. E. 1964. The nature of belief systems in mass publics. Pp. 206-61 in *Ideology and Discontent,* ed. D. E. Apter. New York: Free Press.

Cormford, F. M. 1908. *Microcosmographia Academia.* Cambridge: Bowes and Bowes.

Crick, B. 1962. *In Defence of Politics.* London: Weidenfeld and Nicholson.

Dahl, R. A. 1957. The concept of power. *Behavioral Science, 2:* 201-15.

Dahrendore, R. 1959. *Class and Class Conflict in Industrial Society.* Stanford, Calif.: Stanford University Press.

Deutsch, K. 1963. *The Nerves of Government.* Glencoe, Ill.: Free Press.

Dierkes, M., and Biervert, B., eds. 1992. *European Social Science in Transition,* Frankfurt am Main/Boulder, Colo.: Campus Verlag/ Westview.

Dryzek, J.; Farr, J.; and Leonard, S., eds. 1995. *Political Science in History.* Cambridge: Cambridge University Press.

Duverger, M. 1954. *Political Parties,* trans. B. and R. North. London: Methuen; originally published 1951.

Easton, D. 1965. *A Systems Analysis of Political Life.* New York: Wiley.

Edelman, M. 1964. *The Symbolic Uses of Politics.* Urbana: University of Illinois Press.

Eulau, H., and Wahlke, J. C., *et al* 1978. *The Politics of Representation.* Beverly Hills, Calif.: Sage.

Fenno, R. 1978. *Home Style.* Boston: Little, Brown.

Ferejohn, J.A. 1974. *Pork Barrel Politics.* Stanford, Calif.: Stanford University Press.

Florina, M.P. 1981. *Retrospective Voting in American National Elections.* New Haven, Conn.: Yale University Press.

Flora, P., ed. 1986. *Growth to Limits. 4* vols. Berlin: de Gruyter.

Foucault, M. 1977. *Discipline and Punish,* trans. A. Sheridan. Harmondsworth, Mddx.: Alien Lane.

Freedman, L 1981. *The Evolution of Nuclear Strategy.* London: Macmillan.

Galtung, J. 1967. *Theory and Methods of Social Research. Oslo:* Universitetsforlaget.

Goodin, R. E. 1976. Possessive individualism again. *Political Studies, 24:* 488-501.

Graber, Doris. 1993. Political communication: scope, progress, promise. Pp. 305-34 in *Political Science: The State of the Discipline, H,* ed. A. Finifter. Washington, D.C. American Political Science Association.

Granovetter, M. 1985. Economic action and social structure: the problem of embeddedness. *American Journal of Sociology,* 91: 481-510.

Greenstein, F. I., and Polsby, N. W., eds. 1975. *Handbook of Political Science.* 8 vols.

Reading, Mass.: Addison-Wesley.

Hart, H. L A. 1961. *The Concept of Law.* Oxford: Clarendon Press.

Hirschman, A. O. 1970. *Exit, Voice and Loyalty.* Cambridge, Mass.: Harvard University Press.

Hollis, M. 1977. *Models of Man.* Cambridge: Cambridge University Press.

Hughes, E. C. 1958. *Men and their Work.* Glencoe, 111.: Free Press.

Huntington, S. P. 1968. *Political Order in Changing Societies.* New Haven, Conn: Yale University Press.

Inglehart, R. 1977. *The Silent Revolution.* Princeton, N.J.: Princeton University Press.

Jennings, M. K., and Niemi, R. G. 1981. *Generations and Politics.* Princeton, N.J.: Princeton University Press.

Jervis, R. 1976. *Perception and Misperception in International Politics.* Princeton, N.J.: Princeton University Press.

Johnson, N. 1989. *The Limits of Political Science.* Oxford: Clarendon Press.

Jouvenel, B. De. 1948. On *Power,* trans. J. F. Huntington. London: Hutchinson; originally published 1945.

Kaase, M.; Newton, K.; and Scarebough, E., eds. 1995. *Beliefs in Government. 5* vols. Oxford: Oxford University Press.

Katznelson, I. 1981. *City Trenches.* Chicago: University of Chicago Press.

Key, V. O. Jr. 1942. *Politics, Parties and Pressure Groups.* New York: Crowell.

Kiewiet, D. R. 1983. *Micropolitics and Macroeconomics.* Chicago: University of Chicago Press.

King, g. Keohane, R.D., and Verba, S. 1994. *Designing Social Inquiry.* Princeton, N.J.: Princeton University Press.

Klingemann, H.D. 1986. Ranking the graduate departments in the 1980s: toward objective qualitative indicators. *PS*, 29: 651-61.

Laclau, E., and Mouffe, C. 1985. *Hegemony and Socialist Strategy.* London: Verso.

Lane, R. E. 1962. *Political Ideology.* Glencoe, 111.: Free Press.

Lasswell, H. D; 1950. *Politics: Who Gets What, When,* how? New York: P. Smith.

Lindblom, C. E. 1965. *The Intelligence of Democracy.* New York: Free Press.

Lipset, S. M. 1960. *Political Man.* New York: Doubleday.

Lowi, T. J. 1964. American business, public policy, case-studies and political theory. *World Politics.* 16: 676-715.

Lukes, S. 1974. *Power A Radical View.* London: Macmillan.

Mansbridge, J. J., ed. 1990. *Beyond Self-interest.* Chicago: University of Chicago Press.

March, J. G. 1972. Model bias in social action. *Review of Educational Research,* 42: 413-29.

Marshall, G. 1990. *In Praise of Sociology.* London: Unwin Hyman.

Marx, K. 1972a. The civil war in France. Pp. 526-77 in *The Marx-Engels Reader,* ed. R. C. Tucker. New York: Norton; originally published 1871.

McCoy, C. A., and Playford, J., eds. 1968. *Apolitical Politics: A Critique of Behavioralism.* New York; Thomas Y. Crowell.

Medawar, P. B. 1979. *Advice to a Young Scientist.* New York: Harper & Row.

Merton, R. K. 1936. The unintended consequences of purposive social action. *American Sociological Review* 1: 894-904.

Mitchell, W. C. 1969. The shape of political theory to come: from political sociology to political economy. Pp. 101-36 in *Politics and the Social Sciences,* ed. S. M. Lipset. New York: Oxford University Press.

Monroe, K.R., ed. 1991. *The Economic Approach to Politics.* New York HarperCollins.

Moon, J. D. 1975. The logic of political inquiry: a synthesis of opposed perspectives. In Greenstein and Polsby 1975: vol. i, pp. 131-228.

Moore, B., Jr. 1966. *The Social Origins of Dictatorship and Democracy.* Boston: Beacon.

Nelson, B. J., and Chowdhury, N., eds. 1994. *Women and Politics Worldwide.* New Haven, Conn.: Yale University Press.

Neurath, O.; Carnap, R.; and Morris, C. L, eds. 1955. *International Encyclopedia of Unified Science: Foundations of the Unity of Science. 1* vols. Chicago: University of Chicago Press.

Neustadt, R. E. 1960. *Presidential Power.* New York: Wiley.

Nimmo, D. D., and sanders, K. R., eds. 1981. *Handbook of Political Communication.* Beverly Hills, Calif.: Sage.

Nordlinger, E. A. 1981. *On the Autonomy of the Democratic State.* Cambridge, Mass.: Harvard University Press.

North, D. C. 1990. *Institutions, Institutional Change and Economic Performance.* Cambridge: Cambridge University Press.

Nozick, R. 1981. *Philosophical Explanations.* Cambridge, Mass: Harvard University Press.

Oakeshott, M. 1956. Political education. Pp. 1-21 in *Philosophy. Politics and Society.* 1st series. Oxford: Blackwell; originally delivered as an LSE Inaugural Lecture in 1951.

Olsen, I.P. 1972. Public policy-making and theories of organisational choice. *Scandinavian Political Studies,* 7: 45-62.

Olson, M. Jr. 1965. *The Logic of Collective Action.* Cambridge, Mass.: Harvard University Press.

Orren, K. 1991. *Belated Feudalism.* Cambridge: Cambridge University Press.

Ostrom, E. 1990. *Governing the Commons.* Cambridge: Cambridge University Press.

Parsons, T. 1968. Professions. Vol. xii, pp. 536-47 in *International Encyclopedia of the Social Sciences, ed. D.* L Sills. London; Macmillan.

Pateman, C. 1988. *The Sexual Contract.* Oxford: Polity.

Popkin, S. L 1991. *The Reasoning Voter.* Chicago: University of Chicago Press.

Pazeworski, A., and Sprauge, J. 1986. *Paper Stones: A History of Electoral Socialism.* Chicago: University of Chicago Press.

Putnam. R. D. 1993. *Making Democracy Work.* Princeton, N.J.: Princeton University Press. Ranney, A., ed. 1962. *Essays on the Behavioral Study of Politics.* Urbana: University of Illinois Press.

Ridley, F. F. 1975. Political institutions: the script not the play. *Political Studies. 23:* 365-80.

Riker, W. H. 1986. The Art *of Political Manipulation.* New Haven, Conn.: Yale University Press.

Rivlin, A. M. 1971. *Systematic Thinking for Social Action.* Washington, D.C.: Brookings Institution.

Rogowski, R. 1989. Commerce *and Coalitions.* Princeton, N.J.: Princeton University Press.

Rokkam, S., ed. 1979. A *Quarter Century of International Social Science.* New Delhi: Concept, for the International Social Science Council.

Rose R., and Peters, B.G. 1978. *Can Government Go Bankrupt?* New York: Basic.

Russell, B. 1938. Power. London: Alien and Unwin.

Sandel, M. 1982. *Liberalism and the Limits of Justice.* Cambridge: Cambridge University Press.

Schattschneider, E. E. 1960. *The Semi-Sovereign People.* New York: Holt, Rinehart and Winston.

Schelling, T. C. 1960. The *Strategy of Conflict.* Cambridge, Mass.: Harvard University Press.

Schumpeter, J. A. 1943. Capitalism, *Socialism, and Democracy.* London: Alien and Unwin.

Scott, J.C. 1976. *The Moral Economy of the Peasant.* New Haven, Conn.: Yale University Press.

Sen, A. 1977. Rational fools: a critique of the behavioral foundations of economic theory. *Philosophy and Public Affairs,* 6: 317-44.

Shanley, M. L., and Pateman, C., eds. 1991. *Feminist Interpretations and Political Theory.* Oxford: Polity.

Simon, H. A. 1951. *Administrative Behavior.* New York: Macmillan.

Skocpol, T. 1979. State and Social Revolutions. Cambridge: Cambridge University Press.

Somit, A., and Tanenhaus, 1.1967. *The Development of American Political Science.* Boston: Allyn & Bacon.

Stretton, H. 1969. The *Political Sciences.* London: Routledge and Kegan Paul.

Swanson, D. L, and nimmo, D., eds. 1990. New Directions in Political Communication. Newbury Park, Calif.: Sage.

Taylor, C. 1967. Neutrality in political science. Pp. 25-57 in *Philosophy, Politics and Society,* ed. P. Laslett and W. G. Runciman. 3rd series. Oxford: Blackwell. Reprinted in Taylor 1985: vol. ii, pp. 58-90

Tufte, E. R- 1978. *The Political Control of the Economy.* Princeton, N.J.: Princeton University Press.

Verba, S., and Nie, N. H. 1972. *Participation in America.* New York: Harper and Row.

Wagner, P.; Wittrock, B.; and Whitley, R., eds. 1991. *Discourses on Society: The Shaping of the Social Science Disciplines.* Dordrecht: Kluwer.

Waldo, D. 1975. Political science: tradition, discipline, profession science, enterprise. In Greenstein and Polsby 1975: vol. i, pp. 1-130.

Weber, Max. 1946. Politics as a vocation. Pp. 77-128 in From Max *Weber: Essays in Sociology,* ed. H. Gerth and C. W. Mills. New York: Oxford University Press; originally published 1919.

White, S. K. 1991. *Political Theory and Postmodernism.* Cambridge: Cambridge University Press.

2

Political Science and the Other Social Sciences

The discipline of political science is "ill-defined, amorphous and heterogeneous." Twenty years later, the main features of political sciences are: specialisation, fragmentation and hybridisation. Its frontiers are open and moving and need not be defined. The process of specialisation has generated an increasing fragmentation in subfields, which are not "amorphous" but rather well-organised and creative. The "heterogeneity" has been greatly nourished by exchanges with neighbouring disciplines through the building of bridges between specialised fields of the various social sciences. This process of cross-fertilisation is achieved by hybridisation. The relations between political science and the other social sciences are in reality relations between sectors of different disciplines, not between whole disciplines. It is nor an "interdisciplinary" endeavor.

Since there is no progress without specialisation, the creative interchanges occur between specialised subfields, most of the time at the margins of the formal disciplines. The current advancement of the social sciences can be explained in large part by the hybridisation of segments of sciences. It would be impossible to conceive of a history of political science and of its current trends without reference to the other social sciences. A distinction has to be drawn between specialisation within a formal discipline and specialisation at the intersection of monodisciplinary subfields. The latter, hybridisation, can occur only after the former has become fully developed. In the history of science a twofold process can be seen: on the one hand, a fragmentation of formal disciplines and, on the other, a recombination of the specialities resulting from fragmentation. The new hybrid field may become independent, like political economy; or it may continue to claim a dual allegiance, like political geography.

In the latter case, we cannot be sure whether to place a work in the category of geography or of political science. The criterion could be the predominance of one or the other component or the formal affiliation of the author. Political anthropology is a branch of anthropology but also a subfield of political science. Where does historical sociology end and social history begin? We may feel even more unsure when faced with a case of threefold recombination.

As the relative proportions are not always obvious, it remains somewhat arbitrary where the essential affiliation may be said to lie, since the degree of kinship between specialities varies greatly.

Some scholars praise "interdisciplinarity." Such a recommendation often comes from the most creative scientists because they are the first to see the problems caused by gaps between disciplines. But this recommendation is not realistic. Nowadays, it is no longer possible for anyone to have a thorough knowledge of more than one discipline. It is Utopian to want to master two or more whole disciplines. Given that it implies the ability to be familiar with and combine entire disciplines, the idea of interdisciplinary research is illusory. Because it is so difficult for a single scholar to be truly multidisciplinary, some methodologists are led to advocate teamwork.

This is what is proposed by Pierre de Bie in the monumental work published by UNESCO (1970). Teamwork is productive in the big science laboratories, but where the social sciences are concerned it is difficult to achieve in practice. The only examples of successful teamwork concern data production or collection, and very seldom interpretation or synthesis (archaeology being the exception, here). The multidisciplinary approach is illusory because it advocates the slicing up of reality. Some researchers proceed piecemeal, with philological, anthropological, historical, ethnological, psychological and sociological approaches. This alternation of approaches, which almost never allows disciplines to meet, results at best in a useful parallelism—but not in a synthesis.

In fact, research enlisting several disciplines involves a combination of segments of disciplines, of specialities and not whole disciplines. The fruitful point of contact is established between sectors, and not along disciplinary boundaries. Considering the current trends in the social sciences, the word "interdisciplinarity" appears inadequate. It carries a hint of superficiality and dilettantism, and consequently should be avoided and replaced by hybridisation of fragments of sciences.

In Cartesian thought, analysis means breaking things into parts. All sciences, from astronomy to zoology, have made progress from the 16th century on by internal differentiation and cross-stimulation among emergent specialities. Each speciality developed a patrimony of knowledge as its understanding of the world advanced. With the growth of these patrimonies, specialisation became less a choice and more a necessity.

Increasingly focused specialisation has led to the creation of subdisciplines, many of which have gone on to become autonomous. There are in the literature dozens of lamentations and jeremiads about the fragmentation of political science. We cite here just two recent complaints. "Today there is no longer a single, dominant point of view... the discipline is fragmented in its methodological conception . . . students are no longer certain what politics is all about" (Easton and Schelling 1991: 49). In the Nordic countries, "political science showed tendencies to disintegrate into subfields, but these were still subfields of political science. However, the disintegration has continued and has lately taken on different forms which renounce the identity of political science" (Anckar 1987:72).

In fact, fragmentation results from specialisation. The division of the discipline into subfields tends to be institutionalised, as can be seen in the organisation of large departments of political science in many American and European universities. A good indication of the fragmentation of the discipline is the increasing number of specialised journals. In the last twelve years one hundred specialised journals in English relevant to political science have been launched. Most of these journals cross the borders of two or three disciplines, and many of them are located in Europe.

Some other new hybrid journals have appeared in French and in German. European unification has had an impact on the development of cross-national journals focusing on special fields.

Increasing specialisation may have consequences for the role of national professional associations and of the general journals.

> As political scientists have become more specialised, some members [of the American Political Science Association, APSA] have concluded that their interests are better served by other organisations. A comparative government area specialist, for instance, may find that he/she has more in common with economists, sociologists and anthropologists working in the same area than with other political scientists. This may also decrease the value of the *American Political Science Review* . . . Specialisation has devalued the reasons for joining APSA (Lynn 1983: 114-15).

It is pertinent to note that same phenomenon can be observed in Europe. The national professional associations are losing ground in favor of cross-national organisations that represent topical specialisations across disciplines.

It is necessary to stress both parts of the process: fragmentation into special fields and specialisation by hybridisation. It is the interaction of these two processes, and not each one in isolation, that has led to the remarkable advance of the natural as well as the social sciences. The continuous restructuring of political science, like that of the other social sciences, has been the result of these two contending processes.

However, both fragmentation and its correlate, hybridisation, have developed much more recently in political science than elsewhere. In the distant past, hybrid fields were the result of gaps between full disciplines. Today the gaps appear between specialised subfields among neighbouring subdisciplines. As a result, the fragmentation of disciplines into specialised subfields in the last few decades has led to the development of hybrid specialities. The hybrid specialities do not necessarily stand midway between two sovereign disciplines. They maybe enclaves of a section of political science into a sector of another discipline. They combine two delimited domains, not entire disciplines.

These domains do not need to be adjacent. Hybridisation appears in the list of research committees sponsored by the International Political Science Association. Among the forty recognised groups in 1995 a majority are related to specialities of other disciplines and are therefore hybrid: Political Sociology, Political Philosophy, Political Geography, Psycho-politics, Religion and Politics, Political and Social Elites, Armed Forces and Politics, Political Alienation, Politics and Ethnicity, Political Education, International Political Economy, International Economic Order, Comparative Judicial Studies, Biology and Politics, Business and Politics, Science and Politics, Socio-political Pluralism, Health Policy, Sex Roles and Politics, Global Environmental Change. Conceptual and Terminological Analysis, etc. Each of these groups is in contact with specialists belonging formally to other disciplines.

Sociometric studies show that many specialists are more in touch with colleagues who belong officially to other disciplines than with colleagues in their own discipline. The "invisible college" described by Robert Merton, Diana Crane and other sociologists of science is an eminently interdisciplinary institution because it ensures communication not only from one university to another and across all national borders, but also and above all between specialists attached administratively to different disciplines.

The networks of cross-disciplinary influcncc are such that they are obliterating the old classification of the social sciences. II. Borrowing from Neighboring Disciplines

The process of hybridisation consists first of all in borrowing and lending concepts, theories and methods. A review of the lending process would take us too far. I have to forgo to such a review here. In any case, political science has always borrowed much more than it has lent.

For a century and a half, from Sir George Cornewall Lewis' 1832 *The Use and Abuse of Some Political Terms* to Giovanni Sartori's edited collection on *Social Science Concepts* in 1984, numerous scholars have denounced the conceptual confusion and the polysemy of terms in various disciplines and particularly in political science. One of the reasons for this polysemy is indicated by Sartori (1984: 17): "We cannot form a sentence unless we already know the meanings of the words it contains... It is not that words *acquire* their meaning via the sentences in which they are placed, rather, the meaning of a word is *specified* by the sentence in which it is placed."

Another important reason for this semantic problem comes from the peregrination of concepts from one discipline to another. Borrowed concepts need some adaptation to the context of the new discipline, because a concept is not only a term, it is also a notion or an idea.

A recent study of more than 400 concepts used in the social sciences has found few neologisms (de Grolier 1990: 271), and this can be explained by the fact that more concepts are borrowed than created. Some concepts are reanimated after a long oblivion. Max Weber resurrected the concept of charisma after centuries of neglect. David Apter made use of the concept of consociational organisation, which was originally applied to Presbyterian institutions in Scotland. He used it to analyze political conflict in Uganda. Arendt Lijphart and many others have developed it further with respect to small European democracies,

Canada and South Africa. We can neglect the etymology of concepts in order to stress how borrowing fertilises imagination. The word "role" comes from the theatre, but Max Weber gave it a sociological meaning. From sociology this concept spread everywhere.

The word "revolution" was proposed by Copernicus, but it was first applied to politics by Louis XIV. Historians adopted it, sociologists articulated it, before offering it to political science. The patrimony of political science is full of borrowed concepts, which are hybrid in the sense that they were concocted in other disciplines and replanted skilfully in the garden of political science. This discipline has nevertheless generated for its own use a long series of important concepts, the oldest being "power," formulated by Aristotle, and the youngest, "implosion," suggested by the fall of the Soviet Union. In the process of adoption and adaptation many of these concepts have changed their semantic meaning. Political science has borrowed the following important concepts (excluding "lay" terms):

- *From sociology,* accommodation, aggregate, assimilation, elite circulation, clique, cohesion, collective behaviour, hierarchy, ideal-type, individualism, legitimacy, mass media, mass society, militarism, nationalism, pattern variables, Protestant ethic, secular, segregation, social class, social control, social integration, social structure, socialisation, status inconsistency, working class, *Gemeinschaft-Gesellschaft.*
- *From psychology.* affect, alienation, ambivalence, aspiration, attitude, behaviour, consciousness, dependency, empathy, personality, social movement, stereotype, *Gestalt.*

- *From economics:* allocation of resources, cartel, corporatism, diminishing returns, industrial revolution, industrialisation, liberalism, mercantilism, gross national product, scarcity, undeveloped areas.
- *From philosophy and the ancient Greeks:* anarchism, aristocracy, consensus, democracy, faction, freedom, general will, idealism, monarchy, oligarchy, phratry, pluralism, tyranny, value, *Weltanschauung.*
- *From anthropology,* acculturation, affinity, caste, nepotism, patriarchy, plural society, *rites de passage.*
- *From theology,* anomie (disregard of divine law), charisma.
- *From journalists and politicians:* imperialism, internationalism, isolationism, Left and Right, lobbying, neutralism, nihilism, patronage, plebiscite, propaganda, socialism, syndicalism.

Many concepts have multiple origins. Authoritarianism has two roots, one psychological and one ideological. It is often inadvertently interchangeable with despotism, autocracy, absolutism, dictatorship, etc. Authority has been analyzed from different disciplinary perspectives by Malinowski. Weber, Parsons, Lasswell, Kaplan, B. de Jouvenel, and C. J. Fredrich, among others. The concept of culture (civic, political, national) has many variants: cultural convergence, cultural configuration, cultural evolution, cultural integration, cultural lag, cultural parallelism, cultural pluralism, cultural relativity, cultural system, post-materialist culture. In the last two decades political scientists have been very productive in this subfield.

Max Weber and Karl Marx, both hybrid scholars, were the most prolific generators of concepts. Only Aristotle is comparable to them. Almond and Parsons are also the fathers of an impressive number of concepts. Concepts are often germinal grains of theories: structure generates structuralism, system becomes systemism, capital engenders capitalism, and so on.

Paradigm is a word often used or abused in political science, as much as in sociology, instead of the words theory or grand theory. Thomas Kuhn, who concocted this word, has explicitly acknowledged that in the social sciences its use is not justified. He explains in his preface to *The Structure of Scientific Revolutions* (Kuhn 1957: viii) that it was during a stay at Palo Alto Center for Advanced Studies, in the company of social scientists, including political scientists, that he was led to formulate the concept of paradigm with the very aim of making clear the essential difference between natural sciences and the social sciences.

The reason given by Kuhn was the absence of a theoretical consensus in any discipline of social sciences. Today, if someone "wants to legitimate his theory or model as a revolutionary achievement, there are always some who do not rally round the flag" (Weingart 1986:270). Are there in the social sciences instances of paradigmatic upheavals comparable to those created by Copernicus, Newton, Darwin or Einstein? Can the theories of Keynes, Chomsky or Parsons be described as paradigmatic? In the social sciences, does progress occur through paradigmatic revolutions or through cumulative processes? Are there really paradigms in the social sciences? Within a formal discipline, several major theories may cohabit, but there is a paradigm only when one testable theory alone dominates all other theories and is accepted by the entire scientific community. When Pasteur discovered the microbe, the theory of spontaneous generation collapsed: contagion became the new paradigm. In the social sciences, however, we see at best a confrontation between several non-testable theories.

Most of the time there is not even a confrontation but careful mutual avoidance, superb disregard on all sides; this is relatively easy owing to the size of scientific communities, and its division into schools. This is true for all countries, big or small. This mutual disregard is an old practice in the social sciences. At the turn of the century, the great scholars did not communicate, or very little. In the writings of Weber there is no reference to his contemporary Durkheim. Yet Weber was acquainted with Durkheim's journal, *L'Annee sociologique.*

For his part, Durkheim, who could read German, makes only one, fleeting reference to Weber. Yet they worked on a number of the same subjects, such as religion. Durkheim does no more than mention in passing Simmel and Toennies. Harshly criticised by Pareto, Durkheim never alluded to Pareto's work. Pareto's judgment of Durkheim's book on suicide was unfavorable. "Unfortunately," he wrote, "its arguments lack rigour" (quoted in Valade 1990: 207).

Weber seems to have been unaware of Pareto's theory on the circulation of elites and Pareto in his turn says nothing about the Weberian theory of political leadership. Weber and Croce met only once, and that briefly. There was no exchange between Weber and Freud. Ernst Bloch and George Lukacs met regularly with Weber in Heidelberg, but their work shows no sign of his influence. Nor was there any communication between Weber and Spongier.

Of Weber's contemporaries the only one who referred to him was Karl Jaspers, but he was a philosopher (cf. Mommsen and Osterhammel 1987). As was noted by

Raymond Aron, each of the three great scholars followed a "solitary path." Many examples could be cited of scholars co-existing without influencing one another, such as Angus Campbell and Paul Lazarsfeld, who nevertheless devoted a large part of their lives to studying the same political behaviour. The same remark can be made with reference to other topical fields. It is not a bad thing to pit theories one against the other. But there must be debate. There are no paradigms in the social sciences because each discipline is fragmented. For there to be a paradigm, one other condition must be met: theories must refer to essential aspects of social reality. However, the more ambitious a theory is, the less it can be directly tested by the data available. In the social sciences there are no "fundamental discoveries," as there sometimes are in the natural sciences. Instead, unverifiable theories are constructed, partly because social reality itself changes.

Also, and more importantly, the mistakes made by the giants of the natural sciences are most of the time methodological errors; in the social sciences they are basic mistakes.

Consider Malthusianism for instance. Is it a theory or a paradigm? Malthusianism is one of the major theories in the history of the social sciences. Malthus influenced many scientists, primarily Charles Darwin, who acknowledged it to be one of his main sources of inspiration. A host of sociologists, political scientists, demographers and economists took their cue from him, either to agree or to disagree with him. But when demographic conditions changed in the West, his projections were invalidated, and he was condemned as a false prophet.

However, if we consider today the gap between economic

development and population growth in Africa, Asia or Latin America, he could be hailed as a great visionary. We need only agree to an asynchronous comparison between the England of his time and the Third World to admit the asynchronous validity of his theory. Should we go further and talk of a Malthusian paradigm? Is there at least cumulative progress in political science? Clearly, there is such progress since the discipline has its heritage of concepts, methods, theories and praxis. It can soon be recognised whether someone is a professional or an amateur.

There is cumulative progress even in the theoretical field. If a theory becomes outdated, or is invalidated, something nevertheless remains of it, which is incorporated into new theories, for a great deal is learned by making mistakes. We do not repeat a mistake that has been denounced. In recent times, progress in political science has been ensured through a long series of sectoral empirical discoveries.

For example, the correlation established by D. Lerner (1958: 63) between degrees of urbanisation, literacy and communication is a proven fact that remains valid. In these specialised sectors—whether hybrid or monodisciplinary—there is no need for ambitious theories, it is enough for them to be what Merton (1973) has called "middle-range theories."

Let us take a concrete example of a cumulative process. One of the great findings in political science is the influence of electoral techniques on party systems. A bibliography, even a very selective one, on this theme could easily comprise two or three hundred titles in English, not to mention the many varied observations derived from the direct experience of politicians in numerous countries. From Condorcet, Bachofen, John Stuart Mill, Hare and Hondt to Hermens,

Downs, Duverger, Sartori, Lijphart, the theory is based on the contributions and successive improvements made by a very large number of specialists.

It is now recognised that "no paradigm seeks any more to order, and even less to unify, the field of the social sciences" (*Annales* 1989:1322).

The word paradigm should be excluded from the vocabulary of social sciences unless it is placed between quotation marks. Having thus cleared up the apparent theoretical contradiction between hybridisation of specialities and the disciplinary paradigm, let us now look to some hybrid theories. Examples of theoretical cross-fertilisation abound. Interest group theory's most-cited work, David B. Truman's *The Governmental Process,* draws heavily on sociological theories of groups.

Mancur Olson's attack on traditional interest group theory, *The Logic of Collective Action,* was based on economics. Meanwhile, sociologists and economists have borrowed from interest group theories developed by political scientists. The theories of sister disciplines have often confronted one another on the ground of political science, with results beneficial to all concerned. "Rational choice analysis" is a case in point. This approach has proved to be quite impervious to empirical criticism: an argument that a given politician was irrational, for instance, is not usually taken to present a threat to the theory.

Instead, modifications to, or attacks on, rational choice have tended to come either from within or from theoreticians of other disciplines. The strongest criticisms have been the construction of theoretical alternatives. A theory is discredited only by replacing it, usually with the aid of theories from outside the discipline. Psychology has provided the foundation for several of these attacks. Herbert Simon's theory draws not only on economics but also on psychology and on the study of public administration within political science. Theorists of political systems have often used extensive analogies with biological systems. Biology first developed the concept of "system" as a way to organise life and of organic systems as phenomena not reducible to their constituent chemistry.

Some structural functionalists have argued that social systems are like biological systems in that they are self-regulating and homeostatic. These theorists also noted that certain functions have to be performed in any biological system and used the analogy to ask what functions were vital to social systems. "Functionalism was well established in biology in the 1920s and had been used independently in Freudian analysis of the personality and in the study of primitive societies. Thence it spread throughout the social sciences, and with it spread logical scepticism about the exact status of the word function" (Mackenzie 1967: 91).

Systems theory. whether that of David Easton in comparative politics, or of Morton Kaplan, Richard Rosecrance, and Kenneth Waltz in international relations, drew primarily upon such sources for some sectors of sociology.

Theories decay. How old theories are superseded by new ones is a good question. But there is another, raised by Daniel Bell, the phenomenon of theories going wrong or turning into a blind alley: "Why does what was once regarded as an advance become a cul-de-sac?" (D. Bell, in Deutsch *et al.* 1986: 220). One could read today with great interest dozens of political philosophers and grand theorists of the past and cite them with pleasure. But only a handful of theories formulated before World War II are still alive.

Theories survive more easily in linguistics and economics. Castles built on sands by political scientists are ruined at the first rain. In 1912, Gustave Le Bon wrote in *La Psychohgie Politique* that the rules formulated by Machiavelli in *The Prince* were not valid any more because the society observed by the great Florentine no longer existed. But we are not going to make a pilgrimage to the cemetery of political theories. It is sufficient to note that in this necropolis there are fewer tombs in the alley of hybrid theories than in the alley of monodisciplinary theories. Specialised domains need theoretical orientations, but the discipline of political science as a whole cannot have a universal and monopolistic theory.

Methods have a much longer life expectancy and some are even perpetual acquisitions across the boundaries of formal disciplines.

Distinctions should be made between scientific reasoning—in the tradition of J.S. Mill, Durkheim, Claude Bernard or Hubert Blalock—strategy of investigation, method of research and technological ability. All four are cross-disciplinary. I shall concentrate on the borrowing of methods by political scientists, who rarely import directly from logic, mathematics or statistics. Usually they find an intermediary in certain sectors of psychology, economics or sociology, all of which have played a crucial role in the methodological enrichment of political science.

Tabular demonstration, graphic presentation, summation, measures of variability, ratios, rates, sampling distribution, statistical inference, ecological fallacy, binominal distribution, multiple regression, linear correlation, contingency, factor analysis and so on—none of these methods has been imagined by political scientists. All have been imported, and some, after improvement, have been exported in refined forms. The borrowing of methods has not diminished since Oliver Benson admitted, in 1963, that "most mathematical literature relevant to political science is by outsiders, by those who could not identify themselves as primarily students of political phenomena" (Benson 1963: 30).

Borrowing methods is easy. Once the difficult process of invention and initial elaboration is completed, a method can be used by anyone, with or without imagination. A substantial number of political scientists are familiar with scaling methods elaborated by psychologists, path-analysis imported from biology via economics, the multivariate reasoning and measuring of the sociologist Paul Lazarsfeld, the linear structural relation forged by the statistician Joreskog. With the rich methodology of the *American Soldier* edited by Samuel Stouffer many representatives of other disciplines have collaborated. Up to a certain point, the introduction of mathematics into political science has been valuable not only for its own contributions, but as an entree for additional borrowing.

Adoption of these mathematical methods and models has paid several dividends: the rigor necessary for modelling, for example, has also been invaluable in developing compelling and logical arguments, even for work which forgoes mathematical presentation. Because there is no need to obtain a license in order to adopt a method or a research technique, the importation has sometimes been indiscriminate.

What is needed is good sense in applying the method to a new field. Too many political scientists are still confusing scientific reasoning, research strategy and technological tools. Today the main source of disputes among political scientists is not, as many people believe, ideology, but methodology, most of it exogenous to political science. Debates between ideologues are possible, even if often sterile; but between methodological schools, they are inconclusive. The borrowing of statistical methods and techniques is not always beneficial.

Many political scientists who use quantitative methods extend the borders of political knowledge. However, others are motivated mainly by an interest in technique, rather than substance. They routinely build unverifiable models, over-quantify, and over-model. They often choose to discuss minor issues, spending much talent and energy to improve a correlation coefficient, to split a hair into four by factor analysis.

They are productive scholars—any input into the computer will result in an output, mechanically. Few of their papers see the light of day in major mainstream journals, because most are characterised by a painful contrast between highly sophisticated analytical techniques and poor imagination in research design, or data too weak to support the powerful techniques utilised (Dogan 1994). Interdisciplinary free trade methodology needs to be guided by scientific strategy and not by mechanical facilities, particularly in some great universities where many graduate students in political science complain that they are "oppressed" by a heavy program of imported statistical techniques, to the detriment of scientific reasoning.

Political Psychology

Between psychology and political science there is a hybrid domain flying its own flag: political psychology. This is a third generation hybrid, because psychology itself was born as a hybrid discipline, rooted partly in the natural sciences and partly in the social sciences. Political psychology has two sisters: an older one, social psychology, formally recognised in all major universities of the world; and a younger one, cognitive science, today the best endowed of the young sciences on both sides of the Atlantic. Political psychology rarely meets cognitive science, but is in permanent contact with social psychology.

In a recent survey D. 0. Sears and C. L. Funk (1991:346) write that political psychology, being "an interdisciplinary endeavor, runs the danger of falling between the cracks in academic institutions" because of pressures for "disciplinary orthodoxy induced by bureaucratic inertia." But the inventory they make by showing how political psychology penetrated into political science departments does not justify this fear. The journal *Political Psychology* is a good window onto this hybrid field. In its territory we find the provinces of political socialisation, role theory, alienation, psychobiography, personality analysis, political attitudes and beliefs, small groups, typological analysis of political leaders, national character, mass participation, generations, political dissatisfaction, and a rich methodological area (attitude measurement, sociometric measurement, content analysis, clinical method, quasi-experimental approach, and particularly, survey research).

Very few hybrid domains celebrate a founding father. But American political psychology has one: Harold Lasswell. His progeny include Fred Greenstein, Robert Lane, Herbert Hyman, Erik Erikson, Sidney Verba .md lames C. Davies, among many others. In Western Europe the hybrid field of political psychology is institutionalised in few universities, but the literature related to the field is rich and of great variety as is illustrated in France for instance by the work of Philippe Brand, and in Germany by the contributions of Erwin K. Scheuch to the methodology of sample surveys and the problems of comparability in politics and social psychology. Scheuch has the merit of having discovered the "individualistic fallacy" (Scheuch 1966; 1969). Among the books belonging to the field of political psychology. *Political Action,* edited by Samuel Barnes and Max Kaase, should be singled out. Their typology of protesters, activists, reformists, conformists and inactives is pertinent for many countries.

Political Geography

Geography—a master discipline in the past—today has no core. It is divided into many subfields: biogeography, social geography, urban, historical, economic, political geography. There are multiple encounters between political science and geography: geopolitics, electoral geography, urban politics, territorial bases of federalism, spatial organisation of society, core-periphery, city-hinterland, environmental problems, urban-rural differences, territorial aspects of social mobilisation, etc. Demography is an intervening dimension in political geography.

From the "Geographical Pivot of History" by H. J. Mackinder in 1904 to Stein Rokkan's "conceptual map of Europe" (see the special issue dedicated to his conceptions by *Revue Internationale de Politique Comparee* in 1994), many essays have been published in the field of political geography, and not only in Europe. F.J. Turner's *The Significance of the Frontier in American History* is dealing with geography as much as with history.

In Kasperson and Minghi's collection, *The Structure of Political Geography* (1969), many chapters are of interest even for political scientists who are not oriented toward geography (Ratzel's laws of the spatial growth of states, geopolitical regions, transaction-flow analysis, heartland

and rimland, the impact of negro migration, and so on). The concept of center-periphery obviously has a geographical dimension (Rokkan, Urwin *et al.* 1987) Political science and geography also meet in the domain of electoral geography, particularly for the analysis of aggregate data in countries characterised by a great territorial diversity, and for which information is available at the level of small administrative units.

The privileged countries from this point of view are, or were until recently: France, Italy, Spain, Portugal, Belgium, Norway, Finland, Austria, Canada. Andre Siegfried (1913) did research on the North-West of France, V. 0. Key on *Southern Politics* (1949), Rudolf Herberle (1963) on Schleswig-Holstein during the Weimar Republic. Erik Allardt (1964) on Finland, Mattei Dogan (1968) on Italy, Stein Rokkan and H. Valen (1964) on regional contrasts in Norwegian politics, Juan Linz and Amando de Miguel (1966) on the "Eight Spains," R.E. De Smet and R. Evalenko (1956) and Frognier *et al.* (1974) on Belgium.

This geographical approach has, however, been challenged in an analysis by deciles, where the territory disappears in favor of a sociological reordering of the territorial units and of the variables (Dogan and Derivry 1988). This hybrid field has a series of specialised journals which are interdisciplinary bridges: *Economic Geography, Urban Geography, International Journal of Urban and Regional Research* and, particularly. *Political Geography.*

Interestingly, political scientists are still adopting the nation-state as a unit of analysis at a time when there are in the world more giant cities with over four million inhabitants than independent states which reach this level. The world is increasingly dominated by giant cities (Dogan and Kasarda 1988).

Geographers and urbanists are in this domain at the front rank, proposing theoretical frameworks, concepts and methods of measurement. Urban studies are expanding; they may soon become an independent discipline. Today in almost all countries, advanced and developing, the number of specialists in "urbanology" is higher than the number of political scientists. "Urban politics" is a growing field.

Political Sociology

Political science and sociology have a condominium: political sociology. This is an old hybrid, recognised as early as the 1950s, as was testified by Neil Smelser:

> In the newer branches of political science that have grouped loosely under the heading of behavioural approach, the methods of research are, except for relative emphasis, almost indistinguishable from the methods of sociology ... political scientists have employed a vast array of methods of data gathering, statistical manipulation and comparative methods that are also commonly used in sociology (Smelser 1967:27).

Today political economy tends to weaken the privileged relations between sociology and political science. Giovanni Sartori makes a distinction between political sociology and the sociology of politics. For him, the latter is a branch of sociology, like the .sociology of religion. A dividing line could be traced by considering the emphasis on the dependent or on the independent variables. "The independent variables—causes, determinants or factors—of the sociologist are, basically, *social* structures, while the independent variables of the political scientist are, basically *political* structures" (Sartori 1969:67).

He concludes that "political sociology is an interdisciplinary hybrid attempting to combine social and political explanatory variables, i.e. the inputs suggested by the sociologist with inputs suggested by the political scientist" (Sartori 1969:69). Many of the best-known scholars in political science are leading sociologists. Quite a number of scholars have or have had a dual appointment in political science and in sociology, among them R. Aron, S.M. Lipset, R. Bendix, J. Linz, G. Sartori, M. Kaase, J. D. Stephens. Mildred A. Schwartz, Ch. Ragin, and M. Dogan.

Some economists advocate an "imperialistic expansion of economics into the traditional domains of sociology, political science, anthropology, law and social biology" (Hirschleifer 1985:53). Several of these imperialists are famous scholars, including a few Nobel laureates. A kind of manifesto has been published in the *American Economic Review,* which is worth quoting:

> It is ultimately impossible to carve off a distinct territory for economics, bordering upon but separated from other social disciplines. Economics interpenetrates them all, and is reciprocally penetrated by them. There is only one social science. What gives economics its imperialist invasive power is that our analytical categories—scarcity, cost, preferences, opportunities, etc.—are truly universal in applicability . . . Thus economics really does constitute the universal grammar of social science. But there is a flip side to this. While scientific work in anthropology and sociology and political science and the like will become increasingly indistinguishable from economics, economists will reciprocally have to become aware of how constraining has been their function. Ultimately, good economics will also have to be good anthropology and sociology and political science and psychology (Hirschleifer 1985:53).

This view is anachronistic, and contrasts with the perception of economics as a shrinking discipline: "Economics as a formal discipline is suffering because its main achievements—conceptualisation, theory, modelling and mathematisation—have been accompanied by an excessive isolation from the other social sciences" (Beaud 1991:157).

In reality, the recent history of the social sciences shows that enormous areas of scientific knowledge have been abandoned by the science of economics. These areas have been taken over by neighboring disciplines. At one particular moment, economics reached a fork in the path: it could have chosen intellectual expansion, the penetration of other disciplines, at the cost of diversification, and at the risk of dispersal (a risk taken by political science); instead it chose to remain unflinchingly pure, true to itself, thereby forfeiting vast territories.

Yet many economists consider that the choice of purity, methodological rigor and hermetic terminology was the right choice. It is thus clear that self-sufficiency, to use a word familiar to economists, leads sooner or later to a shrinking of borders. But this does not imply general impoverishment, since the lands abandoned by the economists were soon cultivated by others.

Those abandoned lands now have their own flags: management, political economy, development science, the comparative study of Third World countries, economic and social history. The position of economics in the constellation of the social sciences might have been more enviable today had it not withdrawn into itself.

This situation is particularly surprising, in that few classical scholars— from Marx and Weber to Schumpeter, Polanyi, Parsons and Smelser (Martinelli and Smelser, 1990), not forgetting Pareto—have failed to assign a central place in their theories to the relationship between economy, society and politics.

A whole army of famous American economists have given priority to the study of political phenomena, even if they have kept one foot in economics. Among them are Kenneth Arrow, Anthony Downs, Kenneth Boulding, Charles Lindblom, James Buchanan, Gordon Tullock, Albert Hirschman, John Harsanyi, Herbert Simon, Duncan Black, Jerome Rothenberg, Thomas Schelling, Richard Musgrave, Mancur Olson and others. Some eclectic economists denounce the reductionism advocated by others, particularly with reference to research on development: development is reduced to economic development; this is reduced to growth; which in turn is reduced to investment, in other words to accumulation. It has taken several decades to dethrone per capita GDP as a composite indicator of development.

Gunnar Myrdal railed against economists who were in favor of undisciplinary models. In many countries large numbers of economists have locked themselves up in an ivory tower, and as a result whole areas have escaped their scrutiny. Their contribution to the problem of the development of the Third World, for instance, is rather modest when compared with the work of political scientists and sociologists.

This is particularly true in the United States, Latin America and India. If a discipline has a tendency to turn in upon itself, if it does not open up enough, if its specialities do not hybridise, the neighboring territories do not remain barren. Many economists have had a somewhat condescending attitude towards political science.

This has resulted in the development, alongside and in competition with economics, of a new corporate body, with an extremely active and large membership in the United States, the UK and Scandinavia: political economy was protected by only one of its parents and renamed through the revival of an old name from the French nomenclature of the sciences.

Political economy is currently one of the main provinces of American political science—with a large output and renowned journals. It is one of the most popular sectors among Ph.D. students in political science. Political science is the greatest beneficiary of the monodisciplinary self-confinement of economics. Many years ago F. A. Hayek wrote that "nobody can be a great economist who is only an economist—and I am even tempted to add that the economist who is only an economist is likely to become a nuisance if not a positive danger" (Hayek 1956:463). It may now be too late for economics to reconquer the territories conquered by political science, sociology, economic history and particularly by political economy.

Some economists are still hoping: "It is necessary to reduce the use of the clause *ceteris paribus,* to adopt an interdisciplinary approach, that is to say to open economics to multidimensionality" (Bartoli 1991: 490). Abandonment of reasoning by assumptions and by theorems would not be enough, because the reality has changed: "economic issues become politicised and political systems become increasingly preoccupied with economic affairs" (Frieden and Lake 1991:5).

From Political Anthropology to Hybrid Area Studies

In a few years towards the end of the 1950s and the beginning of the 1960s, about fifty colonies achieved national independence. At that time some three thousand American social scientists, among them many political scientists, were sent—with the financial help of American foundations—to Asia, Africa and Latin America in order to study the newly independent nation-states. They covered the planet with hundreds of books and articles. They have become area specialists.

They have replaced the European scholars who returned home after the withdrawal of Britain, France, Belgium, the Netherlands and Portugal from their colonies. This spontaneous generation of area specialists was born hybrid. The topics of their research blurred the disciplinary boundaries. They and their successors were confined to non-Western underdeveloped countries, to stateless societies, to what Joel S. Migdal calls "weak states and strong societies"—which is to say, to the privileged territory of an old discipline, anthropology, which had flourished in Western Europe around the turn of the century.

The European anthropologists had discovered these "primitive" societies long before the American area specialists had done so. There is a basic difference between the two. The European anthropologists were monodisciplinary scholars with a clear identity, vocabulary and theoretical framework. They were exporters of knowledge to the entire spectrum of social sciences.

Some of them had imperialistic ambitions, proclaiming that anthropology was the master science. All other disciplines, including political science and sociology, were considered by these academic imperialists as provinces of anthropology. But when the European empires which covered half of the planet started to disintegrate, these anthropologists lost their research fields. Anthropology shrank. The abandoned territories were delivered to specialists in area studies. In contrast to their predecessors, the new invaders did not come under a disciplinary flag. Few of them were trained in anthropology, and most of them were neither theoreticians nor methodologists. The most famous exceptions are David Apter, Leonard Binder, James Coleman, Lucian Pye, Fred Riggs, Dankwart Rustow, Richard Sklar and Myron Wiener. David Easton was then eager to establish a new subfield: political anthropology.

He published an essay under this title in 1959. Retrospectively it can be said that this was a sickly child, born at a moment when the new hegemonic power needed non-disciplinary specialists of these new countries—not experts in anthropology, a discipline which began to be colonised by other disciplines. It is significant that at the same moment Margaret Mead (1961: 475) was frightened of seeing her discipline "swallowed" and "isolated from me community of scientists and scholars." Good old anthropology fell from imperialism to being an "unsuitable scientific repository" (Mead 1961:476). Political anthropology does not flourish today, because it is too anthropological and insufficiently political, at a time when the poor countries are developing, except in Africa, and are experiencing an increasing internal diversification in facing the global economic world. The seminal essay by Lucian Pye in 1958 "The Non-Western Political Process" needs a serious updating by reducing the scale of dichotomies. The field of political anthropology seems to be the only hybrid field in decline.

Meanwhile, a French demographer-economist-sociologist Alfred Sauvy (1952; 1956) suggested calling these underpriviledged new countries "the Third World," by analogy with the Third Estate before the French Revolution. This label has survived even though the "second world" imploded in 1989. It is probable that sooner or later this label will be abandoned, because it includes an enormous variety of countries: old civilisations like China and artificial states in Africa; rich countries like Saudi Arabia and extremely poor ones. Which discipline will propose the new labels? Area studies in the Third World give priority to topics which seem important to understanding a particular country. "They do not respect disciplinary boundaries" (Lambert 1991:190).

In the area studies, humanities are well represented. "Area specialists who are in the social sciences are likely to have a great deal more contact and shared intellectual activity with human sciences than do most of their non-area-oriented disciplinary colleagues"; it is at the conjunction of anthropology, history, literature and political science that "much of the genuinely interdisciplinary work in area studies occurs" (Lambert 1991:192). Describing the struggle between the conventional disciplines and area studies, which has affected the self-identity of scholars, Lucian W. Pye (1975: 3) writes: "The emergence of area specialisation has changed perspectives and raised questions which go to the foundations of the social sciences." These foundations have been altered much more by the hybrid fields at the interstices of disciplines than by the transversal hybrid area studies.

Natural and Social Sciences

The geographical distribution of various types of political regime is a striking phenomenon. But it has been absent from the literature during the last few decades, as a reaction against the exaggerations of the sociologist Ellsworth Huntington, who was severely and rightly criticised by the sociologist Pitirim Sorokin in 1928. This criticism dissuaded an entire generation of American sociologists and political scientists from taking into consideration environmental and climatic factors. But many prominent economists did not remain silent. In 1955, W. Arthur Lewis noted in his *Theory of Economic Growth:* "It is important to identify the reasons why tropical countries have lagged during the last two hundred years in the process of modern economic growth" (Lewis 1955:53). John Kenneth Galbraith wrote in 1951: "If one marks off a belt a couple of thousand miles in width encircling the earth at the equator one finds within it no developed countries... Everywhere the standard of living is low and the span of human life is short" (Galbraith 1951: 39—41).

Charles Kindleberger (1965: 78) wrote some fifteen years later: "The fact remains that no tropical country in modern times has achieved a high state of economic development." Kenneth Boulding (1970: 409) goes one step further: "The principal failure of economics, certainly in the last generation, has been in the field of economic development [which} has been very much a temperate zone product." These economists are cited by Andrew Kamarck, director of the Economic Development Institute of the World Bank, in his *The Tropics and Economic Development* (1976). There is no reference at all to politics in that book, but it nevertheless manages to challenge our perception of politics in tropical areas. Trypanosomiasis, carried by the tsetse fly, prevented much of Africa from progressing beyond subsistence level: "For centuries, by killing transport animals, it abetted the isolation of tropical Africa from the rest of the world and the isolation of the various African peoples from one another" (Kamarck 1976: 38). Twenty years ago an area of Africa greater than that of the United States was thereby denied to cattle (Kamarck 1976: 39). Agricultural production in humid tropics is limited by the condition of the soil, which has become laterite (Kamarck 1976:25). Surveys in the 1960s by the World Health Organisation and by the World Food Organisation estimated that parasitic worms infected over one billion people throughout the tropics and sub-tropics. Hookworm disease, characterised by anemia, weakness and fever, infected 500 million in these areas (Kamarck 1976:75). These ecological factors are confirmed by a considerable amount of research in tropical areas during the last two decades by geologists, geographers, biologists, zoologists, botanists, agronomists, epidemiologists, parasitologists, climatologists, experts of the World Bank and several agencies of the United Nations, and also by hybrid political scientists well-versed in tropical agriculture, the exploitation of minerals, and sanitary conditions of these countries.

The situation has improved during the last generation, according to dozens of reports prepared by international organisations.

Translating these economic and social conditions into political terms, it is worth asking questions such as these:

- Why are almost all pluralist industrial democracies in temperate zones?
- Why has India—which according to some theories "should not be democratic," and which is a relatively poor tropical country—nevertheless had, for a long period, a democratic regime?
- Is there any relationship between the fact that most of the 30 million square kilometers of continental Africa (excluding the Mediterranean rim) are in the tropics, and the facts that this continent is the poorest and is without a single truly pluralist democracy capable of surviving more than a few years?
- To what extent should ecological factors be included in the parameters of economic, social and political development?

Such questions can be asked not only by the old "school of development," but also by its successor, the new "school of transition." One team (G. O'Donnell, P.C. Schmitter and L. Whitehead) gave to their book the prudent title: *Transitions from Authoritarian Rule,* which does not indicate the final outcome. Another team (led by L. Diamond, J.J. Linz and S.M. Upset) took a risk by suggesting, in the title of their book *Democracy in Developing Countries,* that democratic institutions are indeed taking root in these countries, which were previously considered by one of these co-editors as not responding to the "requisites of democracy."

Neither of these two teams make an explicit and functional distinction between the genuine pluralist democracy, Dahl's polyarchy, and the limited, partial, facade or embryonic kind of democracy. Processes of democratisation, stages of modernisation, liberalisation, electoral games, respect for human rights are only steps toward the "western model." Today the word "democracy" without an adjective can be misleading.

As anyone would admit there is a large variety of democratic regimes. Democracy comes by degrees, as is shown by the data collected by Raymond Gastil in h is series *Freedom in the World.* Only by a clear distinction between types of democracy would it be possible to frame a tentative reply to the first question asked above: why until now have truly advanced democracies tended to flourish in temperate zones? India as a democratic country is a clinical case, a scientific "anomaly" in the sense given to this word by Thomas Kuhn. Comparativists interested in this case should proceed as biologists do when they have the good fortune to discover an abnormality, they could follow the advice of Claude Bernard in *Introduction a la medecine experimentale* (1865), which is still a pertinent book. They could start with one of the best indicators that we have in comparative politics: small agricultural ownership. The Indian peasant is poor, but he is a proprietor! Concerning tropical Africa and other similar areas, natural sciences and demography should be brought into the picture when asking, as Samuel Huntington does: how many countries will become democratic? Dependency theory may be of some help for Latin America and Eastern Europe, but it is much less so for tropical Africa. The literature on the ecological parameters of the tropics can be contrasted with the literature about the transfer of flora and fauna from one temperate zone to another.

If the eminent comparativist Charles Darwin were still alive, he would criticise monodisciplinarity, in particular W. W. Rostow whose theory of "stages of growth" does not admit any physical or environmental constraints on growth.

Comparative Politics

The process of hybridisation appears not only in exchanges of concepts, theories and methods among disciplines and between subfields. It is also evident in exchanges of information, substance, indicators, statistical data and in the daily praxis of empirical research. This trade is excedentary for some disciplines and deficitary for others. Social geography borrows information from physical geography, which borrows in turn from geology, rather than the reverse.

Political science has contracted an enormous foreign debt, because politics cannot be explained exclusively by politics. Political phenomena are never produced *in vitro,* artificially in the laboratory. They are always related to a variety of factors behind politics. Dozens of non-political variables are used to explain politics. This is one of the main reasons why political science is interwoven with the other social sciences. The storage of information produced by other social sciences is particularly important in the domain of comparative politics, to such a degree that it could be said that a comparison across nations necessarily encompasses several disciplines. In the history of comparative politics there was a privileged time of co-operation and convergence during the 1960s.

During the fifteen years between 1958 and 1972, three dozen important books and articles were published, which shared three characteristics: comparison by quantification, by hybridisation and by cumulative knowledge. "Such a combination had never previously been achieved in the history of political science" (Dogan 1994: 39).

This privileged moment also marks a break with European classical comparisons in the sociological style of Tocqueville, J. S. Mill, Marx, Spencer, Weber and Pareto. At that particular moment sociology was no longer at the center of the constellation of social sciences. For the first time in the history of social sciences, it was political science. In the new constellation a number stars are visible—it is unnecessary to name them. "What should be emphasised is the process of cumulative knowledge, in which several dozen specialised scholars and experts have participated.

The alarm concerning the parochial state of comparative politics—after the subjugation of all social sciences during the period of totalitarianism in Europe (Scheuch 1991) and before their renaissance in the United States— was raised by Roy Macridis in 1955. Around the same time (1954) the Statistical Bureau of the United Nations started to publish "social statistics," none of which was political. They concerned demographic variables, income, standard of living, social mobility, sanitary conditions, nutrition, housing, education, work, criminality. In 1957, *Reports on the World Social Situation* began to be published by the Department of Economic and Social Affairs of the United Nations. Chapters in these publications on "The Interrelations of Social and Economic Development and the Problem of Balance" (in the 1961 volume) or on "Social-economic Patterns" (in the 1963 volume) are contributions that can be read today with great interest, even if the political data so important for comparative politics are absent from these analyses. Two years after that series began came Upset's Political *Man* (1959), the most cited book by political scientists for two decades. In fact, however, this book borrows from all social sciences and very little from political science. One year later Karl Deutsch produced his "manifesto" (Deutsch 1960), followed by a seminal article a few months later (Deutsch 1961). Both articles deal with indicators which are not directly political.

The following year an important article by Phillip Outright (1963) was published which appears in retrospective to have been prophetic: it is the only article of that time to give priority to political variables. In the same year Arthur Banks and Robert Textor published their *A Cross-Polity Survey* (1963) in which the majority of the fifty-seven variables proposed and analyzed are not political Shortly thereafter, the first *World Handbook of Political and Social Indicators* (Russett *et al.* 1965) discussed seventy-five variables, of which only twelve are strictly political and eight others economic-cum-political.

Remarkably, year later G. Almond and G. Bingham Powell published a fundamental book. *Comparative Politics* (1966), in which several social sciences, particularly social anthropology, are seen in the background. From that moment on the field of international comparisons becomes bifurcated. One road continues with quantitative research, in which contributors constantly use non political factors in their analysis of "correlates of democracy." An important recent input comes again from the Development Program of the United Nations, the *Human Development Report* (1990 *et seq.)*. In this publication GNP per capita is dethroned and is replaced by a new indicator: Purchasing Power Parity (PPP). The other road gave priority to sectoral comparisons, for instance the eight volumes on political development, published by Princeton University Press, where politics is for most of the time a dependent variable explained by non-political factors. There are several good reviews of the "political development" school (Almond 1990; Wiarda 1989).

Today this school seems to have reached its limits, to be out of steam, to have exhausted the theme. It is a good example of crowded fields subjected, after a period of productivity, to diminishing marginal returns: "the higher the density of scholars in a given field, the less likely innovation is per capita" (Dogan and Pahre 1990: 36). This "paradox of density" designates creative marginality as the opposite of density of scholars.

Notably, in the recent period, the field of comparative politics has expanded in all directions, penetrating into the territories of other disciplines: transition to democracy, values and beliefs, crisis of confidence, public corruption, ungovernability, limits to growth and so on. (These new directions figure throughout many other chapters of the *New Handbook.)* Is the field of comparative politics becoming imperialistic?

As we can see, comparative politics does not consist only in cross-national analysis. It is also necessarily a cross-disciplinary endeavor, because in comparative research we are crossing units (nations) and variables (numerical or nominal). The variables are usually more numerous than the units. The relations between variables are often more important for theoretical explanations than the discovery of analogies and differences between nations. In comparative politics there is no single major book that attempts to explain politics strictly by political variables—except in constitutional matters. But of course the dose of hybridisation varies according to the subject and to the ability of the author to leave in the shadow what should be implicitly admitted.

For instance, in their comparisons of political systems, scholars like Klaus von Beyme or Giovanni Sartori might not need to discuss at length social structure or cultural diversity. By contrast, Arend Lijphart (in his comparison of consociational democracies) and Ronald Inglehart (in his analysis of beliefs and values) do have to stress the importance of social, religious, linguistic and historical variables.

In these cases, Lijphart and Inglehart cross the disciplinary boundaries more than von Beyme and Sartori do. Comparative politics across disciplines means first of all crossing history. The relation between comparative history and comparative politics merits a lengthy discussion. Here it is sufficient to admit that the two sub-fields do not co-operate along their common frontiers, but only at certain Hates, and usually on the territory of other hybrid fields: historical sociology, social history, economic history, cultural history, asynchronic comparisons. Some of the most important books in comparative politics also belong to this "hyphened history," from Dumont's *Homo Hierarchicus,* Bairoch's *De Jericho H Mexico, villa et economic dans I'histoire,* Wittfogel's *Oriental Despotism,* Wallerstein's

Modern World System, to Upset's *The First New Nation* or Bendix's *Kings or People.*

Different disciplines may proceed to examine the same phenomenon from different foci. This implies a division of territories between disciplines. On the contrary, hybridisation implies an overlapping of segments of disciplines, a recombination of knowledge in new specialised fields. Innovation in the various sectors of political science depends largely on exchanges with other fields belonging to other disciplines. At the highest levels of the pyramid of political science, most researchers belong to a hybrid subdiscipline: political sociology, political economy, political psychology, political philosophy, political geography, public administration, area studies and so on.

Alternatively, they may belong to a hybrid field or subfield: mass behaviour (related to social psychology), elite recruitment (related to sociology and history), urban politics (related to social geography), welfare states (related to social economy and social history), values (related to philosophy, ethics, and social psychology), governmental capabilities (related to law and economics), poverty in tropical countries (related to agronomy, climatology and economic geography), development (related to all social sciences and to several natural sciences). There is probably as much communication with outsiders as between internal subfields. For instance, a political psychologist who studies protest movements and alienation interacts only a little with the colleague who uses game theory to study the same topic.

He may find intellectual common ground with the social historian who studies the phenomenon in previous times, or with the sociologist who studies the impact of unemployment or immigration on violence and delegitimation in some European countries.

There is no communication between two political scientists analysing the crisis of the social security system, one by abstract modelling, the other in vernacular language. The first is in contact with modellers in economics, and the second cites scholars from other disciplines. All major issues are crossing the formal borders of disciplines: breakdown of democracy, anarchy, war and peace, generational change, the freedom-equality nexus, individualism in advanced societies, fundamentalism in traditional societies, ruling class, public opinion. Most specialists are not located in the so-called core of the discipline.

They are in the outer rings, in contact with specialists of other disciplines. They borrow and lend at the frontiers. They are hybrid scholars. The number of "general" political scientists is rapidly decreasing. Everyone tends to specialise in one or several domains. When two political scientists meet for the first time, the spontaneous question they ask each other is: "What is your field?" This is true also for other disciplines. *Al* professional congresses, scholars meet according to specialities. Congresses that bring together crowds of people who have little in common consume a lot of energy which could be better invested in the organisation of meetings by fields bringing together specialists from various disciplines.

Suppose it were possible to select, from all political scientists in the various countries, the five or six hundred scholars who are doing the most creative research, those who advance knowledge, the most renowned of them. Suppose further that we except from this upper-stratum of eminence the scholars who specialise in the study of constitutional matters and the governmental process of their own country, some of whom are famous in their own field. After making this double delimitation, we would discover that among this body of scholars, the majority are not "pure" political scientists. They are specialists of a research domain which is not exclusively political. Those who shut themselves within the traditional frontiers of political science are narrowing their perspective and reducing their opportunities to innovate—except in constitutional matters and the organisation of the state apparatus.

At the other extreme are the enthusiastic imitators. In some domains borrowing is too much simple imitation and not enough imaginative adaptation. If it were possible to rank the various subfields and schools on a scale of eclecticism it would appear that sophisticated statistical analysis and economic heuristic assumptions are the two most imitative schools. I have commented already about the over-quantifiers.

To conclude, political science lives in symbiosis with the other social sciences, and will continue to be a creative science only if it remains extrovert. In fact, this science has no choice, because it is genetically programmed to generate grandchildren who will talk different tongues and who will sit, as Almond says, "at distant tables." These tables are distant because they are placed at the interstices of disciplines in the enormous hinterland of political science.

REFERENCES

Almond, G.A. 1990. *A Discipline Divided: Schools and Sects in Political Science.* Newbury Park, Calif.: Sage.

Anckar, D. 1987. Political science in the Nordic countries. *International Political Science Review. 8:*73-84.

Andrews, W.G. 1982. *International Handbook of Political Science.* Westport, Conn.: Greenwood Press.

Andrain, C.A. 1980. *Politics and Economic Policy in Western Democracies.* Belmont, Calif.: Wadsworth.

Apter, D. E. 1968. *Conceptual Approaches to the Study of Modernisation.* Englewood Cliffs, NJ.: Prentice-Hall.

Bairoch, P. 1988. *De Jericho a Mexico, villes et economic dans I'histoire (Cities and Economic Development),* trans. C. Braider. Chicago: University of Chicago Press.

Banks, A. S., and textor, R. B. 1963. A *Cross-Polity* Survey. Cambridge, Mass.: MIT Press.

Barnes, S. H.; kaase, M.; *et ai* 1979. *Political Action, Mass Participation in Five Western Democracies.* Beverly Hill, Calif.: Sage Publications.

Bartoli, H. 1991. *L'Economie Unidimensionnelle.* Paris: Economica.

Beaud, M. 1991. Economie, theorie, histoire: essai de clarification. *Revue Economique, 2:* 155-72.

Bendix, R., ed., 1968. *State and Society: A Reader in Comparative Political Sociology.* Boston: Little, Brown.

—— 1978. *Kings or People.* Berkeley: University of California Press.

Benson, O. 1963. The mathematical approach to political science. Pp. 30-57 in *Mathematics and the Social Sciences,* ed. J. Charlesworth. New York: American Academy of Political and Social Science.

Bernard, C. 1865. *Introduction a la Medecine Experimentale.* Various editions.

Beyme, K. von. 1979. *Die Parlamentarischen Regierungssysteme in Europe.* Munich: Piper.

—— 1985. *Political Parties in Western Democracies.* Aldershot: Gower.

Boulding, K. 1970. Is economics culture-bound? *American Economic Review (Papers and Proceedings),* 60 (May): 406-11.

Cardoso, F. H., and enzo faletto, E. 1979. *Dependencia y desarrollo en America Latina (Dependency and Development in Latin America),* trans. M. M. Urquidi. Berkeley: University of California Press.

Clastres, P. 1974. *La Societe centre l'Etat, Recherches d'anthropologie politique.* Paris: Editions Minuit.

CNRS. 1990. *Carrefour des Sciences: L'Interdisciplinarite.* Paris: CNRS.

Cutright, P. 1963. National political development: measurement and analysis. *American Sociological Review, 28*:253-64.

Dahl, R. A , and lindblom, C. E. 1953. *Politics, Economics and Welfare.* New York: Harper and Row.

Deutsch, K. W. 1960. Toward an inventory of basic trends and patterns in comparative and international politics. *American Political Science Review,* 54: 34-56.

—— 1961. Social mobilisation and political development. *American Political Science Review,* 55: 493-514.

—— Markovits, A. S.; and platt, J., eds. 1986. *Advances in the Social Sciences.* New York: University Press of America.

Diamant, A. 1990. If everybody innovates, will we all sit at separate tables? Paper presented to the World Congress of the International Sociological Association, Madrid.

Diamond, L; linz, J.; and lipset, S. M., eds. 1988. *Democracy in Developing Countries.* 3 vols. Boulder, Colo.: Lynne Rienner.

Dogan, M. 1968. Un fenomeno di atassia politica. Pp. 465-88 in *Partiti Politici e Strutture Sociali in Italia, ed.* M. Dogan and O.M. Petracca. Milano: Edizioni Comunita.

—— 1994. Limits to quantification in comparative politics. Pp. 35-71 in *Comparing Nations,* ed. M. Dogan and A. Kazancigil. Oxford: Blackwell.

Dowse. R. E., and Hughes. J. A. 1975. *Political Sociology.* New York: Wiley.

Dumont, L. 1966. *Homo Hierarchicus: Le Systems des Castes et ses Implications.* Paris: Gallimard.

Easton, D. 1959. Political anthropology. Pp. 211-62 in *Biennial Review of Anthropology,* ed. B.J. Siegel. Stanford, Calif.: Stanford University Press.

—— and Schelling, C. S., eds. 1991. *Divided Knowledge Across Disciplines, Across Cultures.* Newbury Park, Calif.: Sage.

—— Gunnell, J. G.; and Graziano, L., eds. 1991. *The Development of Political Science.* London: Routledge.

Finifter, A. W., ed. 1983. *Political Science: The State of the Discipline.* Washington, D.C.: American Political Science Association.

Frieden, J.A., and Lake, D.A. 1991. *International Political Economy.* New York: St. Martin.

Frognier, A. P., *et al.* 1974. *Vote, Clivages Socio-Politiques.* Louvain: Vander.

Galbraith, J. K. 1951. Conditions for economic change in underdeveloped countries. *Journal of Farm Economics,* 33 (.November): 255-69.

Gastil, R. 1980-1989. *Freedom in the World.* New York: Freedom House. Greenstein, F. I., and lerner, M. 1971. A *Source Book for the Study of Personality and Politics.* Chicago: Markham.

—— and Polsby, N.W., eds. 1975. *Handbook of Political Science.* Reading, Mass.: Addison- Wesley.

Grolier, E. de. 1990. Des theories aux concepts et des fails aux mots. *Revue Internationale des Sciences Sociales,* 124: 269-79.

Hayek, F. A. 1956. The dilemma of specialisation. Pp. 462-73 in *The State of the Social Sciences,* ed. L. White. Chicago: University of Chicago Press.

Heberle, R. 1963. *Landbevolkerung und Nationalsozialismus: Eine Soziologische Untersuchung der Politischen Willensbildung in Schleswig-Holstein.* Stuttgart: Deutsche Vcrlagsanstalt.

Hirschleifer, *J.* 1985. The expanding domain of economics. *American Economic Review (Papers and Proceedings), 75* (#6): 53-68.

Hoogerwerf, A. 1982. The Netherlands. In Andrews 1982:127-45.

Huntington, E. 1924. *Civilisation and Climate.* New Haven, Conn.: Yale University Press.

Huntington, S. 1984. Will more countries become democratic? *Political Science Quarterly,* 99:193-218.

Inglehart, R. 1990. *Culture Shift in Advanced Industrial Society.* Princeton, N.J.: Princeton University Press.

Intriligator, M. D. 1991. Some reflections about the interactions between the behavioural sciences. *Structural Changes and Economic Dynamics,* 1:1-9.

Johnston, R. I. 1994. Geography journals for political scientists. *Political Studies,* 42: 310-17.

Kamarck, A. M. 1976. *The Tropics and Economic Development.* Baltimore, Md.: Johns Hopkins University Press for the World Bank.

Kasperson. R.E., and Minghi, J.V., eds. 1969. *The Structure of Political Geography.* Chicago: Aldine.

Kavanagh. D. 1991. Why political science needs history. *Political Studies,* 39:479-95.

Key. V.O. 1950. *Southern Politico.* New York. Knopf.

Kindleberberger, C. P. 1965. *Economic Development.* 2nd edn. New York: McGraw-Hill.

Knutson, J. N., ed. 1973. *Handbook of Political Psychology.* San Francisco, Calif.: Jossey-Bass.

Konig, R. 1973. *Handbook der Empirischen Sozialforschung. 3rd* edn. Stuttgart: Enke.

Kuhn. T. S. 1957. *The Structure of Scientific Revolutions.* 1962 edn. Chicago: University of Chicago Press.

Kuhnle, S. 1982. Norway. In Andrews 1982:256-74.

Lambert, R.D., 1991. Blurring the disciplinary boundaries: area studies in the United States. In Easton and Schelling 1991:171-94.

Laponce, J. 1989. Political science: an import-export analysis of Journals and footnotes. *Political Studies, 28:*401-19.

Le Bon, G. 1912. *La Psychologie Politique.* Paris: Flammarion.

Leca, J. La science politique en France. *Revue Francaise de science politique,* 32/4:653-18.

Lepsius, R. M., ed. 1981. *Soziologie in Deutschland und Osterreich.* Opiaden: Westdeutscher Verlag.

Lerner, D. 1958. *The Passing of Traditional Society.* New York: Free Press.

Lewis, G. C. 1832. *Remarks on the Use and Abuse of Some Political Terms.* London: B. Fellowes.

Lewis, W. A. 1955. *The Theory of Economic Growth* Homewood, III.: Irwin.

Linz, J. J., and Miguei, A. de. 1966. Within-nation differences and comparisons: the eight Spains. Pp. 267-320 in *Comparing Nations: The Use of Quantitative Data in Cross-National Research, R. L.* Merritt and S. Rokkan. New Haven, Conn.: Yale University Press.

Lipset, S. M. 1959. *Political Man.* New York: Doubleday.

—— ed. 1969. *Politics and the Social Sciences.* New York: Oxford University Press.

——1979. *The First New Nation: The United States in Historical and Comparative Perspective.* New York: Norton.

—— and Hofstadter, R. 1968. *Sociology and History: Methods.* New York: Basic.

Loewenberg, P. 1983. *Decoding the Past: The Psychohistorical Approach.* New York: Knopf.

Lynn, N.B. 1983. Self-portrait: profile of political scientists. In Finifter 1983:114-15.

Mackenzie, W.J.M. 1967. *Politics and the Social Sciences.* Harmondsworth: Penguin.

Mackinder, H.J. 1904 The geographical pivot of history. *Geographical Journal,* 23:421-37; reprinted in *The Scope and Methods of Geography, and The Geographical Pivot of History,* ed. E. W. Gilbert. London: Royal Geographical Society, 1951.

Macridis, R.C. 1955. *The Study of Comparative Government.* New York: Random House.

Martinelli, A., and smelser, N. J. 1990. Economic sociology. *Current Sociology,* 38 (#2): 1-49.

Marvick, D., ed. 1977. *Harold Lasswell on Political Sociology.* Chicago: University of Chicago Press.

Mead, M. 1961. Anthropology among the sciences. *American Anthropologist,* 63:475-82.

Merton, R.M. 1973. *The Sociology of Science.* Chicago: University of Chicago Press.

Migdal, J. S. 1983. Studying the politics of development and change: the state of the art. In Finifter 1983:309-38.

Mitchell, W. C. 1969. The shape of political theory to come: from political sociology to political economy. In Lipset 1969:101-36.

Mommsen, W. J., and osterhammel, J. 1987. *Max Weber and His Contemporaries.* London: Alien and Unwin.

Narain, L, and mathur, P. C. 1982. India. In Andrews 1982:194-206.

O'Donnell, G.; Schmitter, P.; and whitehead, L, eds. 1986. *Transitions from Authoritarian Rule. 4 vols.* Baltimore, Md.: Johns Hopkins University Press.

Olson, M. 1965. *The Lope of Collective Action.* Cambridge, Mass.: Harvard University Press.

Organisation for economic cooperation and development (OECD). 1972. *Interdisciplinarity, Problems of Teaching and Research in Universities.* Paris: OECD.

Pye, L. W. 1958. The non-western political process. *Journal of Politics,* 20:468-86.

Radnitzky, G., and Bernholz, P., eds. 1986. *Economic Imperialism: The Economic Approach Outside the Traditional Areas of Economics.* New York: Paragon House.

Randall, V. 1991. Feminism and political analysis. *Political Studies,* 39:513-32.

Rokkan, S., et al 1995. Special issue dedicated to Rokkan's geo-economic-political model. *Revue Internationale de Politique Comparee,* 2(#1): 5-170.

Rostow, W.W. 1963. *The Stages of Economic Growth.* Cambridge: Cambridge University Press.

Ruin, O. 1982. Sweden. In Andrews 1982: 299-319.

Russett, B. M., *et al* 1965. *World Handbook of Political and Social Indicators.* New Haven, Conn.: Yale University Press.

Sartori, G. 1969. From the sociology of politics to political sociology. In Lipset 1969: 65-100.

Scheuch, E. K. 1966. Cross-national comparison using aggregate data. Pp. 131-67 in *Comparing Nations,* ed. R. Merritt and S. Rokkan. New Haven, Conn.: Yale University Press.

Sears, D.O., and funk, C.L. 1991. Graduate education in political psychology. *Political Psychology,* 2:345-62.

Siegfried, A. 1913. *Tableau Politique de la France de l'Ouest sous la III Republique.* Paris: Colin.

Sills, D.L., ed. 1968. *International Encyclopaedia of Social Sciences.* New York: Macmillan.

Simon, H.A. 1982. *Models of Bounded Rationality.* Cambridge, Mass.: MIT Press.

Smelser, N.J. 1967. Sociology and the other social sciences. Pp. 3-44 in *The Uses of Sociology, ed.* P. Lazarsfdd, W. H. Sewell, H. L. Wilensky. New York Basic.

Stouffer, S. A. 1950. *American Soldier.* Princeton, NJ: Princeton University Press.

Tonnies, F. 1887. *Gemeinschaft und Gesellschaft.* Berlin: **Curtius.**

Trent, I. E. 1979. Political science beyond political boundaries. In Rokkan 1979:181-99.

Truman, D.B. 1955. *The Governmental Process.* New York: Knopf.

Turner, F.J. 1959. *The Significance of the Frontier in American History.* Gloucester, Mass.:

P. Smith; originally published 1893.

United Nations. Department of International Economic and Social Affairs. 1957 *et seq. Reports on the World Social Situation.* New York: United Nations.

Valade, B. 1990. *Pareto: La naissance d'une autre sociologie.* Paris: P.U.F.

Vanhanen. T. 1984. *The Emergence of Democracy: A Comparative Study of 119 States, 1850-1979.* Helsinki: Finnish Society of Sciences and Letters.

Wallerstein, I. 1974. *Modem World System.* New York: Academic Press.

Weingart, P. 1986. T. S. Kuhn: revolutionnary or agent provocateur. In Deutsch *et al.*

1986:265-85.

Wiarda, H.J. 1989. Rethinking political development: a look backward over thirty years and a look ahead. *Studies in Comparative International Development,* 24 (#4): 65-82.

Wiese, L. von. 1926. *Soziologie, Geschichte und Hauptprobleme.* Berlin: De Gruyter.

3

Political History

An important branch of Political history is the narrative and analysis of political events, ideas, movements, and leaders. It is usually structured arounds thes nation states. Its is distincts froms, but related to, other fields of history such as social history, economic history, and military history.

Generally, political history focuses on events relating to nation-states and the formal political process. According to Hegel, Political History "is an idea of the state with a moral and spiritual force beyond the material interests of its subjects: it followed that the state was the main agent of historical change" This contrasts with one, for instance, social history, which focuses predominantly on the actions and lifestyles of ordinary people, or people's history, which is historical work from the perspective of common people.

Diplomatic history, sometimes referred to as "Rankian History" in honor of Leopold von Ranke, focuses on politics, politicians and other high rulers and views them as being the driving force of continuity and change in history. This type of *political history* is the study of the conduct of international relations between states or across state boundaries over time. This is the most common form of history and is often the classical and popular belief of what history should be.

Diplomatic history is the past aggregate of the art and practice of conducting negotiations between accredited persons representing groups or nations. Occurring in succession leading from the past to the present and even into the future regarding diplomacy, the conduct of state relations through the intercession of individuals with regard to issues of peace-making, culture, economics, trade and war. Diplomatic history records or narrates events relating to or characteristic of diplomacy.

Various Aspects

The first "scientific" political history was written by Leopold von Ranke in Germany in the 19th century. His methodologies profoundly affected the way historians critically examine sources; see historiography for a more complete analysis of the methodology of various approaches to history. An important aspect of political history is the study of ideology as a force for historical change. One author asserts that "political history as a whole cannot exist without the study of ideological differences and their implications." Studies of political history typically centre around a single nation and its political change and development.

Some historians identify the growing trend towards narrow specialization in political history during recent decades: "while a college professor in the 1940s sought to identify himself as a "historian", by the 1950s "American historian" was the designation." From the 1970s onwards, new movements sought to challenge traditional approaches to political history.

The development of social history and women's history shifted the emphasis away from the study of leaders and national decisions, and towards the role of ordinary citizens;

"...by the 1970s "the new social history" began replacing the older style. Emphasis shifted to a broader spectrum of American life, including such topics as the history of urban life, public health, ethnicity, the media, and poverty." As such, political history is sometimes seen as the more 'traditional' kind of history, in contrast with the more 'modern' approaches of other fields of history.

Political World History

The political history of the world is the history of the various political entities created by the Human race throughout their existence on Earth and the way these states define their borders.. The history of political thinking goes back to antiquity. Political history, and thus the history of political thinking throughout human existence stretches though up to Medieval period and the Renaissance. In the Age of Enlightenment, political entities expanded from basic systems of self-governance and monarchy to the complex democratic and communist systems that exist of the Industrialied and the Modern Era, in parallel, political systems have expanded from vaguely defined frontier-type boundaries, to the definite boundaries existing today.

Early Developments

Although much of existing written history might be classified as diplomatic history - Thucydides, certainly, is among other things, highly concerned with the relations among states - the modern form of diplomatic history was codified in the 19th century by Leopold von Ranke, a German historian. Ranke wrote largely on the history of Early Modern Europe, using the diplomatic archives of the European powers (particularly the Venetians) to construct a detailed understanding of the history of Europe *wie es eigentlich gewesen* ("as it actually happened.") Ranke saw diplomatic history as the most important kind of history to write because of his idea of the "Primacy of Foreign Affairs" (*Primat der Aussenpolitik*), arguing that the concerns of international relations drive the internal development of the state. Ranke's understanding of diplomatic history relied on the large number of official documents produced by modern western governments as sources.

Remarkably, Ranke's understanding of the dominance of foreign policy, and hence an emphasis on diplomatic history, remained the dominant paradigm in historical writing through the first half of the twentieth century. This emphasis, combined with the effects of the War Guilt Clause in the Treaty of Versailles (1919) which ended the First World War, led to a huge amount of historical writing on the subject of the origins of the war in 1914, with the involved governments printing huge, carefully edited, collections of documents and numerous historians writing multi-volume histories of the origins of the war. In general, the early works in this vein, including Fritz Fischer's controversial (at the time) 1961 thesis that German goals of "world power" were the principal cause of the war, fit fairly comfortably into Ranke's emphasis on *Aussenpolitik*.

Modern Developments

In the course of the 1960s, however, some German historians (notably Hans-Ulrich Wehler and his cohort) began to rebel against this idea, instead suggesting a "Primacy of Domestic Politics" (*Primat der Innenpolitik*), in which the insecurities of (in this case German) domestic policy drove the creation of foreign policy. This led to a considerable body of work interpreting the domestic policies of various states and the ways this influenced their conduct of foreign policy. At the same time, the middle of the twentieth century began to see a general de-emphasis on diplomatic history.

The French *Annales School* had already put an emphasis on the role of geography and economics on history, and of the importance of broad, slow cycles rather than the constant apparent movement of the "history of events" of high politics. The most important work of the *Annales* school, Fernand Braudel's *The Mediterranean and the Mediterranean World in the Age of Philip II*, contains a traditional Rankean diplomatic history of Philip II's Mediterranean policy, but only as the third and shortest section of a work largely focusing on the broad cycles of history in the *longue durée* ("long term"). The *Annales* were broadly influential, leading to a turning away from diplomatic and other forms of political history towards an emphasis on broader trends of economic and environmental change.

In the 1960s and 1970s, an increasing emphasis on giving a voice to the voiceless and writing the history of the underclasses, whether by using the quantitative statistical methods of social history or the more qualitative assessments of cultural history, also undermined the centrality of diplomatic history to the historical discipline. Nevertheless, diplomatic history has always remained a historical field with a great interest to the general public, and considerable amounts of work are still done in the field, often in much the same way that Ranke pioneered in the middle years of the 19th century.

REFERENCES

1. Brunner, Borgna, "The History of Women's History".
2. Burke, P. (1992). New perspectives on historical writing. University Park, Pa: Pennsylvania State University Press. Page 3.

3. Parthasarathi, Prasannan, "The State and Social History.
4. Politics: The historical development of economic, legal, and political ideas and institutions, ideologies and movements. In *The Dictionary of the History of Ideas*.
5. Richard J. Jensen, Historiography of American Political History. In Jack Greene, ed., *Encyclopedia of American Political History* (New York: Scribner's, 1984), vol 1. pp 1-25.
6. Tosh, John: *The Pursuit of History*, 2nd edition, London Group UK Limited, USA, 1991, pg.74

4

Political Economy

"Those who have finished by making all others think with them, have usually been those who began by daring to think with themselves."

—Charles C. Colton

Political Economy is rather recent offshoot of political science Traditionally, economic behaviour meant people making utility-maximising exchanges, and political behaviour meant people voting and joining interest groups. Of course, there were institutions. Exchanges took place in markets, which are institutions. Voting and lobbying suggest and existence of legislatures and majoritarian procedures. But the institutions were all *exogenous* and moreover, the economic and political institutions were seen as *separate,* not as part of the same overall structure surrounding human interactions.

It uses an economic approach, constrained maximising and strategic behaviour by self-interested agents, to explain the origins and maintenance of political processes and institutions and the formulation and implementation of public policies. At the same time, by focussing on how political and economic institutions constrain, direct, and reflect individual behaviour, it stresses the political context in which market phenomena take place and attempts to explain collective outcomes like production, resource allocation, and public policy in a unified fashion. In contrast to either economics or political science in isolation, this positive political economy emphasises both "economic" behaviour in the political process and "political" behaviour in the marketplace. Accordingly, we organise this review around institutions and policy. The *Handbook of Political Science* had no chapter entitled "political economy," though it did include ones on collective choice by Michael Taylor and on formal theory by Gerald Kramer and Joseph Hertzberg (1975).

> The major topics of what might be called modern political economy: the theory of preference and individual choice behaviour underlying much of formal theory; the notion of a multiperson behavioural equilibrium, and some of the mathematical tools needed to investigate it; some aspects of social choice theory, and related normative questions; and finally, some of the work on the theoretical analyses of political institutions (Kramer and Hertzberg 1975:354).

Remarkably, the rapid growth of the field of political economy in the last two decades is reflected in the fact that one of our topics, the theoretical study of institution formation, was then little more than an afterthought, while the other, the positive analysis of public policy, did not make the list of "major topics" at all. We devote the first half of this review to the origins, evolution, and maintenance of institutions, emphasising Congress-style legislatures, government formation in parliamentary systems, and bureaucracies.

This research program built on concepts from a generation of earlier "classic" works available by the time the *Handbook* appeared. They include Arrow's (1951/1963) discussion of cycles in majority voting and Black's (1958) median voter theorem, key elements of subsequent work on the *stabilising properties of voting institutions.* Downs's (1957) discussion of party competition and Riker's (1962) theory of coalition formation laid the groundwork for contemporary models of *the role of distributive politics in government formation.* Coase's (1937; 1960) costly transactions, Schelling's (1960) co-ordination games, and Buchanan and Tullock's (1962) relationship between supermajorities and externalities are at the heart of recent analyses of how economic and political institutions enable actors to *capture the gains from exchange,* just as Niskanen's (1971) bureaucratic information advantages foreshadow the analysis of *agency costs* in inter—and intra-institutional relationships.

The attempt to provide an integrated rational approach to the origins and policy consequences of political institutions brought new answers to older questions about institutional stability and fragility, the sources and effects of information asymmetries, and the over- all importance of institutions for the allocation of scarce and valued resources. The second half reviews the political economy of public policy, mostly economic and fiscal. We focus on the "new political economy" that grew at the intersection of macroeconomics, game theory, and social choice theory by making policy choice endogenous, rather than treating policy as either exogenous or chosen by the mythical "social planner."

On the contrary, policy is the result of some interaction between citizen-voters and policy- makers within institutions having certain characteristics. This literature has literally exploded in a variety of directions.

The Political Economy of Institutions

It is remarkable that Institutions help individuals deal

with certain fundamental problems of exchange, collective choice, and collective action. If nothing were ever chosen by vote, there would be no problem of cyclical instability. If there were no social (i.e.. Prisoners') Dilemmas, we would have less need to deal with problems of communication, co-operation, or co-ordination.

If information were freely available, specialisation and delegation would not produce agency costs. If there were no non-simultaneous exchange, *ex post* opportunism would not be a concern. However, all these problems exist, and institutions ubiquitously deal with the tradeoffs they create, providing opportunities for beneficial transactions that would not take place in the absence of the institutions. Political economists largely agree that in the presence of these problems, institutions increase predictability, reduce uncertainty, or induce stability in human interactions. This view of institutions echoes one of the rare occasions when the *Handbook* did address rational choice approaches, though even in Dennis Palumbo's chapter on organisation theory, the theory seemed too restrictive to be useful: "Many—perhaps most—decisions in organisations cannot be understood in terms of rational choice... They involve a great deal of uncertainty" (Palumbo 1975:361).

By contrast, today's political economist would ask how, if the uncertainty were so costly, rational individuals might redesign the organisation or help it evolve in a direction which would reduce uncertainty. Exactly that sort of question, how institutional changes affect the possibility of profitable transactions, is central to many recent analyses of economic and political institutions alike.

It is remarkable that is a sharp division between those who model institutions as (1) *equilibria* in some underlying social game and (2) rules, procedures, and choice *mechanisms* taken as pre-existing. Within the second, we connect two approaches to institutions as formal procedures to an ongoing debate about the relationship between transactions costs, institutions, and efficiency. In fact, since all of these share a transactions-costs approach to institutions, in the first half of this chapter we use this framework to examine recent research on legislatures.

Approaches to Institutions

Some, like Schotter (1981), define institutions as equilibria in an underlying social game. This approach emphasises the *self-enforcing* characteristic and *co-ordinating* function of institutions. If self-enforcing, they avoid the instabilities in collective choice and collective action which they are supposed to ameliorate. Models of such institutions focus on the conditions regarding common knowledge, shared information, and enforcement strategies which must be satisfied (Calvert 1995).

If institutions as equilibria solve *co-operation* problems by being self-enforcing, they solve *coordination* problems by fostering "focal points." Kreps (1990) shows how co-ordination of beliefs offers an equilibrium strategy for dealing with unforeseen contingencies in repeated interactions. Ideally, the formal analysis of self-enforcing regimes or constitutions would treat both aspects.

Notably, others take institutions as pre-existing, and define them to include diverse things like informal norms, complex formal organisations, and a variety of rules, procedures, and choice mechanisms that channel political and economic activity. A key insight motivating tills *procedural* analysis of institutions is that if individuals could make costless enforceable exchanges whenever they wished, there would often be no equilibria, and some beneficial transactions would not take place. Two particularly influential contributions are the structure-induced equilibrium (see Shepsle and Weingast 1987) and the Romer-Rosenthal "setter model" (Rosenthal 1990).

In the former approach, vetoes, gate-keeping, or agenda power arise in jurisdictions, which are specified domains of responsibility or control, like divisions in firms or specialised committees in legislatures, perhaps backed by further rules requiring self-restraint by other actors.

These institutional features are sources of friction which prevent certain comparisons from being made socially, or otherwise limit the number of enforceable policy outcomes, imposing structure on what would otherwise be disorderly choice processes. The "setter model" has a little more structure: a proposer who places a proposal in play, a defined sequence of moves which result in the proposal being subject to a "take it or leave it" choice, and a "status quo" which is the reversion point if the choice is to "leave it."

This little sketch of political action turns out, like supply and demand curves, to help analysts make straightforward predictions in some institutionally complex situations. Many of the works reviewed below on Congress and bureaucracy, for example, are applications of this model, which is discussed extensively by Weingast .

In all these approaches, the design of economic and political institutions affects how far transactions costs allow or prevent achieving gains from exchange. Transactions costs include the resources consumed in discerning product quality, observing performance, protecting property rights (whether with fences or lawyers), obtaining enforcement of an agreement, or even lobbying.

They include the costs of organisation and bargaining. This sort of transactions cost is incurred within institutions whenever some individuals bargain with or act to influence the holder of a jurisdiction (Milgrom and Roberts 1990) or whenever any group of actors attempts to purchase some property right valuable to them. This second type of cost is as ubiquitous as institutions themselves, but it is not simply a resource cost.

Like the incentive difficulties resulting from principal-agent problems within a firm, the possibility of costly delay or failure to reach an agreement (whether it stems from enforcement depending on laws subject to revision by majorities or specialisation requiring delegation to an agent) often cannot even be overcome by the straightforward application of more resources: From the literature on incentive-compatible mechanisms under asymmetric information we know that there is no way to bring about an outcome to this problem corresponding to the perfect revelation of preferences with-out incurring some efficiency shortfall ... [T]his shortfall ... does not represent the expenditure of resources that could have been put to some next-best use, because the... incentive problem precludes ever doing any better (Calvert 1995).

The argument that differing transactions costs largely frame the choice between different organisational or institutional forms has been a main theme in the study of institutions over the last two decades. It has found many areas of application: the nature, structure, and allocation of property rights, organisational differences and the efficiency of firms, the practice and consequences of regulation, the nature of democratic institutions, and the "Great Debate" itself between central planning of economies and more decentralised capitalistic forms. From starting-points in the works of Coase (1960) and Alchian and Demsetz (1972), Williamson (1993) and others argue that, given a particular structure of transactions costs in some economic activity, there is in principle some best institutional arrangement to minimise the incidence of these costs.

Williamson claims that underlying relationships between types of adaptation, governance structures, and forms of contract law mean that, where it is cost-effective, far-sighted parties will deliberately create bilateral dependencies supported by contractual safeguards of the appropriate sort. For instance, parties making highly specific investments (for example, a power plant located at the mouth of a coal mine, where neither is likely to have good substitute partners) should surround themselves with distinctively contingent contracts. Joskow (1988) reviews some empirical work consistent with this argument. Some believe that market-like forces drive emerging institutions to the form necessary to achieve this "best" realistic-institutional level of economic activity (Posner 1977).

Others propose evolutionary mechanisms by which such efficient institutions emerge (Rubin 1977; Nelson and Winter 1982), analogous to evolutionary mechanisms for cultural transmission where learning is costly (Boyd and Richerson 1994). However, limited systematic empirical evidence, some experiments, and a lot of historical analysis suggest that the actual evolution of institutions looks nothing like the aggregate purposive implementation or even decentralised natural selection of efficient forms (North 1990). Once institutions have been created (for whatever reason), they generate constituencies of support in government, business, and even the public and become difficult to dislodge or improve.

The property-rights literature is replete with examples

of institutions which reduce efficiency and whose main effect is to redistribute, as varied as rent control in Hong Kong (Cheung 1975) and salmon-fishing rights in Washington (Higgs 1982). Moreover, even an initially efficient institution may be impossible to alter, even if changing conditions make it dysfunctional, as David's (1985) account of the QWERTY typewriter keyboard standard suggests. Political changes also have economic effects. Rosenthal (1989) shows how an "unintended" consequence of the French Revolution was to allow a lot of "efficient" water projects which had previously been politically impossible. Levi (1988) shows how the incentives of French governments in creating economic institutions worked against efficiency for long periods.

However, any so-called "inefficiency" of these institutions arises from the "costliness" of the collective action that would be necessary to change them, which is itself partly determined by other political institutions. It is precisely this costliness of change that insures that institutions can last long enough to have effects on economic and political outcomes. This division over whether institutions are efficient has been tran-scended by those in investigating the construction of *durable* institutions, which are designed to enforce *some* distributional outcome (and thus inefficiency" relative to some normative standard) over time by making credible the commitment of the "enacting coalition" to this distribution. This literature extends a familiar theme in a new direction. Contracts have to be enforced, but conveying to individuals the power to enforce also conveys the power to extract.

Under what circumstances will rational individual so empowered refrain from extracting? How can the commitment to refrain be made credible? Ostrom (1990) describes a variety of transparent, simple, self-enforcing, durable arrangements for the exploitation of common-pool resources. Weingast's chapter (above: chap. 5) discusses other cases where reputation and decentralisation are key elements of durable institutions.

The Political Economy of Legislatures

It is remarkable that three "camps" of political economy theories about legislative institutions, all based on the U.S. Congress, all involving some aspect of costly exchange or information, respectively explain institutional adaptation to secure costly but beneficial exchanges, to alleviate social dilemmas and to disperse the gains from specialisation among legislators, who are assumed to have different purposes which reflect their concerns about re-election, personal views of good public policy, institutional ambitions, and also the influence of others (Shepsle and Weingast 1994).

Weingast and Marshall (1988) describe how such *heterogeneous tastes* make the exchange of support necessary if legislators are to achieve their objectives. An immense, highly successful theoretical and empirical literature described how the American Congress developed to facilitate exchanges, to deal with imperfect information, to co-ordinate members' activities, and to contain agency problems (Shepsle and Weingast 1994).

There are possible gains from exchange when the value a legislator places on the benefits from his or her own projects exceeds the burdens he or she must bear in supporting the projects of other legislators as part of a deal. But partners need to be identified, and deals need to be enforced, to have extended lives, and to have future benefit flows secured against unanticipated events. Replacing repeated "spot-market-like" one-at-a-time exchanges of support with an institutionalised form of deal-making economises on these transaction costs, in Fiorina's (1987) words:

> Thus legislatures establish committees with specialised jurisdictions, permit their members to self-select positions on committees with greatest interest..., and adopt "norms" that lubricate the gears of the system... [which] allows members to exercise disproportionate influence on the formulation and implementation of policies important for their electoral interest and provides a variety of opportunities to claim political credit....

To work, such a committee system must foster self-selection by legislators (honor individual preferences in the committee assignment process), retain extraordinary influence in their respective policy areas (combining gate-keeping and proposal power, relatively restrictive amendment rules, control over conference committee proceedings, and oversight authority), and adapt to the rise of new issues and changing legislative interests.

However, decentralised jurisdictions can also create *market imperfections* like social dilemmas. For example, decoupling taxes and spending produces deficits (Kiewiet and McCubbins 1991). Such problems in turn stimulate institutional developments which smooth out the imperfections and expand the opportunities for co-operation. Thus, individual legislators facing a collective dilemma (by acting alone they cannot capture the gains from legislation for their district) will devise mechanisms to capture potential gains. This is how to explain the development and importance to the larger institution of leadership and party organisation (Cox and McCubbins 1993). Cox and McCubbins (1993) ask: Why and with what effects are parties the basis of legislative organisation?

How do they interact with the committee structure and affect public policy-making?

While legislators' tastes are heterogeneous, on many aspects of policy they broadly agree. The majority party, if united in political purpose, can seize legislative authority and (re)design legislative institutions and practices (like the committee system) to pursue its political agenda. Congressional parties are a sort of legislative cartel. To gain from party labels (a collective reputation from which individual legislators can benefit), party members must create collective mechanisms for resolving disputes. Committee composition via assignments, the production and scheduling of committee products, and the control of the floor fall come under party control.

Parties will permit less self-selection and scrutinise appointments more carefully to those committees whose policies entail greater externalities for the re-election prospects of many partisans. Cox and McCubbins (1993) present extensive empirical evidence to support their view of the representativeness of committees.

Political economy also provides an alternative, *informational rationale* for legislative organisation. All members stand to benefit from the provision of information by experts, and committees provide that expertise. Thus, as Shepsle and Weingast (1994) put it, committees are not only transactions-cost-economising agents of distribution but are also specialised factors of production. Committees serve as specialised bodies of experts that collect and reveal information bearing on the relation between public policies and social outcomes. The point, as set forth in Krehbiel's (1991) book and a series of papers summarised in Gilligan (1993), is that if legislators do not know the precise relationship between the policy instruments they select and the outcomes these instruments subsequently produce, they would like to update and improve their beliefs by collecting new information. Then institutional arrangements reflect the need to acquire and disseminate information in addition to (or instead of) the need to solve distributional issues.

Majorities will provide incentives and convey resources to specialised committees who invest in becoming experts. Committees maybe powerful in a legislature not (only) because they monopolise agenda power, but (also) because they monopolise information and expertise. When such new information is disseminated, it can, in turn, affect the policy choices of the whole legislature. A host of empirically-testable implications follow. First, to limit the potential agency losses (to the legislature as a whole) from specialisation, committees should in general not be composed chiefly of preference outliers (legislators far from the center of opinion in the legislature) but rather should reflect a more centrist, median position.

Similarly, conference committees (those resolving disputes between chambers) should reflect majoritarian sentiments. Gilligan and Krehbiel also suggest that to provide committees with incentives to become expert, majorities will often want to impose restrictive procedures on themselves to prevent tampering with committee outputs by the floor. Such self-imposed constraints should be more likely, and more likely to be effective, the more representative committees are of the parent body. Many of these implications are directly in conflict with those of the other "camps," and so the next few years' empirical work will be decisive. This literature is dominated by the study of the U.S. Congress: it is therefore excellent but narrow. There is a parallel literature on relations between Congress,

President, and bureaucracy (Moe 1984; 1990) which we discuss below, and we describe a policy model which explicitly takes into account the wishes of the President (Alesina and Rosenthal 1995). There is a nascent political economy literature on how transactions costs affect the organisation of parliamentary legislatures, but with what economic consequences (Palmer 1995; Moe and Caldwell 1994; Spolaore 1993).

After a quiet period, there has also been a recent resurgence of interest in the relationship between party policies, political institutions, and the process of forming governments.

The Political Economy of Government Formation

Early coalition models, of which Riker (1962) is the exemplar, treated coalition formation as a game played between parties for a prize denominated in Cabinet seats. Nearly all the early game-theoretic approaches assumed parties were *office*-seeking rather than policy-motivated. They also took a co-operative approach by assuming that any deals which were struck were exogenously enforced, avoiding the need to confront and model transactions costs.

Moreover, the lack of actors' subsequent opportunism (desire to renege on an agreement) gave these models a myopic quality. In addition, few contained any descriptions of ways in which institutions impinged on the process of government formation, in spite of rich descriptions which were readily available (Laver and Schofield 1990). Finally, even those coalition theories based on an assumption of policy-seeking politicians assumed that a winning coalition, if it existed, could form at any point in the policy space. Just recently, however, there has been an proliferation of models and approaches. Some of these advance formalisations in the older, spatial-model, co-operative-game tradition.

Others, however, introduce sophisticated agents and costly transactions in a variety of forms, including specific sequences in play imposed by institutions, restriction to self-enforcing (rather than exogenously enforced) bargains, indivisibilities in policy outcomes, and politicians' desire to make credible commitments in order to attract electoral support. These models attack precisely the problems of collective choice and collective action which are at the heart of the newer political economy approach.

Schofield (1992; 1993) applies theoretical conditions for the existence of spatial equilibrium points in a weighted majority-rule setting to government formation in legislatures with political parties of various sizes. He establishes necessary and sufficient conditions for the existence of structurally stable majority cores, majority cores that are robust to small perturbations in parties' ideal points. He shows that in a multidimensional policy space in which party ideal points are located, for any minimum winning coalition of parties there is a coalition's *compromise set,* bounded by the lines connecting party ideal points, die set of policy points from which departure to any other point harms at least one of the coalition parties. A policy point is a core point if and only if it lies in the compromise set of *every* minimum-winning coalition. If the intersection of these compromise sets is empty, then there is no core. A "core party" is a party whose ideal *-policy* is a core point. When such a party exists, the government which forms will contain it, maybe as a single-policy minority government or as a coalition with other parties. Either way, policy will reflect the core party's ideal point.

When a core party does not exist, as is often the case, Schofield's theory predicts an outcome in the cycle set, the region of the space within which cycles amongst coalitions and policies are likely to be located. Either the core or the cycle set must exist. Hopefully, the latter is reasonably compact, so that testable predictions of outcomes can be made.

Austen-Smith and Banks (1988) provide a formal model of government formation in which parties (based on size) take turns attempting to form coalitions (an institutionally imposed sequence of moves), actors are not myopic, and their expectations take into account a reversion point if each attempt fails, and parties suffer a subsequent electoral penalty based on how far from their promises they stray in order to form a coalition.

The model leads to predictions of coalitions between large and small parties. Baron (1991) uses a similar setup, with an explicit vote of confidence mechanism determining when a government forms. An important feature of these non-co-operative approaches is that any "co-operative" ventures such as forming coalitions or making policy compromises which do arise do so because it is in every co-operators' interest to stick to the deal they have negotiated.

The models we have reviewed so far concentrate on the equilibrium collective policy that emerges given the balance and distribution of party strengths in the parliament. It is also possible to think of governments as collections of ministers with individual jurisdictions, rather than as a body collectively responsible for a single outcome. In the case where ministers have jurisdictions, the outcome is a bundle of individual party-preferred policies, rather than an average of spatial locations, depending on which party receives which portfolio. Jurisdiction makes a party's promises credible to its electors, for it can carry them out (only) if it receives the relevant ministry.

At the same time portfolio allocation monitors party behaviour, for the party receiving a portfolio has no excuse for not carrying out its preferred policy, and thus no incentives to misrepresent its desires. This approach to ministerial specialisation potentially opens up models of government formation to the considerations of the costs and benefits of specialisation and delegation, discussed in other sections. Laver and Shepsle (1996) analyse a portfolio-based model of government formation, based on a constitutionally established sequence of proposals from a historically determined status quo. They see bargaining taking place among rationally foresighted policy-motivated parties, each of which has an explicit veto over every cabinet in which it could participate, in a lattice of feasible governments (rather than a continuous space) in which every actual or potential government is a discrete entity with a particular forecast policy output.

The only effective way for legislators to control a government is to credibly threaten to or actually replace it with another government. Their predictions give important roles to a "strong" party, one which participates in (and can thus veto) every cabinet preferred by a majority over its ideal, the cabinet in which the strong party takes all portfolios.

Even though comparing predictions of policy outcomes with predictions of portfolio allocations is difficult, there now appear to exist significant possibilities for empirical evaluations of these contending models.

Political Economy of Bureaucracy

Remarkably, Niskanen (1971) models the bureaucracy

as a monopoly seller of services, with private information about its costs, diminishing returns to scale, the maximisation of agency budgets as its source of utility, and a quiescent legislature as the buyer of its output. Each of these assumptions can be relaxed, and Niskanen's conclusion that bureaucracy grows in a democracy changes accordingly. Miller and Moe (1983) activated the legislature to highlight the information revelation that could take place in a bargaining situation. This drew scholarly attention to the question of whether the legislature or bureaucracy was "dominant."

This was a somewhat black-and-white way to ask how the costs and benefits were actually shared in a situation in which some "slack" or "drift" between goals and outcomes was inevitable. However, choices over institutional design affect the extent and distribution of slack, and design choices themselves depend on assumption about what agents maximise. Since largely the same functions were performed by state-owned enterprises in some countries and by private firms regulated by commissions in others, such choices clearly exist, and follow the same principles we have discussed above.

As in the "informational rationale for committees," issue complexity and the inherent consequent desire to take advantage of specialisation leads representative assemblies to rely on the opinions and actions of experts.

Rather than bear the costs of becoming informed, legislators *who* want to develop effective policies but lack the needed expertise often delegate the jobs of fact-finding and policy development to others like bureaucrats, presidents, government ministers, party leaders, as well as to legislative committees. Delegation to an expert can be an effective substitute for the acquisition of expertise.

However, it can involve "agency costs" since the experts can use their expertise to take actions whose consequences are both unknown to legislators and detrimental to legislative interests. In short, experts can use their expertise to seize control of the policy-making process from legislators.

Thus, legislators face the problem of how to realise the potential benefits of delegation without abdicating their control over policy (Lupia and McCubbins 1994). Moreover, the exchange between legislators and constituents is typically not simultaneous. The flow of benefits to legislators is usually more immediate than the flow of benefits to constituents.

Constituents run the risk that this or subsequent legislative coalitions might undermine the benefits of legislation, quite legally, and without any prospects of compensation (Moe 1990). This is also a problem for legislators because forward-looking constituents will assess the durability of future legislative benefits and costs and reflect that assessment in the degree of electoral support that they are willing to offer."

In short, the expected net benefit flow from the legislation will be capitalised into present value of the legislation and therefore into the net political support offered to the enacting coalition. It is often assumed that although legislatures cannot be bound, the enacting coalition can influence the costs that subsequent coalitions must incur to modify a deal at the legislative level as well as the administrative level.

The real threat to the durability of the enacting coalition's deal is that future legislators will undermine the value of the legislation by altering the way it is administered or enforced. In particular, the enacting coalition can try to add to the durability of their deal with constituents by reducing the scope of delegated authority and by delegating that authority to an agent, like the court, that is relatively independent of the incumbent legislature (Landes and Posner 1975). However, an agency problem arises again here. The enacting coalition and its constituents must delegate to implement their arrangement, but their agents do not necessarily share the objectives of the enacting coalition and its constituents, and so the enacting coalition cannot be sure that its administrative agent will administer the legislation in the manner intended at enactment.

It is difficult to monitor these agents and create a system of ex *post* rewards and sanctions that will insure they act to protect the interests represented at enactment. Even imperfectly faithful implementation can only be secured with significant agency costs that include the costs of selecting administrators and monitoring their compliance (but legislative oversight is time-consuming), using *ex post* corrective devices (rewards, sanctions and subsequent legislative direction), and the cost of any residual non-compliance that produces a difference between the policy enacted and what is implemented (since the agent knows more about the merits of alternative administrative decisions than either the enacting legislature or its constituents).

Precisely in this spirit, McCubbins, Noll, and Weingast (1987; 1989) argue that the creation of a new agency (or new mission for an agency) is a principal-agent problem between the enacting coalition, which seeks to have a durable arrangement implemented, and the bureaucratic entity will that implement the arrangement. While imperfect monitoring, the need to give agents some discretion, and the possibility that agents' preferences differ from those of the principals mean that there will always be agency losses, they stress how these costs can be limited (not eliminated) by features of the appointment process and by a variety of procedural controls. Analyses of some systems characterised as legislator-dominant (the U.S. in some treatments; see Weingast and Moran 1984) and others as bureaucrat-dominant are appearing. Horn (1995) theorises that legislators generally decide the type of organisation that will be used (for example, state-owned enterprises for sales-financed production rather than bureaus for tax-financed production; courts rather than regulatory commissions) by minimising the sum of the 'transactions costs they face in any given situation.

The costs are those of reaching a decision (as in "legislatures," above), agency, commitment (durability), and uncertainty (inherent in all arrangements). The key dimensions along which institutional choices are made include the extent to which decisions are delegated (especially the degree of legislative vagueness), the governance structure of the administrative agent (especially the way senior personnel are selected, the degree of statutory independence from the legislature and the jurisdiction of the administrative agent), the rules that specify the procedures that must be followed in administrative decision-making (including the rights of constituents to participate in the administrative process), the nature and degree of legislative monitoring and the ability to use *ex post* rewards and sanctions, and the "rules" governing the allocation and use of capital and labour; in particular, the extent to which agencies are financed by sales revenues rather than taxes and the administrators' employment conditions.

Horn reviews case study evidence which is consistent with many of his conjectures, but exciting opportunities for systematic empirical work clearly exist here.

Political Economy of Public Policy

Now coming to the effects of institutions on public policy, in a political economy framework. For the most part, we treat the institutions as exogenous, even though the first half of this chapter was about how institutions can be endogenous. However, assuming institutional exogeneity is justified if institutions are either self-enforcing or, at least, difficult to change because of significant costs of collective choice or collective action, at least in the short term.

Political Business Cycles

Remarkably, literature on political business cycles developed in two phases. First, in the mid-1970s, Nordhaus (1975) and Hibbs (1977) identified two different types of cycles. Nordhaus emphasised an "opportunistic" cycle according to which incumbent politicians of any party stimulate the economy before each election, in order to win and continue in office. Hibbs identified a "partisan" cycle in which the Left fights unemployment even at the cost of increasing inflation, while the Right fights inflation even at the cost of higher unemployment. Both these opportunistic and partisan models were based upon a traditional, pre-rational expectations approach to macroeconomics. The second phase took off in the mid-1980s as a branch of the game-theoretic approach to the positive theory of macroeconomic policy. "Rational" versions of both opportunistic and partisan models appeared.

This second generation of models departs from its predecessors in two important ways. First, the assumption of rational expectations makes real economic activity less directly and predictably influenced by economic policy in general, and monetary policy in particular. Second, rationality implies that the voters cannot be systematically fooled in equilibrium.

This approach is (or used to be) the most popular type of "political business cycle" model. The most famous contribution is due to Nordhaus (1975), whose model hinges on three crucial assumptions: (i) the economy is characterised by an exploitable Phillips curve with backward-looking expectations; (ii) politicians only care about winning elections; and (iii) voters are retrospective and naive; they reward the incumbent if the economy is "doing well" (i.e., growth is high) in the period immediately before the election. Under these assumptions, Nordhaus derives the following implications: (i) every government follows the same policy; (ii) towards the end of his term of office, the incumbent stimulates the economy, to take advantage of the "short run" more favourable Phillips curve; (iii) the rate of inflation increases around the election time as a result of the pre-electoral economic expansion; after the election, inflation is reduced with contractionary policies. Thus, one should observe high growth and low unemployment before every election and a recession after even.- election.

One line of research maintains the assumption of opportunistic politicians in "political business cycle" models in which voters are rational but imperfectly informed about some characteristic of incumbents, in particular, about their "competence" in handling the economy. The competence of policy-makers is defined as their ability to reduce waste in the budget process (Rogoff 1990; Rogoff and Sibert 1988), to promote growth without inflation (Persson and Tabellini 1990) or to insulate the economy from random shocks (Cukierman and Meltzer 1986).

If policy-makers are more informed than the citizens

about their own competence but try to appear as competent as possible, they behave in ways leading to a Nordhaus-style political business cycle. However, voters' rationality and awareness of politicians' incentives limit politicians' "opportunistic" behaviour.

In fact, if politicians appear too openly opportunistic, they are punished by the electorate. Thus, the political cycles in these rational models are more short-lived, smaller in magnitude, and less regular than in Nordhaus's model, and more likely to be observed in policy instruments than in policy outcomes.

A "strong" version of the partisan model (Hibbs 1977; 1987) holds that different parties can take advantage of an exploitable Phillips curve to bring about their desired outcomes. Thus, the Left chooses a point on the Phillips curve with less unemployment and more inflation; the Right chooses a point with the opposite combination. These different preferences are due to the distributional consequences of macroeconomic outcomes. These differences in macroeconomic outcomes are thus permanent, lasting for the entire term of office of the different parties.

Alesina (1987) proposed a model which later became known as the "rational partisan theory." He retains Hibbs's assumption that different parties have different preferences over inflation and unemployment, but he embodies this assumption in a rational expectation model with nominal wage stickiness. This model generates a political cycle if nominal wage contracts are signed at discrete intervals and electoral outcomes are uncertain.

Given the sluggishness in wage adjustments, changes in the inflation rate associated with changes in governments create temporary deviations of real economic activity from its natural level. In fact, uncertainty about electoral outcomes creates post-election unexpected inflation shocks. The model has the following implications: (i) at the beginning of a Right (Left) government, output growth is below (above) its natural level, and unemployment is above (below) its natural level; (ii) after expectations, prices, and wages adjust, output and unemployment return to their natural level, and after this adjustment period (which lasts for no more than a couple of years) the level of economic activity is independent of the party in office; (iii) the rate of inflation should remain higher throughout the term of a Left government. The inflation rate remains higher when the Left is in office even after the level of economic activity returns to its natural level partly because of a credibility problem. In sum, this rational partisan model differs from the traditional one because it emphasises how the differences in growth and unemployment associated with changes of government are only temporary.

It is pertinent to note that a vast literature has explored the empirical implications of these models, with data from the United States and from other industrial economies. It finds that:

1) "Nordhaus's model is generally and unambiguously rejected regarding its implications about unemployment and growth;
2) consistent with the "rational" version of the opportunistic model, one observes occasional short-run manipulations of policy instruments (monetary and fiscal) around elections, but these effects are small and do *not* imply regular cycles in unemployment as predicted by the traditional model;
3) partisan effects on growth and unemployment are

widespread but are not persistent; they disappear about two years after the election of a new government;

4) left-wing governments are associated with permanently higher inflation right-wing ones.

First, the new theories of political cycles based on the paradigm of rational choice and rational expectations, are more successful empirically than their predecessors. Second, the partisan model out-performs the opportunistic model as an explanation of politically induced macroeconomic fluctuations of GNP growth, unemployment, and inflation.

Moreover, political business cycle models in general, and partisan models in particular, are more applicable and in fact perform better in two-party or two-bloc systems. The evidence from the U.S. is consistent with that of other two-party or two-bloc party systems.

The important differences are *not* but between the U.S. and parliamentary democracies in general, but between two-party or two-bloc systems and countries typically governed by "middle-of-the-road" coalition governments.

A large, convincing, empirical literature shows that the state of the economy in an election year has strong effects on election results. This observation raises two puzzles. First, why, if a strong growth performance in election years increases the probability of re-electing the incumbent, do incumbents not achieve a higher than average growth rate in election years (as argued in the previous subsection)?

Then there is the effect of the economy on presidential and congressional elections in the U.S., which is much stronger on the former than on the latter. Furthermore, the President's party always loses support in mid-term congressional elections, even when growth is high in the first two years. The second puzzle is why this is so, and moreover, why even Democratic presidents suffer a mid-term loss despite their high growth performance in the first two years. In order to answer these puzzles, Alesina and Rosenthal (1995) provide a model in which the macroeconomic cycle and electoral results are jointly determined. This model has several key building-blocks.

First, the two parties are politically motivated, and the economy is described as in the rational partisan model above. Second, administrative competence influences the growth performance. Voters also have ideological preferences *and,* in addition, prefer more to less competent administrations. Therefore, it is rational for the voters to judge the incumbent's competence by observing the pre-electoral growth of the economy and by (rationally) trying to disentangle the effects of competence from those of "luck," that is, favourable exogenous shocks.

Third, there is no asymmetry of information between policy-makers and voters. This assumption rules out opportunistic behaviour by policy-makers. Fourth, policy outcomes depend upon which party holds the presidency, and upon the partisan composition of Congress. With a Republican president, for instance, the larger the share of the Democratic party in Congress, the more policy is pulled toward the ideal policy of the Democratic party, and vice-versa. Fifth, middle of the road voters use "institutional balancing" to bring about moderate policies.

Since policy must reflect a compromise between President and Congress, moderate voters (those with preferences in between those of the two parties) balance by turning to the party opposite that of the President in congressional elections. The following example (written before the 1994 elections!) illustrates the model. Suppose that a Democratic president, who was a slight favourite according to the polls, is elected. This tilts the electorate in favour of the Republican party in the next Home elections in order to moderate the favoured Democratic candidate to the White House.

The Democratic administration follows expansionary policies, which lead to an upsurge of growth in the first two years of the term, and to an increase in inflation. Therefore, in mid-term, the electorate further balances the Democratic administration by turning to the Republican party: the voters want to insure themselves against excessive inflation. This voting behaviour implies a non-obvious correlation, that strong economic growth in the first half of the Democratic administration is accompanied by a poor showing of this party in midterm. Empirical work by Alesina and Rosenthal (1995) shows that this whole model performs remarkably well through the period 1915-89.

This model is consistent with many regularities of the American political economy and provides a coherent framework which encompasses *all the* following observations, which earlier literature typically studied one at a time:

1) The vote share of the incumbent president party's presidential candidate increases with the rate of GNP growth in the election year.
2) Congressional elections are less sensitive to economic conditions; the economy influences these elections only through its effect on presidential votes.
3) There is a mid-term cycle where the party holding the White House loses votes in mid-term.

4) GNP growth exhibits a partisan cycle with short-run post-electoral deviations from average growth.
5) the rate of GNP growth in election years is not systematically different from average.

Political Economy of Budget Deficits

The subject of budget deficits has been a center of attention of the "public choice" literature for decades. The recent impetus to this area of research comes from the emergence of very large peacetime public debt in several, but not all, OECD economies. In fact, Grilli, Masciandaro, and Tabellini (1991) show that OECD countries can be divided into two clearly identifiable groups. In one group, including Belgium, Ireland, Italy, Greece, the Netherlands, and Spain, the ratio of total public debt to GNP is very high and/or increasing rapidly. In another group, which includes Australia, France, Germany, the United Kingdom, Japan, and Denmark, debt to GNP ratios are much lower and stable. By international standards the United States belongs to the second group of relatively low debt countries. However, even in the United States, the rapid increase in the debt/GNP ratio in the 1980s reversed a downward trend which started at the end of the Second World War.

The difference in the debt to GNP ratios in otherwise relatively similar OECD economies is staggering. Belgium, Ireland, and Italy owe more than 100 percent of a year's GDP; Italy is currently pushing toward 120 percent The debt/GNP ratio of several countries in the low debt group is about one *fourth* of that value.

These large differences across OECD countries are relatively recent They started to appear in the mid-1970s and have increased since then. We examine how far political economy approaches have been able to answer two questions, namely: why do we observe large peacetime deficits and debt, and why did they appear "now," namely in the last twenty years? Why do we observe large public debts in some countries but not in others?

Tax Smoothing Theory

A point of departure is the normative theory of public debt, known as "tax smoothing" theory (Barro 1979). The principle of tax smoothing is simple, but quite powerful. Budget deficits and surpluses should be used to minimise the distortionary effects of taxation, given a certain path of government spending. The implication is that tax rates should be kept approximately constant and budget deficits (surpluses) should be used as a buffer to compensate for temporary fluctuations of tax revenues (due to fluctuations in income) and spending.

Thus, one should observe deficits during recessions and during periods of exceptionally high (and temporary) spending, for instance, during wars. To be sure, the tax smoothing theory goes a long-way toward explaining the long run trend of public debt in the United States and United Kingdom. However, it cannot answer the two questions raised above. In particular, the tax smoothing theory has very little to say on the second question.

It is very hard to explain the very large cross-country variance is debt purely based upon a tax smoothing argument. Under perfect information, tax smoothing can minimise long-run costs of adjusting fiscal policy. Politico-economic approaches, seeking to ground positive models which encompass strategic behaviour, depart from the tax smoothing theory by pointing out the possible consequences of imperfect information, social dilemmas and institutional processes, beyond the purely economic factors emphasised by the tax-smoothing model.

We describe four different approaches which combine asymmetric information and collective action problems in different ways: (i) fiscal illusion; (ii) intergenerational redistribution; (iii) political conflict and instability; and (iv) institutional processes.

Intergenerational Redistribution

In models where the "Ricardian equivalence" does not hold, public debt generates intergenerational redistributions if the generation that is alive today, and votes, leaves the burden of the debt to future generations. Cukierman and Meltzer (1989) argue that public debt can be a way for those in the current generation who are "poor" to leave negative bequests to their offspring, since private negative bequests are not permissible. The idea that public debt redistributes in favour of the current generation, the only generation that the political influence, is quite powerful, at leas at first sight. However, again, this overlapping generation model cannot explain "why now?" (we always had parents and children) nor "why is certain countries and not in others?" (parents and children are everywhere).

Fiscal Illusion

The "public choice" school of Buchanan, Tullock and their associates (Buchanan and Wagner 1977; Buchanan, Rowley and Tollison 1986) made the concept of "fiscal illusion" central in their models of budget deficits. In a nutshell, the idea is that voters overestimate the benefits of current expenditures and underestimate the burden of future taxation. They do not internalise the government's budget constraint. Opportunistic politicians take advantage of this illusion by raising spending more than taxes. However, "fiscal illusion" theory does not answer either of the two-questions above. The theory implies that any democracy at any point in time should be in deficit. This contradicts the evidence. Moreover, fiscal illusion theory in unconvincing in that it relies heavily on a particular form of voter irrationality, a specific bias in vote perceptions. Recent politico-economic literature on budget deficits, as well as modern political economy more generally, relies on standard notions of "rational choice."

Political Conflicts and Instability

These models emphasise socio-political conflicts, partisan politics, and government fragility as determinants of public debt. They separate in treating debt sometimes as a *commitment* and sometimes as the result of *government fragmentation.* In the first case, commitment, debt is used by current partisan governments to constrain and influence the choice of future governments with different preference. Public debt is increased in polarised situations by partisan governments that expect to be followed by opponents from the opposite end of the political spectrum. A high public debt limits the choices of future governments, since a larger fraction of tax revenues must be committed to servicing the debt.

Empirically, this line of research implies that frequent government changes back and forth between polarised parties should be associated with large public debts. While this approach can potentially answer both questions, the evidence, though seeming generally to go in the "right direction," is often anecdotal and unsystematic. A different way of looking at political conflict emphasises fragmentation within the government, rather than polarisation between one government and the next. Alesina and Drazen (1991) formalise a "war of attrition" model of delayed fiscal adjustment which occurs only when one group stops using their veto power.

Delays in adjustment and debt accumulation are "rational" in this social dilemma model, since the passage of time is necessary to establish which group(s) is (are) the weakest, though costs can be avoided if all groups can agree at the outset on an equitable, co-operative rule to share the burden of adjustment. This model implies that coalition governments are more likely than single party governments to run into fiscal imbalances (Spolaore 1993). Moreover, coalition governments (and, generally, fragmented and short-lived governments) do not *create* deficits, but rather postpone adjustment through legislative deadlock. This approach can also answer both our basic questions, and apparently does so, at least to some extent. Empirical work on OECD economies by Roubini and Sachs (1989*a*; 1989*b*) and Grilli, Masciandaro, and Tabellini (1991) shows that measures of government fragmentation are strongly associated with measure of public debt. This is a reasonable answer to the second question.

As for the first question on timing, the point is that cross-country differences appeared after the major shocks of the early 1970s. Single party governments seem to have been more capable to adjusting than coalition governments. In the U.S., the equivalent of coalition government is the common situation of divided government. Although Alesina and Rosenthal (1995) regard divided government as a balancing device, others believe that it can cause co-ordination problems with inefficient policy delays. A lively debate has sprung up within and outside academia over whether divided government in the 1980s is responsible for the rapid growth of public debt.

While the evidence at the federal level is weak and rather questionable, Alt and Lowry (1994) and Poterba (1994) find much more convincing evidence at the state level, showing that states with divided government are slower in adjusting to fiscal shocks than states with unified governments, resulting in growing deficits in recessions where party control is divided. The similarity between these results and those for OECD countries (after allowing for the obvious institutional differences) is quite amazing.

Institutional Process

Congress scholars have analysed in great detail how the legislature's rules influence policy outcomes in general, and fiscal policy in particular. This literature usually focuses on the level of spending, rather than deficits. In fact, its models are generally static rather than dynamic. In an influential contribution of this sort, Weingast, Shepsle, and Johnsen (1981) argue that representatives with geographically based constituencies overestimate the benefits of public projects in their districts relative to the costs of financing them which are distributed nationwide. The consequence is an oversupply of public projects. No doubt, legislative procedures have important implications for outcomes.

In order to apply the insights of this typically "American" literature to issues of public debt in industrial economies, one has to tackle three issues. First, formal models need to be made explicitly dynamic to study not only the level of spending, but also the budget balance. Second, the American models focus on geographically based public "pork barrel" projects, but in fact purely redistributive programs are a larger and larger fraction of the public budgets of OECD countries.

Third, one has to take into account the effects of different electoral systems and other legislative institutions in different countries. Research in this area is in an embryonic stage but in our view is quite promising. It is reinforced by other studies which show that specific debt-limiting features of constitutions affect the speed with which state governments respond to fiscal shocks (Alt and Lowry 1994; Poterba 1994). Most important, this is again a point of direct contact between the study of institutions and the study of policy.

To conclude, fundamental to the rational choice-based approach to the evolution and policy consequences of institutions around which we wove our selective review was a broad notion of costly transactions. The costs involve not just the problems of monitoring and enforcing contracts but the various aspects of organising and bargaining which inevitably arise in the process of forming agreements through collective action and choice. Thirty years ago, the foundations of this approach existed, but not very much systematic, positive, empirical work had been done. Now a great deal has. Out of it has come an increased understanding of the interrelationships between delegation, jurisdiction, and agenda power on the one hand, and of the nature of politico-economic cycles on the other.

Other areas in which this approach seems to be on the verge of a takeoff include trade policy, energised by a recent debate over the consequences of institutions and factor mobility for collective action and coalition formation, and whether cross-country differences in investment and economic growth are influenced by democratic institutions, political instability, income inequality and/or social polarisation.

Since evidence in these other areas is only just beginning to accumulate, rather than summarising only some parts of the possible literature we recommend two recent reviews, and we look forward to future opportunities for further analysis.

REFERENCES

Alchian, A., and Demzetz, H. 1972. Production, information costs, and economic organisation. *American Economic Review,* 62:777-95.

Alesina, A. 1987. Macroeconomic policy in a two-party system as a repeated game. *Quarterly Journal of Economics.* 101:651-78.

Alt, J. 1985. Political parties, world demand, and unemployment: domestic and international sources of economic activity. American PoKricaiSciewe review, 79: 1016—40.

——and Gilligan, M. 1994. The political economy of trading states. *Journal of Political Phihsophy. 2:*165-92.

——and Lowry, R. 1994. Divided government, fiscal institutions, and budget deficits: evidence for the states. *American Political Science Review,* 88:811-28.

——and Shepsle, K., eds. 1990. *Perspectives on Positive Political Economy.* New York: Cambridge University Press.

Arrow, K. 1951. *Social Choice and Individual Values.* 2nd edn. New Haven, Conn.: Yale University Press, 1963.

Austen-Smith, D., and banks, J. 1988. Elections, coalitions and legislative outcomes. *American Political Science Review,* 82:407-22.

Baron, D. 1991. A spatial bargaining theory of government formation in parliamentary systems. *American Political Science Review.* 85:137-65.

——1993. Government formation and endogenous parties.' *American Political Science Review,* 87:34-47.

——and Ferejohn, J. 1989. Bargaining in legislatures. *American Political ScisniX Review,* 83:1181-206.

Barro, R. 1979. On the determination of public debt. *Journal of Political Economy,* 87: 940-7.

Black, D. 1958. *Theory of Committees and Elections.* Cambridge: Cambridge University Press.

Boyd, R., and Richerson, P. 1994. The evolution of norms. *Journal of Institutional and Theoretical Economics,* 150:72-87.

Buchanan, J., Rowley, C.; and Tollison, R. 1986. *Deficits.* Oxford: Blackwell.

——and Tullock, G. 1962. *The Calculus of Consent.* Ann Arbor: University of Michigan Press.

——and Wagner, R. 1977. *Democracy in Deficit.* New York: Academic Press.

Calvert, R. 1995. The rational choice theory of social institutions. Pp. 216-67 in *Modem Political Economy,* ed. J. Banks and E. Hanushek. New York: Cambridge University Press.

Chappell, H., and Keech, W. 1988. The unemployment consequences of partisan monetary policy. *Southern Economic Journal,* 55:107-22.

Cheung, S. 1975. Roofs or stars: the stated intents and actual effects of a rents ordinance. *Economic Inquiry,* 13:1-21.

Coase, R. 1937. The nature of the firm. *Economica,* 4:386-405.

——1960. The problem of social cost. *Journal of Law and Economics,* 3:1—44.

Cox, G., and McCubbins, M. 1993. *Legislative Leviathan.* Berkeley: University of California Press.

Cowhey, p., and McCubbins, M. 1995. *Structure and Policy in Japan and the United States.* New York: Cambridge University Press,

Cukierman, A., and Meltzer, A. 1986. A positive theory of discretionary policy, the cost of a democratic government and the benefits of a constitution. *Economic Inquiry,* 24: :367-88.

——1989. A political theory of government debt and deficits in a neo-Ricardian framework. *American Economic Review,* 79:713-33.

David, P. 1985. Clio and the econometrics of QWERTY. *American Economic Review,* 75: 332-7.

Downs, A. 1957. *An Economic Theory of Democracy.* New York Harper.

Eggertsson, T. 1990. *Economic Behaviour and Institutions.* Cambridge: Cambridge University Press.

Erikson, R. 1988. The puzzle of midterm loss. *Journal ofPolitics,* 50:1012-29.

Fair, R. 1988. The effect of economic events on votes for president: 1984 update. *Political Behaviour,* 10:168-79.

Fiorina, M. 1981. *Retrospective Voting in American National Elections.* New Haven, Conn.: Yale University Press.

——1987. Alternative rationales for restrictive procedures. *Journal of Law, Economics, and Organisation,* 3:337-45.

Gilligan, T. 1993. Information and the allocation of legislative authority. *Journal of Institutional and Theoretical Economics,* 149:321-41.

Grilli, V.; Masciandaro, D.; and Tabellini, G. 1991. Political and monetary institutions and public finance policies in the industrial democracies. *Economic Policy, 6:*341-92.

Hibbs, D. 1977. Political parties and macroeconomic policy. *American Political Science Review, 7:*1467-87.

——1987. *The American Political Economy.* Cambridge, Mass.: Harvard University Press.

Higgs, R. 1982. Legally induced technical regress in the Washington Salmon fishery. *Research in Economic History. 7:*55-85.

Horn, M. 1995. *The Political Economy of Public Administration.* New Yorfc Cambridge University Press.

Huntington, S. 1968. *Political Order in Changing Societies.* New Haven, Conn.: Yale University Press.

Jenson, M. 1983. Organisation theory and methodology. *Accounting Review,* 8:319-39.

Joskow, P. 1988. Asset specificity and the structure of vertical relationships: empirical evidence. *Journal of Law, Economics, and Organisation,* 4:95-117.

Keech, W., and pak, K. 1989. Electoral cycles and budgetary growth in Veterans' Benefit programs. *American Journal of Political Science,* 33:901-12.

Kiewiet, R., and McCubbins, M. 1991. *The Logic of Delegation.* Chicago: University of Chicago Press.

Kramer, G., and Hertzberg, J. 1975. Formal theory. Vol. vii, pp. 351-403 in *Handbook of Political Science,* ed. F. Greenstein and N. Polsby. New Yorfc Addison-Wesley.

Krehbiel, K. 1991. *Information and Legislative Organisation.* Ann Arbor University of Michigan Press.

Kreps, D. 1990. Corporate culture and economic theory. In Alt and Shepsle 1990:90-143.

Landes, D., and Posner, R. 1975. The independent judiciary in an interest group perspective. *Journal of Law and Economics,* 18:875-901.

Laver, M., and Schofield, N. 1990. *Multiparty Governments.* Oxford: Oxford University Press.

—— and Shepsle K. 1996. *Making and Breaking Governments.* New York: Cambridge University Press.

Levi, M. 1988. *Of Rule and Revenue.* Berkeley: University of California Press. Lewis-Beck, M. 1988. *Economics and Elections.* Ann Arbor University of Michigan Press.

Lupia, A., and McCubbins, M. 1994. Designing bureaucratic accountability. *Law and Contemporary Problems,* 57:91-126.

McCubbins, M., and Sullivan, T., eds. 1987. *Congress.* New York: Cambridge University Press.

Milest-Ferretti, G. M., and Spolaore, E. 1994. How cynical can an incumbent be? Strategic policy in a model of government spending. *Journal of Public Economics,* 55: 121-40.

Milgrom, P., and Roberts, J. 1990. Bargaining costs, influence costs, and the organisation of economic activity. In Alt and Shepsle 1990:57-89.

Miller, G., and mob, T. 1983. Bureaucrats, legislators, and the size of government *American Political Science Review, 77:297-* 322.

Moe, T. 1984. The new economics organisation. *American Journal of Political Science,* 28: 739-77.

Nelson, R., and Winter, S. 1982. *An Evolutionary Theory of Economic Change.* Cambridge, Mass.: Harvard University Press.

Niskanen, W. 1971. *Bureaucracy and Representative Government* Chicago: Aldine-Atherton.

Nordhaus, w. 1975. The political business cycle. *Review of Economic Studies,* 42:169-90.

North, D. 1981. *Structure and Change in Economic History.* New York: Norton.

——1990. *Institutions, Institutional Change and Economic Performance.* New York Cambridge University Press.

Ostrom, E. 1990. *Governing the Commons.* New York: Cambridge University Press.

Paldam, M. 1991. Politics matter after all: testing Alesina's theory of RE partisan cycles. Pp. 369-98 in *Business Cycles, ed.* N. Thygesen, K. Velupillai and H. Zombelli. London: Maonillan.

Paimer, M. 1995. Toward an economics of comparative political organisation: examining ministerial responsibility. *Journal of Law, Economics and Organisation, 1*1:164-88. palumbo, D. 1975. Organisation theory and political science. Vol. ii, pp. 319-69 in *Handbook of Political Science,* ed. F. Greenstein and N. Polsby. New York: Addison-Wesley.

Persson T., and Svensson, L 1989. Checks and balances on the government budget. *Quarterly Journal of Economics,* 104:325-46.

——-and Tabellini, G. 1990. *Macroeconomic Policy, Credibility and Politics.* Chur, Switzerland: Harwood.

Poole, K., and Rosenthal, H. 1991. On dimensionalising roll call votes in the US Congress. *American Political Science Review,* 85:955-60.

Posner, R. 1977. *The Economics of Law* 2nd edn. Boston: Little, Brown.

Poterba, J. 1994. State responses to fiscal crises: the effects of budgetary institutions and politics. *Journal ofPolitical Economy,* 102:799-821.

Powell, G. B., and Whitten, G. 1993. A cross-national analysis of economic voting. American *Journal ofPolitical Science,* 37:391-414.

Riker, W. 1962. *The Theory of Political Coalitions.* New Haven, Conn.: Yale University

Rogoff, K. 1990. Equilibrium political budget *cycles. American Economic Review,* 80: 21-36.

—— and Sibert, A. 1988. Equilibrium political business cycles. *Review of Economic Studies,* 55:1-16.

Rosenthal, H. 1990. The Setter Model. Pp. 199-230 in *Advances in the Spatial Theory of Voting,* ed. J. Enelow and N. Hinich. Cambridge: Cambridge University Press.

Rosenthal, J.-L. 1989. *The Fruits of Revolution.* New York: Cambridge University Press.

Roubini, N., and Sachs, J. 1989a. Political and economic determinants of budget deficits in the industrial democracies. *European Economic Review,* 33:903—33.

Rubin, P. 1977. Why is the common law efficient? *Journal of Legal Studies,* 6:51-63.

Schelling, T. 1960. *The Strategy of Conflict.* Oxford: Oxford University Press. Schofield, N. 1992. A theory of coalition government in a spatial model of voting. Working Paper, Center in Political Economy, Washington University.

—— 1993. Political competition and multiparty coalition governments. *European Journal of Political Research,* 23:1-33.

Schotter, A. 1981. *The Economic Theory of Social Institutions.* Cambridge: Cambridge University Press.

Shepsle, K., and Weingast, B. 1987. The institutional foundations of committee power. *American Political Science Review,* 81:85-104.

———1994. Positive theories of legislative institutions. *Legislative Studies Quarterly,* 19:149-79.

Spolaore, E. 1993. *Macroeconomic Policy, Institutions and Efficiency.* Cambridge, Mass.: Ph.D. dissertation. Department of Economics, Harvard University.

Tabellini, G., and Alesina, A. 1990. Voting on the budget deficit. *American Economic Review,* 80:17-32.

Taylor, M. 1975. The theory of collective choice. Vol. iii, pp. 413-82 in *Handbook of Political Science, ed.* F. Greenstein and N. Polsby. Reading, Mass.: Addison-Wesley.

Weingast, B. 1984. The congressional-bureaucratic system: a principal-agent perspective. *Public Choice,* 44:147-91.

Williamson, O. 1993. The emerging science of organisation. *Journal of Institutional and Theoretical Economics,* 149: 36-63.

5

Major Elements

> "The manner in which a man wins life's battles shows something of his character. The manner in whihc he loses shows all."
>
> —***Artemus Calloway***

In the present chapter we will put light on major issues and key elements of political science.

I. DEEP POLITICS

Deep politics is a phrase coined by researcher and academic Peter Dale Scott, which he describes thus:

> "My notion of deep politics... posits that in every culture and society there are facts which tend to be suppressed collectively, because of the social and psychological costs of not doing so. Like all other observers, I too have involuntarily suppressed facts and even memories about the drug traffic that were too provocative to be retained with equanimity."

Scott has spent an enormous amount of time researching political processes that fly under the radar of conscious political activity, are omitted from discourse on the right and the left, and are many times intertwined with global drug traffic.

Here is Scott's definition of "parapolitics";

> para politics, n. 1. a system or practice of politics in which accountability is consciously diminished. 2. generally, covert politics, the conduct of public affairs not by rational debate and responsible decision-making but by indirection, collusion, and deceit... 3. the political exploitation of irresponsible agencies or parastructures, such as intelligence agencies... Ex. 1. 'The Nixon doctrine, viewed in retrospect, represented the application of parapolitics on a hitherto unprecedented scale.' 2. 'Democracy and parapolitics, even in foreign affairs, are ultimately incompatible.'

No doubt, valuable, Scott ultimately found the label of parapolitics too limiting;

> "...the investigation of parapolitics, which I defined (with the CIA in mind) as a 'system or practice of politics in which accountability is consciously diminished.' . . . I still see value in this definition and mode of analysis. But parapolitics as thus defined is itself too narrowly conscious and intentional . . . it describes at best only an intervening layer of the irrationality under our political culture's rational surface. Thus I now refer to parapolitics as only one manifestation of deep politics, all those political practices and arrangements, deliberate or not, which are usually repressed rather than acknowledged."

David MacGregor is another academic who applies the ideas of parapolitics and deep politics to his own research. Here are some of his observations;

> "Deep politics is a revision of Scott's original concept of parapolitics first developed in The War Conspiracy. It responds to criticism that political conspiracies, like the murder of Kennedy, are too difficult to arrange and keep hidden..."

> "Scott came to see parapolitics as "too narrowly conscious and intentional to describe the deeper irrational movements which culminated collectively in the murder of the

> President." In contrast deep political analysis presupposes "an open system with divergent power centers and goals" The collapse of the First Italian Republic in the mid-1990s, involving large-scale criminal influence in government, offers a telling example. It originated as an American parapolitical operation to suborn the threat of communism which parachuted prominent U.S. Mafia hoods into power in post-war Italy "[B]y the 1980s this . . . strategem had helped spawn a deep political system of corruption exceeding Tammany's, and (as we know from the Andreotti trial of 1995) beyond the ability of anyone to call it off". Another example... is the CIA-financed jihad against Russian occupiers in Afghanistan that flooded Europe with opium and helped create Osama bin Laden, a modern version of the Old Man of the Mountains, who's 11th Century followers – the Assassins – "sacrificed for him in order to perpetuate his crimes."

II. PUBLIC OPINION

Public opinion is the aggregate of individual attitudes or beliefs held by the adult population. Public opinion can also be defined as the complex collection of opinions of many different people and the sum of all their views. The principle approaches to the study of public opinion may be divided into four groups:

1. quantitative measurement of opinion distributions;
2. investigation of the internal relationships among the individual opinions that make up public opinion on an issue;
3. description or analysis of the public role of public opinion;
4. study both of the communication media that disseminate the ideas on which opinions are based and of the uses that propagandists and other manipulators make of these media.

Concepts

In fact, Public opinion as a concept gained credence with the rise of "public" in the eighteenth century. The English term "public opinion" dates back to the eighteenth century and has derived from the French *l'opinion publique*, which was first used in 1588 by Montaigne. This concept came about through the process of urbanization and other political and social forces. For the first time, it became important what people thought, as forms of political contention changed. Adam Smith, one of the earliest classical economists, refers to public opinion in his Theory of Moral Sentiments, but it was Jeremy Bentham, the famous utilitarian Philosopher, who fully developed theories of public opinion. He opined that public opinion had the power to ensure that rulers would rule for the greatest happiness of the greater number. He brought in Utilitarian philosophy in order to define theories of public opinion. The German sociologist Ferdinand Tönnies, by using the conceptional tools of his theory of Gemeinschaft and Gesellschaft, argued (1922, "*Kritik der öffentlichen Meinung*"), that 'public opinion' has the equivalent social functions in societies (*Gesellschaften*) which religion has in communities (*Gemeinschaften*).

Notably, the German philosopher Jürgen Habermas contributed the idea of "Public Sphere" to the discussion of public opinion. Public Sphere, according to Habermas, is where "something approaching public opinion can be formed" (2004, p.351). Habermas claimed that it is featured as universal access, rational debate, and disregard for rank. However, he believed that these three features for how public opinion *should* be formed are not in place in western democracy. Public opinion, in western democracy, is highly susceptible to elite manipulation. The American sociologist

Herbert Blumer has proposed an altogether different conception of the "public."

According to Blumer, public opinion is discussed as a form of collective behavior (another specialized term) which is made up of those who are discussing a given public issue at any one time. Given this definition, there are many publics; each of them comes into being when an issue arises and ceases to exist when the issue is resolved. Blumer claims that people participate in public in different capacities and to different degrees. So, public opinion polling cannot measure the public. An educated individual's participation is more important than that of a drunk. The "mass," in which people independently make decisions about, for example, which brand of toothpaste to buy, is a form of collective behavior different from the public. Public opinion plays an important role in the political sphere. Cutting across all aspects of relationship between government and public opinion are studies of voting behavior. These have registered the distribution of opinions on a wide variety of issues, have explored the impact of special interest groups on election outcomes and have contributed to our knowledge about the effects of government propaganda and policy.

Three communities of people who form Public Opinion 1: Public Leaders and Thinker 2: Common Educated Class 3: Common People

Private Opinion and Public Policy

The most pervasive issue dividing theories of the opinion-policy relation bears a striking resemblance to the problem of monism-pluralism in the history of philosophy. The controversy deals with the question of whether the structure of socio-political action should be viewed as a more or less centralized process of acts and decisions by a class of key leaders, representing integrated hierarchies of influence in society or whether it is more accurately envisaged as several sets of relatively autonomous opinion and influence groups, interacting with representative decisionmakers in an official structure of differentiated governmental authority.

The former assumption interprets individual, group and official action as part of a single system and reduces politics and governmental policies to a derivative of three basic analytical terms: society, culture and personality.

Applied Public Opinion Studies

It is pertinent to note that rapid spread of public opinion measurement around the world is reflection of the number of uses to which it can be put. Governments have increasingly found surveys to be useful tools for guiding their public information and propaganda programs and occasionally for helping in the formulation of other kinds of policies.

The US Department of Agriculture was one of the first government agencies to sponsor systematic and large scale surveys. It was followed by many other federal bodies, including the US information agency which has conducted opinion research in all parts of the world. Public opinion can be influenced by public relations and the political media. Additionally, mass media utilizes a wide variety of advertising techniques to get their message out and change the minds of people.

A continuously used technique is propaganda. The tide of public opinion becomes more and more crucial during political elections, most importantly elections determining the national executive. Some think the Overton window is a method for shifting or describing shifts in public opinion.

It is frequently measured using the method of survey sampling.

III. POLITICAL SOCIOLOGY

Remarkably, political sociology is the study of the relations between state and society. The discipline draws on comparative history to analyze socio-political trends. A typical research question in this area might be: "Why do so few American citizens choose to vote?" The field developed from the work of Max Weber, Barrington Moore, Jr., and Moisey Ostrogorsky.

Theory

Notably, there are four main areas of research focus in contemporary political sociology:

1. The socio-political formation of the modern state.
2. "Who rules"? How social inequality between groups (class, race, gender, etc.) influences politics.
3. How public personalities, social movements and trends outside of the formal institutions of political power affect politics, and
4. Power relationships within and between social groups (e.g. families, workplaces, bureaucracy, media, etc). Contemporary theorists include Robert A. Dahl, Seymour Martin Lipset, Theda Skocpol, Luc Boltanski and Nicos Poulantzas.

Political sociology looks at how major social trends can affect the political process, as well as exploring how various social forces work together to change political policies. Political sociologists apply several theories to substantive issues. Three major theoretical frameworks are pluralism, elite or managerial theory and class analysis which overlaps with Marxist analysis. Pluralism sees politics primarily as a contest among competing interest groups. Elite or managerial theory is sometimes called a state-centered approach. It explains what the state does by looking at constraints from organizational structure, semiautonomous state managers, and interests that arise from the state as a unique, power concentrating organization.

A leading representative is Theda Skocpol. Social class theory analysis emphasizes the political power of capitalist elites. The theory emerged from Marxism in the 1850s based primarily on the premise of economic exploitation of one class by another. It split into two parts: one is the power structure or instrumentalist approach, another is the structuralist approach. The power structure approach focuses on Who Rules? and its most well-known representative is G. William Domhoff.

The structuralist approach emphasizes how the very way a capitalist economy operates only allows and encourages the state to do some things but not others. Its best known representative was Nicos Poulantzas. Important innovations in the field come from the French Pragmatism and particularly from the Political and Moral Sociology elaborated by Luc Boltanski and Laurent Thévenot. Political sociology also concerns the play of power and personality, for instance, the impact of globalization upon identity: "The fragmentation and pluralization of values and life-styles, with the growth of mass media and consumerism and decline of stable occupations and communities, all means that previously taken for granted social identities have become *politicized*."

IV. POLITICAL ANTHROPOLOGY

Political anthropology concerns the structure of political

systems, looked at from the basis of the structure of societies. Political anthropologists include Pierre Clastres, E. E. Evans-Pritchard, Meyer Fortes, Georges Balandier, Fredrik Bailey, Jeremy Boissevain, Marc Abélès, Jocelyne Streiff-Fenart, Ted C. Lewellen, Robert L. Carneiro, John Borneman and Joan Vincent. Political anthropology developed as a recognizable, well-defined branch of anthropology only in the 1940s and 1950s, as it became a main focus of the British functionalist schools, heavily inspired by Radcliffe-Brown, and openly reacting against evolutionism and historicism. The approach was empirical, with the main bulk of work carried out in colonial Africa. The British structural-functionalist school was institutionalised with African Political Systems, edited by Fortes and Evans Pritchard (1940).

A similar degree of institutionalization of a distinctive political anthropology never took place in post-war America, partly due to the Parsonian view of the sciences which artificially relegated anthropology to the sphere of culture and symbolism. The very strong stress on social equilibrium, which was so evident in Evans-Pritchard's approach, was quickly questioned in a series of works that focused more on conflict and change (Leach 1954). These works attempted to show how individuals acted within political structures, and that changes took place both due to internal and external pressures.

Contradictions and conflict came to the fore. A special version of conflict oriented political anthropology was developed in the so-called 'Manchester school', started by [Max Gluckman]. Gluckman focused on social process and an analysis of structures and systems based on their relative stability. In his view, conflict maintained the stability of political systems through the establishment and re-establishment of crosscutting ties among social actors. Gluckman even suggested that a certain degree of conflict was necessary to uphold society, and that conflict was constitutive of social and political order. From the 1960s a 'process approach' developed, stressing the role of agents (Bailey 1969; Barth 1969). It was a meaningful development as anthropologists started to work in situations where the colonial system was dismantling. The focus on conflict and social reproduction was carried over into Marxist approaches that came to dominate French political anthropology from the 1960s Pierre Bourdieu's work on the Kabyle (1977) was strongly inspired by this development, and his early work was a marriage between French post-structuralism, Marxism and process approach.

From Stateless Anthropology to an Anthropology in and of the State

While for a whole century (1860 to 1960 roughly) political anthropology developed as a discipline concerned primarily with politics in stateless societies, a new development started from the 1960s, and is still unfolding: anthropologists started increasingly to study more "complex" social settings in which the presence of states, bureaucracies and markets entered both ethnographic accounts and analysis of local phenomena. This was not the result of a sudden development or any sudden "discovery" of contextuality.

From the 1950s anthropologists who studied peasant societies in Latin America and Asia, had increasingly started to incorporate their local setting (the village) into its larger context, as in Redfield's famous distinction between 'small' and 'big' traditions (Redfield 1941). The 1970s also witnessed the emergence of Europe as a category of anthropological investigation. Boissevain's essay, "towards an anthropology of Europe" (Boissevain and Friedl 1975) was perhaps the first systematic attempt to launch a comparative study of cultural forms in Europe; an anthropology not only carried out in Europe, but an anthropology of Europe. The turn toward the study of complex society made anthropology inherently more political. First, it was no longer possible to carry out fieldwork in say, Spain, Greece, Italy, Mexico, Algeria or India without taking into account the way in which all aspects of local society were tied to state and market. It is true that early ethnographies in Europe had sometimes done just that: carried out fieldwork in villages of Southern Europe, as if they were isolated units or 'islands'.

However, from the 1970s that tendency was openly criticised, and Jeremy Boissevain (Boissevain and Friedl 1975) said it most clearly: anthropologists had "tribalised Europe" and if they wanted to produce relevant ethnography they could no longer afford to do so. Contrary to what is often heard from colleagues in the political and social sciences, anthropologists have for nearly half a century been very careful to link their ethnographic focus to wider social, economic and political structures.

This, of course, does not mean to abandon an ethnographic focus on very local phenomena, the care for detail. In a more direct way, the turn towards complex society also signified that political themes increasingly were taken up as the main focus of study, and at two main levels. First of all, anthropologists continued to study political organization and political phenomena that lay outside the state-regulated sphere (as in patron-client relations or tribal political organization). Second of all, anthropologists slowly started to develop a disciplinary concern with states and their institutions (and of course on the relationship between formal and informal political institutions). An anthropology of the state developed, and it is a most thriving field today. Geertz' comparative work on the Bali state is an early, famous example. There is today a rich canon of anthropological studies of the state.

Notably, from the 1980s a heavy focus on ethnicity and nationalism developed. 'Identity' and 'identity politics' soon became defining themes of the discipline, partially replacing earlier focus on kinship and social organization. This of course made anthropology even more obviously political. Nationalism is to some extent simply state-produced culture, and to be studied as such. And ethnicity is to some extent simply the political organization of cultural difference (Barth 1969). The interest in cultural/political identity construction also went beyond the nation-state dimension. By now, several ethnographies have been carried out in the international organizations (like the EU) studying the *fonctionnaires* as a cultural group with special codes of conduct, dressing, interaction etc.

Increasingly, anthropological fieldwork is today carried out inside bureaucratic structures or in companies. And bureaucracy can in fact only be studied by living in it – it is far from the rational system we and the practitioners like to think, as Weber himself had indeed pointed out long ago (Herzfeld 1992). The concern with political institutions has also fostered a focus on institutionally driven political agency. There is now an anthropology of policy making (Shore and Wright 1997). This focus has been most evident in Development anthropology or the anthropology of development, which over the last decades has established as one of the discipline's largest subfields. Political actors like states, governmental institutions, NGOs, International Organizations or business corporations are here the primary subjects of analysis. In their ethnographic work anthropologists have cast a critical eye on discourses and practices produced by institutional agents of development in their encounter with 'local culture'.

Development anthropology is tied to global political economy and economic anthropology as it concerns the management and redistribution of both ideational and real resources. In this vein, Escobar (1995) famously argued that international development largely helped to reproduce the former colonial power structures. Many other themes have over the last two decades been opened up which, taken together, are making anthropology increasingly political: post-colonialism, post-communism, gender, multiculturalism, migration, not to forget the umbrella term of globalization. It thus makes sense to say that while anthropology was always to some extent about politics, this is even more evidently the case today.

V. POLITICAL COMMUNICATIONS

Basically, political communication is a field of communications that is concerned with politics. Communication often influences political decisions and vice versa.

It is remarkable that the field of political communication concern 2 main areas:

- Election campaigns - Political communications involved in campaigning for elections.
- Government operations - This role is usually fulfilled by a Ministry of Communications, Information Technology or similar political entity. Such an entity is in charge of maintaining communication legislation and would be responsible for setting telecommunications policy and regulations as well as issuing broadcasting licenses, comments press releases, etc...

According to James Chesebro, there are five critical approaches to contemporary Political communications:

1. Machiavellian - ie power relationships.
2. Iconic - symbols are important.
3. Ritualistic - Redundant and superficial nature of political acts - manipulation of symbols.
4. Confirmation - political aspects looked at as people we endorse.
5. Dramatistic - politics is symbolically constructed. (Kenneth Burke).

VI. POLITICAL PSYCHOLOGY

Basically, Political psychology is an interdisciplinary academic field dedicated to the relationship between psychology and political science, with a focus on the role of human thought, emotion, and behavior in politics.

It analyzes political science as related to entities such as voters, lawmakers, local and national governments and administrations, international organizations, political parties, and associations. While the grammar of "political psychology" tends to stress psychology as the central field, the discipline could also be accurately labeled "the psychology of politics," so as to more evenly recognize the interdisciplinary nature of the field.

Also not fully conveyed by the label is the wide scope of the disciplines from which political psychology draws, including anthropology, cognitive and personality psychology, sociology, psychiatry, international relations, and other more distant fields such as economics, philosophy, and the arts.

The cross-fertilization between political science and

psychology has risen to a modestly active level since its beginnings in the 1940s, though both fields have traditionally had a wider magnitude of collaboration with other disciplines, such as history with political science, and sociology with psychology.

Prominent Political Psychologists

- James David Barber
- Eugene Borgida
- Christopher Federico
- Ofer Feldman
- Stanley Feldman
- Margaret Hermann
- Leonie Huddy
- Shanto Iyengar
- John Krosnick
- Harold Lasswell
- Howard Lavine
- Jack Levy
- Milton Lodge
- George Marcus
- Rose McDermott
- Kathleen McGraw
- Diana Mutz
- Ashis Nandy
- Steve Reicher
- Virginia Sapiro
- David Sears

- John Sullivan
- Charles Taber
- Philip Tetlock
- Vamýk Volkan
- Dana Ward
- Jim Sidanius
- James Kuklinski

VII. POLITICAL SCIENCE OF RELIGION

Political Science of Religion (also referred to as Politicology of Religion or Politology of Religion) can be defined as one of the youngest disciplines in the political sciences that deals with a study of influence that religion has on politics and vice versa with a focus on the relationship between the subjects (actors) in politics in the narrow sense: government, political parties, pressure groups, and religious communities. It was established in the last decades of the twentieth century.

Major Research Areas

Its basic research areas are:

1. All aspects of religious teachings and practices that have direct political contents and messages, such as religious understanding of government, power, political authority, Sovereign state, political organizing, war, peace, etc;
2. All aspects of religious behavior and practice that don't have direct political contents and messages but do have direct political consequences, such as building of religious edifices, pilgrimages, etc.;
3. Attitudes and positions of political subjects in the

narrow sense towards religion and religious communities, such as that of political parties and pressure groups towards religion and religious communities;

4. Everything within apparently completely secular public behavior with no religious motives that causes religious consequences, such as an economic monopoly achieved by a religious group within a multi-confessional society – it cannot but cause political consequences.

These fields of research are in constant development. Political Science of Religion is studied at almost all universities and political science departments in the US. American Political Science Association has a section "Religion and Politics". In Europe there is a growth of this discipline and in the Balkans and Eastern Europe it was founded for the first time in 1993 at the Faculty of Political Science of the University of Belgrade, Serbia.

Also, but this time globally, it was in Belgrade, Serbia, that the first biannual *"Politics and Religion"* Journal , was founded in 2007 and its first issue appeared in February '07. It is published by the Center for Study of Religion and Religious Tolerance. Its spiritus movens and Editor in Chief is Dr. Miroljub Jevtic, professor at the Faculty of Political Science, University of Belgrade, Serbia

VIII. POLITICAL SOCIALIZATION

Political socialization is a concept concerning the "study of the developmental processes by which children and adolescents acquire political cognition, attitudes and behaviors" (Davidson, 2009, p. 20).

These Agents of Socialization all influence in one degree

or another an individual's political opinions: Family, Media, Friends, Teachers, Religion, Race, Gender, Age, Geography, etc. These factors and many others that people are introduced to as they are growing up will affect their political views throughout the rest of their lives. Most political opinions are formed during childhood. Many Political Ideas are passed down from Parents to young Adults through them expressing their beliefs.

Major Factors

The agents a child surrounds him/herself with during childhood are crucial to the child's development of future voting behaviors. Some of these agents include:

1. Family: Glass et al. (1986) recognizes family (1) as a primary influence in the development of a child's political orientation, mainly due to constant relationship between parents and child.
2. Schools: Most influential of all agents, after the family, due to the child's extended exposure to a variety of political beliefs, such as friends and teachers, both respected sources of information for students.
3. Mass Media: Becker et al. (1975) argue that the media (2) functions as a political information-giver to adolescents and young children.
4. Religion: Religious tradition can have a strong effect on someones political views. For example, Protestants tend to be more conservative.
5. Political Parties: Scholars such as Campbell (1960) note that political parties (3) have very little direct influence on a child due to a contrast of social factors such as age, context, power, etc.

IX. PUBLIC LAW

Public law is a theory of law governing the relationship between individuals (citizens, companies) and the state. Under this theory, constitutional law, administrative law and criminal law are sub-divisions of public law. This theory is at odds with the concept of Constitutional law, which requires all laws to be specifically enabled, and thereby sub-divisions, of a Constitution. Generally speaking, private law is the area of law in a society that affects the relationships between individuals or groups without the intervention of the state or government. In many cases the public/private law distinction is confounded by laws that regulate private relations while having been passed by legislative enactment. In some cases these public statutes are known as laws of public order, as private individuals do not have the right to break them and any attempt to circumvent such laws is void as against public policy.

Areas of Public Law

- Constitutional law *deals with the relationship between the state and individual, and the relationships between different branches of the state, such as the executive, the legislative and the judiciary.* In most legal systems, these relationships are specified within a written constitutional document. However, in the United Kingdom of Great Britain and Northern Ireland (UK), due to historical and political reasons there does not exist one supreme, entrenched written document. The UK has an unwritten constitution—the constitution of this state is usually found in statutes, such as the Magna Carta (see Holt, J.C., *Magna Carta*, 2nd edition 1992), the Petition of Right, the Bill of Rights, The Act of Settlement 1700 and the Parliament Act

1911 and Parliament Act 1949. The constitution is also found in case-law, such as the historical decision in *Entick v. Carrington* (1765) 19 St Tr 1030, and the landmark decision of *M v. Home Office* (1994) 1 AC 377; (1992) QB 270. Due to the lack of a written constitution, the idea of the legislative supremacy of Parliament and the rule of law play an important role in the constitution (see A. V. Dicey, *The Law of the Constitution* (ed. E. C. S. Wade), 10th edition, 1959). Despite all this, in reality, much of the constitution is a political phenomenon, rather than a legal one.

- Administrative law refers to the body of law which regulates bureaucratic managerial procedures and defines the powers of administrative agencies. These laws are enforced by the executive branch of a government rather than the judicial or legislative branches (if they are different in that particular jurisdiction). This body of law regulates international trade, manufacturing, pollution, taxation, and the like. This is sometimes seen as a subcategory of Civil law and sometimes seen as public law as it deals with regulation and public institutions.
- Criminal law involves the state imposing sanctions for defined crimes committed by individuals or businesses, so that society can achieve its brand of justice and a peaceable social order. This differs from Civil law in that civil actions are disputes between two parties that are not of significant public concern.

Public/private Law Distinction in Canada

In the "English" provinces of Canada, the term private law is also known as *English Common Law,* or just *common law*. These are judge-made laws. Public Law is that law which is passed by either the provincial legislatures or by the federal Parliament. In Quebec, private law is basically the civil code of Quebec, considered to be the primary source of private law. These laws are interpreted by judges, but this within the ambit of the codal provisions that have been enunciated by the legislators.

Public/Private Law Distinction

All U.S. states except Louisiana share a heritage with English law, so the private law of most U.S. states is called the common law; indeed, the U.S. Constitution makes specific reference to the common law of England as the fundamental law of the federal United States. Some states, such as New York (owing to its Dutch heritage), have strong civil-law influences, and have enacted laws relating to obligations; e.g., the *General Obligations Law* and the *General Business Law*. The distinction between what is public and what is private in the law is often a hazy one. Many consumer protection laws are of a public law nature, which limits the ability of companies to engage in transactions that fail to respect the rights of consumers. Most laws that impose criminal penalties are considered public law, as these laws are intended to protect all members of society, and this not just in the areas of interaction covered by contract and tort laws. The legal system of Louisiana follows the French legal tradition, especially the Code Napoleon, except where those traditions are effectively overridden by contrary English-based legal principles in the U.S. Constitution.

German-Speaking Countries

In German-language legal literature, there is an extensive discussion distinguishing public law from private law. A variety of theories have been used:

- *Interest theory*: Under this theory, going back to the Roman jurist Ulpian, public law governs legal matters that concern the public interest. This theory may be critiqued to the extent that issues of private law can affect the public interest.
- The *Subjection theory* focuses on explaining the distinction by emphasizing the subordination of private persons to the state: Public law is supposed to govern this relationship, whereas private law is considered to govern relationships where the parties involved meet on a level playing field. This theory fails in areas commonly considered private law which also imply subordination, e.g. in employment law between employer and employee.
- The *Subject theory* considers public law to regulate the conduct of public authorities. This theory arguably fails when the state engages in contracting (for example, when buying office supplies, where regular contract law applies).
- A *combination of the subjection theory and the subject theory* arguably provides a workable distinction: Under this approach, a field of law is considered public law where.
  (a) one actor is a public authority endowed with the power to act unilaterally (*imperium*); and
  (b) this actor uses that *imperium* in the particular relationship.

Under the latter theory, both a contract of situation such as the government buying office supplies are subject to private law. There are areas of law which are mixed under that definition, such as employment law, parts of which are public law (e.g. the activities of an employment inspectorate when investigating workplace safety etc.) and parts of which are private law (e.g. the employment contract). The differentiation is primarily an academic debate, important mainly for the delineation between the competences of the court system and administrative authorities.

A statute will normally include a section stating who is in charge of enforcement. However, under the Austrian constitution the distinction is of some importance, as private law is among the exclusive compentences of federal legislation, whereas public law is partly a matter of state legislation.

As a practical result, the distinction is thus a matter of how the constitution is to be interpreted most accurately.

X. DIGITAL ERA GOVERNANCE

In the public administration debate about New Public Management (NPM), the concept of digital era governance (or DEG) is claimed by Patrick Dunleavy, Helen Margetts and their co-authors as replacing NPM since around 2000-05. DEG has three key elements - reintegration (bringing issues back into government control, like US airport security after 9/11); needs-based holism (reorganizing government around distinct client groups); and digitalization (fully exploiting the potential of digital storage and Internet communications to transform governance).

XI. PERESTROIKA MOVEMENT

The Perestroika Movement in political science is a faction that works towards methodological pluralism and to heighten relevance of political science to people outside the discipline. The movement is against what it sees as dominance for quantitative and mathematical methodology in political science. Such dominance breeds academic isolation and poor quality in scholarship, according to the movement (Schram and Caterino 2006).

The Perestroika Movement began in 2000 with an anonymous e-mail message sent by one "Mr. Perestroika" to the editors of the *American Political Science Review* calling for "a dismantling of the Orwellian system that we have in APSA." The message went to seventeen recipients who quickly forwarded it to others, and within weeks the Perestroika Movement became a force calling for change in the American political science community (Monroe 2005).

In the years that followed, the Perestroika Movement established itself with its own literature, conferences, websites, and blogs. Main books about the movement are Monroe (2005) and Schram and Caterino (2006). Flyvbjerg (2001) has been called a manifesto for the Perestroika Movement.

XII. IMMIGRATION POLICY

An immigration policy is any policy of a state that deals with the transit of persons across its borders, but especially those that intend to work and to remain in the country. Immigration policies can range from allowing no migration at all to allowing most types of migration, such as free immigration. Often, racial or religious bias is tied to immigration policy (for example, a country might only allow commonwealth citizens admission). Ethnic relations policy *within* a county can usually be broadly categorized as either 'assimilationist' or 'multiculturalist'.

Nowadays immigration policy is often closely related to other policies:

- Tax, tariff and trade rules that determine what

goods immigrants may bring with them, what services they may perform while temporarily in the country, etc., and who is allowed to remain, e.g. the European Union has few immigration restrictions within it if any. Any citizen or resident of any of the signatory nations (with the possible exception of a few new member states) may move and seek work anywhere within the E.U. and there is nothing that member states can do to stop it without leaving the E.U. or renegotiating the treaty.

- Investment policy that permits wealthy immigrants to invest in businesses in exchange for favorable treatment, early issuance of passports and permanent resident status.
- Agricultural policy that may make exemptions for migrant farm workers, who typically enter a country only for the harvest season and then return home to a developing nation (such as Mexico or Jamaica which often send such workers to US and Canada respectively).
- Overcrowding which can be blamed for the spread of Tuberculosis or a house price boom
- Birth rates which are low in developed nations

An important aspect of immigration policy is the treatment of refugees, more or less helpless or stateless people who throw themselves on the mercy of the state they enter, seeking refuge from poor treatment in their country of origin. With the rise of terrorism worldwide, another major concern is the national security of nations that let people cross borders. The belief is that terrorists can come from overseas.

These concerns often lead to intrusive security searches

and tighter visa requirements, which can discourage immigration, temporary visitors, and even movement within countries or birth within countries. There is often pressure on nations to loosen immigration policy or inspections to enable tourism and relocation of businesses to a country, from a destabilized region.

REFERENCES

Bentley,Peter,Arnold Rose,Talcott Parsons,and Neil Smelser. "Political Sociological Theories:Theories of the State and Power." 16 Jan.2003.Web.28 Sept 2009.

Bentley,Peter,Arnold Rose,Talcott Parsons,and Neil Smelser. "Political Sociological Theories:Theories of the State and Power." 16 Jan.2003.Web.28 Sept 2009.

Buzzell,Timothy, Betty A. Dobratz,and Lisa K. Waldner." *The Politics of Social Inequality.*"14 Mar. 2001.

Buzzell,Timothy, Betty A. Dobratz,and Lisa K. Waldner." *The Politics of Social Inequality.*"14 Mar. 2001.

Campbell, C. M. (1960). The American Voter. New York: John Wiley.

Deep Politics and the Death of JFK, University of California, 1996, pp.6-7.

Iyengar, Shanto; McGuire, William J. (Eds.) (1993). "Interdisciplinary Cross-Fertilization". *Explorations in Political Psychology*. Duke University Press.

J. Glass, V. B. (1986). Attitude similarity in three generational families: Socialization, status inheritance, or reciprocal influence? American Sociological Review , 685-698.

L.B. Becker, M. M. (1975). Family traditions. In S. C. (ed), Political Communication: Issues and strategies for research (pp. 126–139). New York: Praeger.

Lewis A. Coser.Masters of sociological Thought.Class Theory 1977:48-50 Web.

Lewis A. Coser.Masters of sociological Thought.Class Theory 1977:48-50 Web.

Lipset, S.M. *Introduction: Ostrogorski and the Analytical Approach to the Comparative Study of Political Parties* in M. Ostrogorski, Democracy and the Organization of Political (2 vol, 1964; 1982 ed.)

Lipset, S.M. *Introduction: Ostrogorski and the Analytical Approach to the Comparative Study of Political Parties* in M. Ostrogorski, Democracy and the Organization of Political (2 vol, 1964; 1982 ed.)

McGuire, William J. (1993). "The Poly-Psy Relationship: Three Phases of a Long Affair". in Iyengar, Shanto; McGuire, William J.. *Explorations in Political Psychology*. Duke University Press.

Miroljub Jevtic,Nabozenstvo a politika:Teoreticky Pristup(Religion and Politics:Theoretical Approach)in:*2007 Rocenka Ustavu pre vztahy statu a cirkvi*(Institut for State-Church Relations)Bratislava,2008, Slovakia,pp.104–105.

Miroljub Jevtic,Political Science and Religion,in *Politics and Religion,journal, 1/2007*,Belgrade,pp.63–64.

Miroljub Jevtic,*Religija i politika-Uvod u Politikologiju religije*(Religion and Politics-Introduction into Politology of Religion) ed. Institut for Political Studies and Department of Political Science, Belgrad,2002,pp.15.

Miroljub Jevtic,Religion as a Political Science Research Subject,in *Religion and Politics*,ed. South-West University "Neofit Rilski", Faculty of Law and History, Blagoevgrad , Bulgaria,2005,pp.45–46.

Nachtigal M. Paul."Political Trends Affecting Nonmetropolitan America." Journal of Research in Rural Education Vol.10(1994):161-166.Print.

Nachtigal M. Paul."Political Trends Affecting Nonmetropolitan America." Journal of Research in Rural Education Vol.10(1994):161-166.Print.

Nash, Kate (2000). *Contemporary Political Sociology*. United Kingdom: Wiley-Blackwell. pp. 1–3.

Nash, Kate (2000). *Contemporary Political Sociology*. United Kingdom: Wiley-Blackwell. pp. 2.

Nash, Kate (2000). *Contemporary Political Sociology*. United Kingdom: Wiley-Blackwell. pp. 1–3.

Nash, Kate (2000). *Contemporary Political Sociology*. United Kingdom: Wiley-Blackwell. pp. 2.

Patrick Dunleavy, Helen Margetts et al., Digital Era Governance: IT Corporations,.the State and E-Government (Oxford: Oxford University Press, 2006).

Piven, F. (1988) *Why Americans Don't Vote: And Why Politicians Want it That Way* Pantheon.
Piven, F. (1988) *Why Americans Don't Vote: And Why Politicians Want it That Way* Pantheon.
Powell, L. (2003). Political Socialization: The development of Political Attitudes. In L. Powell, Political Campaign Communication: Inside and Out (p. 20). Birmingham: University of Alabama.

Religion and Foreign Policy Initiative, Council on Foreign Relations, http://www.cfr.org/religion.

Sapiro, Virginia (2001). "Introduction to Political Psychology". http://www.polisci.wisc.edu/users/sapiro/ps267/ps267.htm. Retrieved 19 May 2006.

The Deep Politics of September 11: Political Economy of Concrete Evil, a chapter within: Research in Political Economy Vol.20, Elsevier, 2002.

The Global Drug Meta-Group: Drugs, Managed Violence, and the Russian 9/11, Peter Dale Scott, 10/29/05, http://lobster-magazine.co.uk/articles/global-drug.htm

The War Conspiracy, Bobbs Merrill, 1972, p.173, (chapter epigraph).

6

Political Behaviour

> "Although this may seem a paradox, all exact science is dominated by the idea of approximation. When a man tells you that he knows the exact truth about anything, you are safe in inferring that he is an inexact man."
>
> ***—Bertrand Russel***

Here in this chapter we will discuss the political behaviour in elaborately, illustrating various models and theories.

First it is remarkable to note that the Columbia sociologists were not the only scholars during this general period who turned their focus to the individual citizen. Two other streams of intellectual research, both of which understood democratic politics in the context of individual voters, locate their origins in the same postwar period. The American National Election Study series and the work of Campbell, Converse, Miller and Stokes (1960) trace their origins to fieldwork conducted in the 1948 election. And economic theories of democracy have a genesis which dates, perhaps most notably, to the work of Anthony Downs (1957).

Taken together, these efforts have established three schools of research: the political sociology tradition that flowed from the work of the Bureau of Applied Research at Columbia, the political psychology tradition with origins at the University of Michigan's Center for Survey Research, and the political economy tradition which seriously began to apply concepts of rationality and self-interest to the study of citizen behaviour.

The danger in identifying these separate traditions is that we ignore their commonalities to focus on their differences, thereby missing the forest for the trees. The thesis of this chapter is that each of the three traditions addressed a distinct challenge to democratic theory. Each tradition has made substantial progress in formulating a response to these distinctive challenges, but in moving toward a response, they have also tended to converge on a unified view of the citizen in democratic politics.

We might indeed say that the convergence has produced a new empirical model of the democratic citizen, and hence an updated vision of democratic politics. None of this is meant to suggest that important differences do not continue to exist—much of this chapter will be devoted to an examination of their implications.

We do intend to point out the revolution that the three traditions commonly fostered in the study of electoral politics, the common intellectual problems that they addressed, and the convergence that has marked their development through time. Where do the commonalities originate? Most important, all these studies share a common focus on individual voters—a focus that is enduring in political behaviour research. Moreover, each in a different way called into question the capacity of individual citizens to function in democratic politics, thereby presenting a challenge to democratic theory.

Indeed, it is no exaggeration to say that this challenge has supplied much of the intellectual agenda for political behaviour research during the past 50 years. Political sociologists have been forced to confront social determinism as a challenge to the model of the independent citizen. Political psychologists have confronted the political knowledge vacuum that characterises typical citizens, and the implications that arise for theories of democracy that depend on astute and politically sophisticated citizen decision-makers.

Political economists have posed perhaps the ultimate riddle of citizenship: why would a rational individual invest in the duties of citizenship when the effect of each individual investment is likely to be trivial and unimportant? At the same time that each tradition has addressed a distinctive challenge to the capacity of individual citizens and hence to the potential of democratic politics, all three have produced a high degree of convergence in their responses. Each tradition has arrived at a reconciliation, of sorts, between the capacities of flesh-and-blood citizens and the theoretical requirements imposed by democratic politics.

But in arriving at the reconciliation, a new empirical model of citizenship has evolved which, in many respects, is common across the three traditions. And the point of convergence among the three traditions is the purposeful, instrumentally motivated citizen. The purposeful, instrumentally motivated citizen is, of course, the citizen embodied in political economy traditions. Thus, in a crucial sense, it was this model of citizenship and this tradition of scholarship that posed the fundamental challenge to political behaviour research.

In other words, the political economy tradition encouraged both the political sociology and political psychology traditions to reconsider—and in the process, rediscover—their own roots in the analysis of purposeful citizens and political behaviour.

Perhaps the most fundamental challenge to traditional visions of democratic citizenship was posed by Anthony Downs (1957) in his articulation of an "economic theory of democracy." If citizens act rationally on the basis of individually defined self-interest. Downs showed, they might very well abstain from voting in elections. Rational abstention is a quite sensible response when the benefits that any voter obtains due to participation are compared to the costs of participation, after these benefits are discounted by the microscopically small likelihood that any single voter will play a pivotal role in an election outcome.

Indeed, based on such a calculus, it becomes quite clear that the only reasonable course of action is to refrain from voting. The same calculation can be invoked in the analysis of other citizenship activities as well. Most particularly, the costs of becoming informed about politics are often much higher than the costs of voting, and hence the same underlying analysis comes into play.

Citizens might act more strategically to realise their interests if they based their actions on better, more complete information. But given the minimal likelihood that any single act will be pivotal, what is the use? Why should anyone bother to become informed? Downs's analysis of rational abstention and the costs of becoming informed foreshadowed a more general scholarly assault on a wide range of collective action problems more broadly conceived, most particularly Olson's (1965) analysis of political organisation and the challenge of securing a membership.

Perhaps the ultimate tribute to both analyses is that they have stimulated so much intellectual activity, both within and beyond the political economy tradition. A significant portion of this intellectual effort has been aimed at a reconciliation between the expectations that are generated by the political economy models and the empirical reality as we know it. That is, given the strong individually based incentives for free-riding and shirking responsibility, why does *anyone* participate in elections, join organisations, or stay informed about politics? Perhaps ironically, the task of reconciling theoretical expectations with empirical reality is more readily accomplished with respect to political organisation.

The importance of coercion, selective incentives, and institutional arrangements (Ostrom 1990) for the long-term maintenance and survival of political co-operation is now widely accepted, albeit with some dissenters (Knoke 1990; Chong 1991). The more difficult challenge has arisen with respect to the most widespread and basic citizenship duties—the decision to participate in elections and stay informed about politics. At the same time that Downs makes a persuasive case for rational abstention—and more than a few political scientists have been converted to personal non-participation as a result!—we witness the riddle of relatively widespread participation. Moreover, and particularly in the American case, levels of information and participation are highest among the best educated—those who should be best able to understand and comprehend that the exercise of citizenship duties is not in their own individual best interests.

In short, the simple and persuasive logic of rational abstention runs opposite to some straightforward empirical evidence with respect to the functioning of democratic politics. A great deal of ink has been spilled in the effort to resolve this riddle. Beginning in the 1960s, political economists began an effort to reconcile the facts of widespread participation with the logic of rational abstention—an effort that was perhaps made more urgent by a chorus of critics who viewed the idea of rational citizenship as a crackpot idea. We do not possess the inclination, and this is not the place, to engage in an extensive review of these efforts, except to say that they have mostly failed. Finally and fundamentally, widespread information-seeking and voting in elections cannot be understood from the vantage-point of short-term rational calculation because, as Fiorina (1990) argues, participation and the acquisition of information are activities that are valued intrinsically.

People perform citizenship duties because they like to, or because they feel guilty if they don't, or because it is embarrassing to look stupid during lunchtime conversation. The important point is that the performance of citizenship duties takes on value as an end in itself. Does this mean that voters are not rational? Or more importantly, does it mean that we cannot profitably view the decision to become informed and vote within the context of a rational calculus?

These are fairly absurd questions, and their absurdity might be highlighted by analogy with an example of pure (rational) consumer behaviour.

By demonstrating that rational abstention is the best solution for citizens who base their decision to vote on narrowly defined self-interest, Downs showed us that widespread participation is best understood as a manifestation of an activity that is valued intrinsically. Citizens who read the New *York Times* and vote are not irrational—they just like to vote, or maybe they feel bad when they don't vote. Their preferences are not determinate, however. If the election campaign is particularly nasty, or if the candidates are both unattractive, or if the outcome is a foregone conclusion, or if there is a blizzard on election day, they may stay home.

In short, their preference for voting is not absolute, it is simply one of the factors they take into account when deciding whether to vote. Unfortunately, the discussion of rational citizenship took an unproductive turn that led down a blind alley. Arguments regarding whether citizens are rational tend to be very unproductive affairs. One measure of the success realised by the political economy tradition is the extent to which it has encouraged other traditions of political behaviour to rediscover their own roots in the analysis of purposeful citizens and political behaviour. Much of the development of these traditions must be seen against the backdrop of the rediscovery of purposeful citizenship by political scientists. Indeed, much of the progress in political behaviour research during the past forty years, beginning with Simon's (1957) work, has come in response to the political economist's challenge—the challenge to rediscover the role of purposeful citizens in the workings of democratic politics.

We are not suggesting that game theory has or should become the vocabulary of choice among political scientists, or that other traditions in political behaviour research have been submerged in a rational choice paradigm. Quite to the contrary, we argue that the other traditions in political behaviour research have relocated the role of purposeful citizens in their own unfolding intellectual histories.

Responses

A central insight of the Columbia school was that social attributes are important not because they translate directly and deterministically to a set of interests and concomitant preferences, but rather because they locate individuals in social structure and hence affect exposure to political information (McPhee *et al.* 1963). While this is a sophisticated argument with powerful consequences, the early Columbia work, and in particular *The People's Choice,* provided its critics with a ready target. Consider the following formulation of the authors' argument: "a person thinks, politically, as he is, socially. Social characteristics determine political preference" (1944:27).

Framed in this way, and perhaps taken out of context, it may be difficult to imagine a more straightforward statement of social determinism. Where did such a statement of the problem leave political science? Was politics simply a residue of social life? Was political science best seen as a subfield within sociology? In their classic response. Key and Munger (1959) seek to establish the unique, independent, and idiosyncratic character of politics. Based on political histories within Indiana counties, they argue that the development of political loyalties takes peculiar and unexpected turns, and hence there is no simple one-to-one correspondence between political preference and social characteristics.

Political preferences are connected to social characteristics in one way at one place, but in quite another way at another place. Hence, politics is not a simple residue of social life, and political preference is not simply and socially determined. The Key and Munger response is often cited as a refutation of the social determinism thought to be inherent in the Columbia studies, but more importantly it provides a political scientist's reconstruction of the political sociological tradition.

The Key and Munger argument is a direct assault on the idea that political preference is the direct consequence of political interest defined in terms of individual characteristics. If we want to understand Indiana voters, the inference becomes, we must understand them where they reside, in the circumstances that surround them, and such an undertaking cannot be accomplished if we study them simply as individuals who are divorced from a place and time. Key's contribution to the political sociological tradition is perhaps best understood with respect to his analysis of white voters in the context of *Southern Politics* (1949). Key provided a compelling account of racial politics in his demonstration that white racial hostility in the south varied as a function of black population concentrations within counties. The central thesis *of Southern Politics was* that the historical unfolding of southern politics depended on the relative dominance of white and black citizens in locally defined populations. But in showing that racial hostility among whites was a direct function of local black population concentrations, how does Key escape his own indictment? What keeps politics in this analysis from becoming a socially determined side-show of social life more broadly defined? Key sees racial conflict as the product of politics and purpose, where the interests of the participants in the conflict are locally defined. In his own words (1949:5) the central problem in the high black concentration counties was "the maintenance of control by a white minority."

In Key's analysis, political self-interest is used to explain racial hostility, even though racial hostility must still be understood with respect to a particular set of socially structured circumstances. Thus, the device that saves Key is individual purpose as it unfolds within a particular time and place. Key takes it as a given that, overall, whites in the postwar south had as a primary goal the maintenance of white political dominance.

The actions taken to realise this goal depended on situational specifics, however. The maintenance of white dominance was assumed in the hill country of Mississippi because there were very few blacks, but it was problematic in the delta where the concentration of black citizens was much higher. In summary, we see the merger of individual purpose and environmental circumstance quite early in the modern emergence of the political sociological tradition—a theme that is carried forward in mere recent studies of the political consequences that arise due to the contexts and networks surrounding individual citizens.

Social Contexts

Understanding the politics of individual citizens within the political and social settings where they are located fits well within the political sociological traditions established by Key and Lazarsfeld and others. Indeed, a significant literature within modern voting studies addresses the contexts and networks of individual citizens—a literature inaugurated by the effects of Warren Miller (1956) and Robert Putnam (1966).

While there is significant overlap in the study of contexts and networks, the fact remains that they present significantly different conceptual devices for understanding the impact of social structure on politics. More recent effects have provided a combined focus on the interplay between networks and contexts, but such a strategy requires that they be understood as separate constructs. Social contexts are politically consequential because they influence the probabilities of social interaction within and across group boundaries, thereby affecting the social flow of politically relevant information.

Hence, social contexts are perhaps best defined in terms of social composition (Eulau 1986), and in this sense, a context can be seen as the social composition of an environment. The environment might be defined on varying bases—a club, a neighborhood, a church, a country, a province—and it has a multitude of defining properties. Some environments are old, big, geographically based, isolated, and attractive, while others are not. Similarly, the social context of an environment can be defined in terms of its various compositional properties—the proportion of inhabitants who are Social Democrats, liberals.

Catholic, politically active, and well educated. Moreover, some efforts have been made to assess the consequences of heterogeneity within contexts, conceived as dispersion around a central compositional tendency.

So, defined in this way, contexts lie beyond the reach of individual control—they are not manufactured by way of individual preference. This is not to say, however, that people do not locate themselves within particular contexts while they avoid others. Indeed, such locational decisions may be strategically motivated on the basis of social, political and economic criteria. The important point is, however, that once a person is located within a context, heroic efforts will be required to change the context.

There are, of course, heroic exemplars: the party worker who delivers his or her precinct, the Jehovah's Witness canvasser who tries to convert his or her neighborhood, and so on. But most of us probably take the contexts as given. Hence, absent the problem of self-selection, contexts are treated as exogenous to the actor. When can the issue of self-selection be ignored? Most particularly, self-selection becomes a less plausible hypothesis when it involves large units of aggregation, when the motive underlying locational or membership choice is politically irrelevant, when the demonstration of contextual effects is linked empirically to a dynamic process, when the contextual effect is linked to a process of social or political conflict, and in general when a more sophisticated mechanism of contextual influence is specified.

First, consider the size of the aggregation unit. In a fascinating study, Erikson, Wright, and McIver (1993) have demonstrated the importance of state-level political cultures for the structure of political coalitions and the behaviour of individual voters. There are a great many other reasons for rejecting self-selection arguments in their work, but at the most basic level, would we really expect that people locate themselves in states (or provinces or counties) for politically relevant reasons? As the units of aggregation become larger, the plausibility of self-selection as an account of contextual effects grows smaller.

Second, an increasing number of studies have turned toward the demonstration of contextual effects in time. Huckfeldt and Sprague (1990; 1995) show that political campaigns enhance contextual effects—the effects are larger at the end of the campaign—and that the magnitude of the enhancement varies in systematic ways across different groups defined in terms of individual characteristics. Grofman *et al.* (1993) and Carmines *et al.* (1995) show that the previously documented "Key effect" can be demonstrated in time.

Both efforts show that the white exodus from the Democratic Party has been accelerated by events of the

1960s in counties where black populations are most concentrated. Dynamic formulations such as these are quite difficult to recast in terms of a self-selection argument: do people relocate themselves between observations in a way that produces the spurious appearance of a time-structured effect? Third, the "Key effect" is insulated from the self-selection argument on another basis as well. When a contextual effect is rooted in social or political hostility, self-selection once again lacks plausibility. If southern whites who live in black counties were racially hostile toward blacks, how can we lay the blame on self-selection? Do racially hostile whites locate in black counties in order to be near the objects of their hostility? In such an instance, the political behaviour is quite clearly predicated, in perhaps complex ways, on the surrounding social context (Huckfeldt, 1986; Huckfeldt and Kohfeld 1989).

Finally, more sophisticated specifications of contextual influence tend in general to undermine the self-selection argument. One of the most important contributions in this regard was made by Erbring and Young (1979), who argued that contextual effects should be seen as the endogenous feedbacks of behavioural interdependence. By focusing on socially communicated information and interdependent behaviour as the medium of contextual influence, the contextual effects literature has moved away from social reference group explanations for contextual influence. Consider Langton and Rapoport's (1975) explanation of support for Allende in 1964 among Santiago workers: workers who lived among other workers came to identify with these workers and hence to support Allende.

In spite of its attractiveness, such an explanation is vulnerable to the self-selection counter explanation: only workers who identify as workers choose to live among workers. As these more recent efforts suggest, there is more to the self-selection dispute than simple issues of temporal precedence. More fundamentally, these are debates regarding the role of individual purpose, the exogeneity of individual preferences, and the form of independent structural effects on individual behaviour.

More complete specifications of contextual influence allow a reconciliation between individual purpose and the independent exogenous effect of social structure. But such an explanation typically involves a marriage between social contexts, social networks, and interdependent citizens who act purposefully on the basis of political goals.

As such, self-selection is not a repudiation of environmental influence. If people decide against joining the local Sierra Club chapter because it is full of knee-jerk environmentalists, it becomes difficult to suggest that political choice is independent of the social context. People choose to be part of some environments, and they avoid others, but neither choice is readily interpreted apart from the intersection of the individual and the environment.

While contexts are structurally defined and external to the individual, social networks are created as a consequence of individuals and their choices. Even though individuals may typically have little control over the political and social composition of their surroundings, they do exercise discretion over the networks of contacts they establish within various settings. In this way the social context serves as an environmental constraint on the individual—particularly on the individual's patterns of social interaction—and citizens make their choices among alternatives that are environmentally imposed.

In some instances individual choice is swamped by

these constraints. At a typical Peoria cocktail party, even committed socialists have little opportunity to talk politics with other socialists. Yet, in other instances, individual choice is imposed quite readily. Consider the empirical results from Finifter's (1974) study of politics and the workplace, where she examined the social interaction patterns of Detroit automobile workers at the factories where they were employed.

The partisan composition of these factories was overwhelmingly Democratic, and the Democratic majority was relatively indiscriminate in their patterns of social interaction and association. In contrast, members of the Republican minority were more likely to turn inward and form friendship groups which served as "protective environments for political deviants" (For parallel findings see Gans (1967) and Berger (1960).) In short, members of the minority imposed their own political preferences on the social context in the creation of networks of social and political relations. In other words, social networks are created as the product of an intersection between the externally imposed social context and the citizen's own exogenous preference. And thus, at this particular level, social structure is neither deterministic nor a simple residue of individual preference (see Boudon 1986).

Moreover, the exercise of individual choice in the construction of a network is contextually conditioned—minorities are more likely to be selective in their associational patterns. Huckfeldt and Sprague engage in a series of analyses aimed at understanding the construction of social and political networks as a process that occurs through time, as individuals (1) realise repeated encounters within particular contexts and (2) make decisions regarding whether to convert these encounters into sources of political information. Such a logic, which is inspired by the work of Coleman (1964) and McPhee *et al.* (1963), takes account of both exogenous preference and independent, structurally imposed constraints on social interaction. People do not roll over and accept whatever political information the environment happens to provide, but neither are they able to wholly escape the consequences of an environmentally supplied stream of information. In keeping with Downs's (1957) early analysis, people reduce the costs of information by seeking out information sources that are biased in keeping with their own political preferences.

The extent to which individuals pursue such a strategy is likely to vary across individuals, depending on their sophistication, attentiveness, majority or minority standing, and so on. But one cannot avoid the conclusion that more politically sophisticated citizens should be more concerned to obtain biased information as opposed to information that is in some sense deemed to be politically objective—a conclusion that is in keeping with the analysis of Calvert (1985).

In short, and perhaps ironically, information which carries a clearly understood political bias is more likely to be useful to the citizen. Political preference is not determinate in the choice of information, however, because it operates within the context of an incoming information stream that is environmentally supplied. That is, the menu of choices lies beyond the control of the individual, and hence individual demand fur information must be understood with respect to environmental supply.

The key elements arc twofold. First, people select information sources on the basis of their own preferences. Second, the individual's set of informational alternatives reflects the bias of an environmental source. People are not unthinking products of their surroundings. Rather, their opinions become the complex products of environmentally biased information and their own pre-existing orientations. The crucial element in recovering the independent citizen is recognising that both individual choice and the environmental supply of information operate probabilistically.

The environment operates probabilistically because social contexts are seldom politically homogeneous. Even families disagree about politics, and hence people obtain information and viewpoints that reflect a less than determinate bias. If you live in a Democratic neighborhood, you are more likely to see Democratic bumper stickers, but on occasion you will see one supporting a Republican candidate. Not the question—why is choice probabilistic? First, individuals form social relationships based on a variety of preferences, not all of which can be easily realised in any single relationship. Moreover, many relationships are less than wholly specialised—we talk politics, sports, and weather with overlapping sets of associates. Everything else being equal. Republican auto-workers would choose to eat lunch with another Republican, but everything else is not equal. If they are also fans of the Chicago Bears, they might prefer to avoid fans of the Detroit Lions, and it may be difficult to find a lunch partner who satisfies both preferences, particularly in a Detroit automobile factory. In other words, realising political preferences in the construction of a social network maybe quite costly, particularly if multiple preferences are being realised in a single choice.

Inevitably, people reduce their costs by compromising their preferences, and hence the control of information flow is incomplete. Second, even if the Republican autoworker is quite careful to avoid political conversation with a Democrat, a great deal of information is unsolicited—the person who works next to our Republican may wear a Democratic lapel pin. And hence, people are exposed to information inadvertently and unwillingly, and much of this exposure carries an environmental bias—people who work in banks see more Republican bumper stickers than people who work in automobile factories. Finally, the choice of information sources is often incomplete because the underlying preference, upon which choice might be based, is uninformed. People often lack preferences, and thus they do not exercise informational control because they have no preference to use in arriving at selection criteria. Indeed, we are at the edge of a "catch-22" conundrum.

Influence Model

How are the political consequences of social and political structure realised? What are the mechanisms that tie together citizens with their surroundings? What are the alternative models of individual influence? Methodological individualism lies at the core of the political sociological tradition we are describing—individual citizens and their political choices constitute the primary objects of study (Przeworski 1985).

The individual actor is not, however, seen in isolation, but rather in the context of surrounding constraints and opportunities that operate on patterns of social interaction, the acquisition of political information, and the formulation of political choice. At the same time, however, the individualistic impulse requires that the pathways of influence between thc individual and the environment be clearly specified. It is not enough, in the case of Tingsten's Swedish workers (1963), to show that those who live among other workers are more likely to vote for the Socialists.

The vehicle of influence must be specified as well. Did these workers vote for the socialists because they talked to their Socialist neighbors or because they talked to the local precinct worker? Why were the neighbors (or party workers) influential? Hence, an important part of the sociological tradition revolves around the development, articulation, and evaluation of alternative models of influence—models of influence that place the individual at the center of the action.

Not surprisingly, many of these models are derived from the political psychology and political economy traditions. And in this sense, the political sociological tradition has become agnostic with respect to epistemological issues regarding individual impulse—there is no official micro-theory that is inseparable from the political sociology tradition. This is not to say that any particular practitioner of the craft lacks an intellectual commitment to a particular individual-level model.

Indeed, those who engage in multi-level analyses connecting citizens and environments include game theorists and cognitive psychologists, rational choice theorists and learning theorists. The tradition does not, however, necessarily dictate a micro-level motor that drives political and social processes.

In other words, the political economist need not denounce rationality and rational actors to invoke a multi-level explanation because particular micro-sociological models might have roots that lie either in political psychology or in political economics. The distinctive feature of micro-theory in the political sociological tradition is its purpose. The explanation of individual behaviour is not an end in itself, but rather a vehicle to attain a quite different goal

—the explanation of interdependence among citizens and a more complete understanding of politics in its collective representations (Eulau 1986).

For political sociologists, the slippery slope of methodological individualism leads to methodological reductionism, and therein lies the antithesis of the political sociological tradition. A commitment to methodological individualism does not negate the sociological impulse, but an analysis that begins and ends either with the individual psyche or with an individual's rational calculation ceases to be sociological.

Remarkably, Boudon (1986) argues for an individualistic tradition in sociology and a micro-sociological model that he traces to the work of Weber (1966). The tradition is individualistic in its emphasis on individual purpose and individual motives, but it is sociological in its focus on the individually external factors that constrain individual behaviour. Hence, Boudon presents a micro-sociological model that places a (more or less) rational actor within a set of macro-sociological constraints. Boudon's individualistic tradition might be illustrated quite well with developments in the models that seek to explain the nature of influence in social relationships. Particularly in the context of path-breaking family socialisation studies (Jennings and Niemi, 1974; 1981), it was perhaps natural for political scientists to adopt a model of social influence that was built upon intimacy and the interaction that occurs within cohesive social groups.

The implicit or explicit assumption is that the influential communication of political information takes place between people who hold one another in high esteem and close personal regard, and these are the factors that make them trusted sources of political information and guidance. According to this view, intimacy and trust become the defining ingredients of political influence among citizens, and hence influence is unrelated to motive and purpose. While this model was enhanced by the political socialisation studies, its history extends to an earlier period. Indeed, the Elmira and Erie County studies articulated social influence in terms which Burt (1987) calls the social cohesion model.

The social cohesion model portrays social influence in politics as occurring among people who hold each other in high personal regard and hence share a normative climate of opinion. Social influence becomes the by-product of close, intimate ties—citizens are more likely to influence one another to the extent that they hold each other in high personal regard, both as friends and as knowledgeable sources of political information (Katz 1957). For many purposes, such a model may be entirely appropriate—there is no reason to expect that intimacy and cohesive social groups are unrelated to important forms of political influence.

At the same time, the intimacy model may disregard important consequences that derive from the social communication of political information across the boundaries of social groups. Moreover, even the family socialisation studies have experienced difficulty in demonstrating the importance of intimacy to the flow of influential political communication (Jennings and Niemi 1974; 1981; Tedin 1974). Burt reanalyses evidence from the medical innovation study (Coleman *et al.* 1966) and calls into question the role of social communication through cliques and cohesive groups in encouraging doctors to adopt a new drug.

Huckfeldt and Sprague (1991) demonstrate that people

engage in political discussion with others who are less than intimate associates, and intimacy does not necessarily translate into higher levels of influence. Findings such as these push for a reconstruction of the micro-theory of political influence arising through social communication.

Burt (1987) advocates a structural equivalence model, conceived in terms of network ties. Two individuals are structurally equivalent if they are similarly located in social structure—if, in network terms, they are connected to the same individuals in the same ways. In terms of politics, such a model might suggest that an individual's capacity for exercising influence is rooted in coincidental interests.

Notably, the distinctive feature of micro-theory in the political sociological tradition is its purpose. The explanation of individual behaviour is not an end in itself, but rather a vehicle to attain a quite different goal —the explanation of interdependence among citizens and a more complete understanding of politics in its collective representations (Eulau 1986). For political sociologists, the slippery slope of methodological individualism leads to methodological reductionism, and therein lies the antithesis of the political sociological tradition.

A commitment to methodological individualism does not negate the sociological impulse, but an analysis that begins and ends either with the individual psyche or with an individual's rational calculation ceases to be sociological. Boudon (1986) argues for an individualistic tradition in sociology and a micro-sociological model that he traces to the work of Weber (1966). The tradition is individualistic in its emphasis on individual purpose and individual motives, but it is sociological in its focus on the individually external factors that constrain individual behaviour.

Hence, Boudon presents a micro-sociological model that places a (more or less) rational actor within a set of macro-sociological constraints. Boudon's individualistic tradition might be illustrated quite well with developments in the models that seek to explain the nature of influence in social relationships. Particularly in the context of path-breaking family socialisation studies (Jennings and Niemi, 1974; 1981), it was perhaps natural for political scientists to adopt a model of social influence that was built upon intimacy and the interaction that occurs within cohesive social groups.

The implicit or explicit assumption is that the influential communication of political information takes place between people who hold one another in high esteem and close personal regard, and these are the factors that make them trusted sources of political information and guidance.

According to this view, intimacy and trust become the denning ingredients of political influence among citizens, and hence influence is unrelated to motive and purpose. While this model was enhanced by the political socialisation studies, its history extends to an earlier period. Indeed, the Elmira and Erie County studies articulated social influence in terms which Burt (1987) calls the social cohesion model.

The social cohesion model portrays social influence in politics as occurring among people who hold each other in high personal regard and hence share a normative climate of opinion. Social influence becomes the by-product of close, intimate ties—citizens are more likely to influence one another to the extent that they hold each other in high personal regard, both as friends and as knowledgeable sources of political information (Katz 1957). For many purposes, such a model may be entirely appropriate—there is no reason to expect that intimacy and cohesive social groups are unrelated to important forms of political influence.

At the same time, the intimacy model may disregard important consequences that derive from the social communication of political information across the boundaries of social groups. Moreover, even the family socialisation studies have experienced difficulty in demonstrating the importance of intimacy to the flow of influential political communication (Jennings and Niemi 1974; 1981; Tedin 1974).

Burt reanalyzes evidence from the medical innovation study (Coleman *et al.* 1966) and calls into question the role of social communication through cliques and cohesive groups in encouraging doctors to adopt a new drug. Huckfeldt and Sprague (1991) demonstrate that people engage in political discussion with others who are less than intimate associates, and intimacy does not necessarily translate into higher levels of influence. Findings such as these push for a reconstruction of the micro-theory of political influence arising through social communication.

Burt (1987) advocates a structural equivalence model, conceived in terms of network ties. Two individuals are structurally equivalent if they are similarly located in social structure—if, in network terms, they are connected to the same individuals in the same ways. In terms of politics, such a model might suggest that an individual's capacity for exercising influence is rooted in coincidental interests.

One citizen is more likely to be influenced by another to the extent that the citizen being influenced recognises the existence of commonalties and shared interests, and hence the existence of a congenial bias (Downs 1957; Huckfeldt and Sprague 1991). But the relevance of communication occurring across the boundaries of cohesive social groups extends beyond the explanation of individual behaviour. If intimacy is a pre-condition for influence, then methodological reductionism is not seriously called into question as a method of political analysis.

It only becomes important to relax the tightly constructed focus on individuals to incorporate a slightly expanded vision of the cohesive social cells that surround voters—their families and their most intimate associates. In contrast, if information is conveyed through less intimate social contacts, important implications arise for the nature and consequence of social communication in politics. First, if social communication beyond cohesive social groups is important, then the focus of political analysis can be profitably expanded to include the multiple and intersecting environments where social communication occurs—workplaces, neighborhoods, and so on. Second, if important political communication occurs beyond the boundaries of cohesive groups, it becomes important to invoke Granovetter's analysis of weak ties (1973).

According to Granovetter, information that is communicated through weak ties travels more widely because it is less likely to feed back to the point of origin. Information obtained from one best friend is likely to be shared with another best friend, who is, in turn, quite likely to report it back to the source. Information obtained from a casual acquaintance might be shared with a second acquaintance, but it is unlikely to find its way back to the source because the source is less likely to be connected to the second acquaintance.

As a consequence, information communicated through weak ties tends to spread and disseminate. In terms of politics, information communicated through weak ties is likely to create a public opinion that is more than a simple aggregation of individual opinions, but instead is a product of complex patterns of social communication.

In nutshell, social communication that occurs through casual, less intimate social interaction is capable of creating a public opinion that is truly public—a public opinion that extends beyond the confines of individual calculation and cohesive social groups (Stimson 1991; MacKuen *et al.* 1989). This is not to suggest that individuals play no role in these public opinion dynamics.

Some citizens play more crucial roles than others in the dissemination of opinion, and an important task is the identification of these individuals. The important point for present purposes is that micro-theoretical constructs such as these have implications that extend beyond the explanation of individual behaviour to include the consequences of behavioural interdependence for the larger political community.

Having seen that the model of the purposeful, instrumentally motivated citizen emerges quite clearly in a wide variety of sociologically oriented studies, we now show that the same citizen has been rediscovered by political psychologists in research as diverse as media studies, racial politics, and heuristically oriented political decision-making.

Media Effects

An important focus of the early Columbia studies was directed toward media effects on individual citizens and their choices. But after nearly twenty years of research,

Klapper (1960) summarised the effort as the "minimal effects model."

Supporters of this general thesis have argued that the political impact of the media is likely to be attenuated for a variety of reasons:

1. Conflicting and intermittent messages tend to cancel out one other.
2. Citizens are not sufficiently attentive to be affected.
3. Any message that does leak through to the individual has been processed through patterns of social interaction and communication.
4. Individual level processes—selective attention and retention based on pre-existing political predispositions—tend to distort media messages and hence nullify their effects.

As such, especially to the extent that patterns of social communication are contained within cohesive social groups that reflect an individual's own interests and characteristics, another element of the external political environment might be safely ignored.

Remarkably much of the early work on the media and media effects focused primarily on the political consequence of bias: How are people's political preferences altered by a biased media? Two interdependent processes—one at the level of individuals and the other at the level of the media—made the pursuit of bias effects a problematic undertaking. First, particularly in the United States, the media has self-consciously moved toward a politically detached and objective style of reporting. In practice this has meant that the partisan press often has been replaced by an adversarial press (Iyengar and Kinder 1987).

Rather than continuing the 19th-century role of partisan champion for particular candidates and parties, the modern press has created the role of the professional, politically detached, critical observer. Such a role frequently places the news media in an adversarial position with respect to both sides in partisan struggles.

Indeed, we might argue that it creates a new bias—the bias of objectivity. Second, and returning to our earlier discussion of the greater utility of biased information for sophisticated individuals, this trend has produced information that is frequently more costly and hence less useful for many citizens.

If information without a well-understood bias is difficult to integrate and incorporate within political decision-making, then the modern media have become increasingly less relevant as they have become increasingly detached and adversarial. The modern newspaper, for example, finds itself in a position where it has no political following, but only an audience of political junkies who are willing and able to pay the high price of sifting, sorting, and evaluating the politically detached information that it presents.

In other words, because the media has come to occupy a permanently adversarial position with respect to *all parties* in the political arena, the citizen cannot use the media as a cost-cutting source of information. And thus it is not surprising that the utility of media reports as sources of political information has tended to decline for many citizens, at the same time that the impact of the media on citizen viewpoints has been difficult to establish.

In short, bias-free information is often less useful and hence less influential. These problems are perhaps illustrated best in the work of Beck (1991). As he shows.

Democratic partisans accuse the press of a Republican bias, and Republican partisans accuse the press of a Democratic bias. Such effects are particularly noteworthy because they operate in an opposite direction from the effects that arise on social communication. At the same time that citizens (often wrongly) project their own partisan preferences onto their associates, they also (often wrongly) project opposite preferences onto their newspapers.

Quite clearly, the price of objectivity is an increase in the level of criticism from both partisan camps. If sophisticated citizens put a high value on information that comes with a we" recognised political bias, such dissatisfaction is perhaps more easily understood. What is less understandable is why, in the modern media age, we should have developed such primitive expectations regarding media effects in the first place. A significant stride forward in media research occurred when scholars began focusing more intently on agenda-setting (Erbring *et al.* 1980; MacKuen 1981).

Efforts aimed at understanding the political consequences of media coverage switched from media bias to media coverage, based on the insight that media influence is not simply a matter of telling people how to vote, but rather a matter of influencing citizen perceptions regarding the importance of various issues and problems. Stated quite simply, the argument suggests that issues covered by the media become the issues that citizens view as important, and hence the connection between the real objective political landscape of policy problems and issues, on the one hand, and people's perceptions of that landscape on the other, depends fundamentally on what the media chooses to report. Erbring *et al.* (1980: 21) made a lasting contribution to the agenda-set-tine literature in their effort to demonstrate "audience-contingent media effects embedded in an issue specific micro model of salience."

They show that citizen perceptions of national problems include an important localised component that is explained on the basis of varying media reports. Even if the variability of local conditions is taken into account, the coverage of various policy problems by the local media has a pronounced impact on what citizens think is important. At the same time, they show that receptivity to the media agenda is "audience contingent"—it is dependent on people's own concerns and preferences. This last point is especially important because it reinforces the emergent trend in political sociology—the intersection between environmentally supplied information and the preferences of individual citizens.

In the case of social communication, citizens attempt to construct patterns of social interaction that minimise their exposure to disagreeable political messages, and in other instances socially communicated messages are either disguised or misperceived in ways that exaggerate agreement (MacKuen *et ai* 1990). The exercise of citizen preference is more problematic in the case of the media for two reasons. First, only a very restricted range of alternative choices is typically available—very few citizens read any newspaper other than the locally supplied alternative.

Second, even when more alternatives are available, such as the case of television news, they are typically quite homogeneous and uniform in the content of their coverage. Nevertheless, individual preference is still invoked in the *interpretation* of environmentally supplied information: people develop a combative stance toward the media by imputing an unfavorable political bias.

And they respond selectively to media coverage—they are not equally likely to think that all issues covered by the media are equally important. Other subtle forms of media influence have been pursued in recent studies by Iyengar and Kinder (1987) and Iyengar (1991). In a series of carefully and creatively constructed experiments, Iyengar and Kinder examine not only the consequences of agenda-setting by the media, but also the impact of media "priming."

Citizens are limited in the amount of information they can employ in rendering political judgments, and hence they make choices based on a limited number of concerns. Correspondingly, the crucial determinant of party and candidate success is often the sets of criteria used by citizens to make their political decisions, and Iyengar and Kinder establish the potential of the media to "prime" citizen decision-making by establishing the basis of evaluation. Once again, the results support the importance of an intersection between environmentally supplied information and the political preferences of those who are exposed to the information source.

In the words of Iyengar and Kinder (1987), "Priming is greatest when viewers are predisposed, by virtue of a well-developed, accessible theory, to see a connection between the president's responsibilities and the condition of the country." And for most citizens, this means that partisan preferences intersect with media reports to determine the extent of media priming effects. In a sequel effort, Iyengar (1991) pursues the importance of media framing—media effects on the attribution of responsibility for policy problems. He argues that television's primary mode of communication—episodic coverage of particular events—encourages the attribution of responsibility for policy problems to individuals rather than to larger social and political forces. As before, we see the importance of the intersection between citizen preference and predisposition on the one hand, and environmentally supplied information on the other.

In particular, partisanship tends to limit the effects of framing. In his own words, "Individuals' partisan affiliations provide them an important resource with which to resist the suggestions of news frames" (126). The extent to which individual citizens play active or passive roles in the acquisition and interpretation of information from the media is open to alternative interpretations. Certainly Downs (1957) would ascribe an important role to individuals as they aggressively pursue the economies that derive from locating information sources that convey a compatible bias.

In contrast, Iyengar and Kinder (1987) see individuals as the victims of a media that lies beyond their control—two of their chapter titles describe citizens as the victims of agenda-setting and priming on the part of the media. Regardless of the particular interpretation given to the role of citizens, media studies almost necessarily focus on the question of whether viewers respond to the media as purposeful, instrumentally motivated consumers of political information.

Politics of Race

It is pertinent to note that the emergent focus on this intersection between the individual and the environment is illustrated quite well with respect to several controversies in the literature on race and politics in the United States. In general, this literature aims to explain the source of racial conflict in politics. In particular, why and under what circumstances do white citizens demonstrate political preferences, choices, and behaviours that are hostile to black citizens? The authors of this chapter have been involved in efforts aimed at connecting the politics of race to political and electoral change. Carmines and Stimson (1989) argue that the evolution of race is responsible for a transformation of American politics.

Beginning in the Congress, filtering through party organisations, and ultimately being demonstrated in elections and voter loyalties, the American political landscape has been reorganised in terms of race. Huckfeldt and Kohfeld (1989) argue that race has not only grown in importance, but its growth has led to a concomitant decline in the importance of class as an organising principle in contemporary American politics.

And thus the importance of class frequently has been eclipsed by the ascendancy of race as the primary line of cleavage in American elections. These efforts share a common viewpoint in which race is understood as one among several possible lines of political conflict. And thus they might be subsumed under what Bobo (1983) and Glaser (1994) refer to as group conflict theories of racial hostility.

The underlying logic is that, under particular social, institutional, and environmental circumstances, race becomes crucial as a line of cleavage in politics. Racial politics is not, in short, something that simply occurs in the heads-of voters. Instead it is a product of time, place, and circumstance, as a particular setting gives rise to the realisation of particularly defined interests and impulses. For Carmines and Stimson this means that the politics of race became ascendant as the result of political elites who chose a propitious moment to place the race issue on the political agenda.

For Huckfeldt and Kohfeld, this means that race

typically grows more important when the political dominance of whites is numerically threatened by the presence of blacks, and when politicians construct coalitional appeals that successfully exploit the racial divide. The first line of resistance to arguments such as these is the assertion that race does not matter, or at least that the political importance of race is radically overstated. The most recent advocate of this position is Abramowitz (1994) who writes in response to Carmines and Stimson (1989).

The general line of argument, which was offered earlier in the work of Wolfinger and Arseneau (1978), is that racial attitudes do a poor job in explaining partisanship differences or voting choices once the effects of other policy opinions are taken into account. Hence, people's attitudes toward civil rights are independent of partisan choice. Several responses are available to the "race does not matter" critique. One response, rooted in cognitive political psychology, argues that for many voters a broad range of issue opinions are organised cognitively with respect to race, and hence race tends to permeate a diverse range of public policy concerns (Hamill, *et al.* 1985).

A second response, rooted in the political sociology of race, argues that the "race does not matter" critique fails the macro-political reality check. If the political consequences of race do not matter, why do 90 percent of voting blacks regularly support. Even among those who accept the premise that race *does* matter, there is significant disagreement regarding the nature of racial effects in politics. Group conflict theorists argue that racial politics is the result of political competition between whites and blacks over scarce resources, and hence is rooted in reality-based assessments on the part of political actors. In contrast, the symbolic racism thesis argues that racial conflict is, in fact, divorced from reality—from the real circumstances and interests of the actors. Rather, racial conflict is rooted in prejudice and hostility toward blacks, and hence it is stimulated and manipulated on the basis of symbolic issues and appeals (Sears *et al.* 1979). Our goal here is not to take sides in these debates—we occupy such an intellectually partisan role in other places! Rather our purpose is to demonstrate the roots of these alternative explanations with respect to enduring traditions in political behaviour research.

Group conflict theories of racial conflict lie in the mainstream of a tradition in political sociology that conceives of macro-political outcomes at the intersection between individual purpose and orientation on the one hand, and the political and social environment on the other. The other two arguments—"race does not matter" and "racial conflict is the same as prejudice"—are both rooted in individualistic conceptions of political behaviour and traditions that seek the explanation of macro-political outcomes in terms of either wholly individualistic impulses or wholly internalised cultural norms.

Notice that the group conflict thesis is essentially noncommittal with respect to the role played by prejudice in racial conflict. Advocates of the group conflict position might argue either that prejudice plays a crucial role in the dynamic of racial conflict, or that it plays a minor role. What the group conflict position does argue is that prejudice alone is not an adequate explanation of racial conflict—racial conflict might exist quite apart from prejudice and, alternatively, prejudice might exist quite apart from racial conflict.

Heuristically Guided Political Decision-making

It is not news that most citizens have only limited

knowledge and information about politics and public affairs. While a minority of citizens are well informed, a majority—and by many accounts, a large majority—lack information about basic facts, salient issues, and significant political figures. If most citizens lack such elementary political information, how can they act as effective political participants? Indeed, how can they formulate meaningful political opinions? And yet plainly most citizens do have political opinions and express them on a vast array of political topics.

Moreover, although these attitudes obviously do not represent reasoned judgments logically derived from full-blown and well-articulated philosophical premises, neither are they capricious or whimsical. Most people seemingly know why they prefer one policy position over another, and this provides at least the potential for effective political action. How is this possible, given their lack of attention to politics and their paucity of information about public affairs? Anthony Downs (1957) was the first analyst to give serious attention to the problem of political information in modern mass democracies. Reasoning that the costs of becoming informed about the details of political issues generally outweigh the relative benefits to bc derived from voting on an informed basis, he argues that it is irrational for most citizens to become fully knowledgeable about public affairs.

Downs (1957: 210) identifies three types of costs involved in becoming informed:

1. Procurement costs are the costs of gathering, selecting, and transmitting data.
2. Analysis costs are the costs of undertaking a factual analysis of data.
3. Evaluative costs are the costs of relating data or

factual analysis to specific goals, i.e., of evaluating them.

Together, these costs constitute a formidable barrier to becoming political informed—too formidable, Downs argues, for most citizens rationally to invest the time, attention, and resources needed to become politically informed. Rather, rational citizens have strong incentives to develop methods of avoiding the substantial costs of information acquisition. They do so by developing a variety of short-cuts in the gathering and use of information. These shortcuts allow citizens to make political decisions and form political preferences without becoming fully informed about the content and details of political issues.

In short, their use leads to minimally informed—but informed nonetheless—citizenry. Since Downs wrote so insightfully about the rational basis of political ignorance, a large literature in cognitive and social psychology focusing on decision-making under conditions of complexity and uncertainty has emerged (for a comprehensive review, see Ottati and Wyer (1990)).

Beginning with Tversky and Kahneman's highly influential paper (1974), this work has disclosed that individuals use a wide variety of heuristics— that is, cognitive shortcuts that reduce complex problem-solving to more simple Judgmental operations—to make many social decisions. Kahneman and Tversky have identified four fundamental heuristic principles that allow individuals to focus on a limited set of information to make decisions rather than engaging in a detailed analysis of all available information.

These principles are availability, representativeness, adjustment, and simulation. Briefly, availability refers to the salient features of a decision-making situation, so that individuals need not attend to all available or even relevant information. For example, in deciding whether to identify oneself as a liberal, citizens may focus only on the most prominent liberal spokesman such as Senator Kennedy or Jesse Jackson rather than considering all those political figures and organisations that fall under the liberal category. Representativeness focuses on the probability that an item or piece of information is part of the appropriate class of all information. Thus, representativeness bears on the typicality of information—whether it possesses the central or defining properties of a given class of information.

A representative heuristic principle would be invoked, for example, if a voter relied on the race of the candidate in a congressional contest between an African -American and a white to estimate which candidate is the Democrat (or Republican). In a racially contested election, African Americans are far more likely to be Democrats than Republicans while whites are Just as likely to be Republicans.

The fact that this is not invariably the case only shows that no heuristic principle, including representativeness, can be employed without a certain probability of error. The final two heuristic principles discussed by Kahneman and Tversky involve more cognitive processing than either the availability or representativeness principles. The adjustment principle refers to the changes that are made in decisions after making an initial, tentative response. The initial or anchoring response is adjusted as relevant new information is brought to bear on the decision.

Thus, in estimating the political ideology of a candidate it might be useful to know that she/he is a Democrat and therefore, , more likely to be a liberal based on this initial piece of information. But this I initial estimate might very well be adjusted if it turns out the candidate opposes all abortions, supports the death penalty, and favors a strict balanced budget.

In other words, the anchoring estimate is altered as more relevant information becomes available. The final heuristic principle studied by Kahneman and Tversky involves still more cognitive processing by the decision-maker. The simulation comes into play when relevant information is lacking and the individual must try to anticipate the consequences of a given decision scenario.

In deciding whether to support a given military project, the Secretary of Defense attempts to decide whether the project is feasible, effective, and worth the investment in terms of providing greater security to the nation. Notice that existing information is only of limited value in this situation because the crucial factor is the probable reaction of your potential adversaries—thus highlighting the substantial amount of cognitive processing involved in the application of the simulation heuristic. Applications of heuristics in political psychology do not usually make use of the specific heuristic principles discussed by Kahneman and Tversky but rather specific political heuristics felt to be more relevant to political decision-making. Yet some of these heuristics can be usefully interpreted within the Kahneman-Tverksy framework. The use of stereotypes to make political judgments, for example, clearly involves the application of the representative heuristic. Poor people, for example, may be seen as lazy and irresponsible—those undeserving of governmental assistance. Alternatively, they may be viewed as hard-working and responsible but unable to find appropriate jobs; this perception is likely to foster greater support for governmental employment programs.

Thus, stereotypical judgments are based on the essential or defining features of a group—their representativeness. Brady and Sniderman (1985; also see Snidermah, *et al.* 1991) discuss what they term a likability heuristic. This heuristic enables citizens to make inferences about the issue orientations of various political groups.

The authors reason that if citizens have an opinion on a given political issue and have affective evaluations of various political groups, then they will attribute their opinion to favored groups, and the opposite opinion to disfavored groups. This turns out to lead to fairly accurate estimates of the issue stands of specific political groups—even though many citizens lack detailed information of the groups' issue positions. As Mondak (1994) has noted, Brady and Sniderman's likability heuristic can be viewed as an application of the adjustment heuristic. The individual's own issue position provides an anchoring for the estimated position of the particular group. Additional information—specifically, their affective evaluation of political groups—leads to the estimates of their issue positions. And this estimate is adjusted as new information becomes available.

Both Carmines and Kuklinski (1990) and Mondak (1993) discuss what "May be termed source cues, a particularly important decision heuristic for politically inattentive and uninformed citizens. Their studies show that citizens, in formulating policy assessments and even in developing their own policy position, often rely on prominent political figures.

Thus, attributing the defense buildup in the 1980s to President Reagan, affected citizens' evaluation of that policy but only among respondents who lacked detailed policy information (1993). Similarly, the experimental studies conducted by Carmines and Kuklinski (1990) indicate that citizens are more likely to form their own opinion on issues if salient political leaders (i.e., Senators Kennedy or Helms) are identified either as proponents or opponents of the issue proposal.

As such by using heuristic principles we see how citizens can make relatively informed judgments about politics on the basis of limited—even minimal —information. In the process, we also see how new developments in political psychology have helped re-establish the role of the citizenry as purposeful, instrumentally motivated actors in the political process.

We are intentionally avoiding the "r" word, and many political economists will not be satisfied with the implementation of citizen purpose as it is typically employed in studies of political behaviour. At the same time, a great many students of political behaviour have come to accept something that approaches Popkin's description of the reasoning voter (1991: 7): "They think about who and what political parties stand for; they think about the meaning of political endorsements; they think about what government can and should do. And the performance of government, parties, and candidates affects their assessments and preferences."

Moreover, and as Popkin points out, such reasoning is accomplished on the basis of "low information rationality"—short-cut methods of collecting and processing information about politics. Perhaps the major controversy surrounding the conception of purposeful citizens concerns whether such a model of instrumental behaviour has any real analytic consequence.

That is, how much analytic purchase has been obtained by beginning with the assumption that citizens act instrumentally on the basis of their own purposes? According to Simon (1985), the assumption (or acknowledgment) of rationality yields very modest analytic reward—simply asserting that citizens are rational takes us very little distance toward a convincing political analysis. Rather, a series of auxiliary assumptions must be made in order to generate analytic utility from the assumption of instrumental citizen behaviour, and it is at this point that the analysis truly begins.

Remarkably, the auxiliary assumptions are important for a variety of reasons. First, they provide meaning to the model of purposeful citizens and instrumental behaviour. One model of purposeful citizens generates analytic utility by suggesting that citizens update their assessments of parties and politicians by reviewing past experience (Fiorina 1981). Another model suggests that instrumental citizens reduce information costs by obtaining information from other citizens (Huckfeldt and Sprague 1994).

Still another model suggests that citizens reduce their information costs through a series of analytic short-cuts, or heuristics (Sniderman *et al.* 1991). These analyses, and many more, are at least partially motivated by the assumption that citizens act in reasonable ways to realise their goals. But beyond that point, they may be radically dissimilar in the models of citizen decision-making that they put forward. Moreover, while the concept of citizen purpose may lie beyond the reach of direct empirical scrutiny, the auxiliary assumptions are often subject to the bright light of empirical evaluation. Thus, the premise of citizen purpose does not mean much until we determine how citizen's purposes are realised.

Therein lies, for example, the contribution of Fiorina's retrospective voting model: it articulates the consequences of purposeful citizens at the same time that it provides a basis for empirical evaluation. Indeed, a great deal of contemporary research in political behaviour is concerned with working out the consequences of citizen purpose. The work of Sniderman *et al.* (1991) provides an exemplar of this general research program: his focus on the manner in which citizens reason about their choices and his articulation of "reasoning chains" are some of the ways that the concept of citizen purpose is given meaning. In short, the citizenship challenge posed by political psychology has been answered, in large part, by turning the challenge on its head.

Rather than focusing on how much citizens fail to know about politics, the new look examines the way in which citizens quite sensibly attempt to contain the costs of acquiring and processing political information. We might also suggest that a "new look" pervades a great deal of political sociology research as well. Rather than focusing on the extent to which individuals are reflections of the environments and contexts and groups within which they are embedded, the new look examines the manner in which citizen purpose is realised or thwarted within particular configurations of time, place, and setting. Rather than seeing individual behaviour as a straightforward product of exogenous determinants, citizen choices are seen as being interdependent with their surroundings.

At the same time that preferences are informed by information taken from an environmentally determined supply, citizens also impress their preferences on the environment by way of their own information sampling criteria. In short, political information is obtained at the intersection between individually denned citizen purpose and environmentally determined information supply. Perhaps unintentionally, students of political economy produced a citizenship challenge which ultimately provided part of the solution to companion challenges posed by political psychology and political sociology.

By recognising the costs as well as the benefits of citizenship, the evolving analysis of political behaviour sees many old problems in a new light. In the attempt to come to grips with citizens who were neither independent nor well informed, a revised model of citizenship has emerged—a model of the citizen as a cost-conscious consumer and processor of political information who, while taking her duties seriously, has successfully reduced the impulse to be consumed by politics and political affairs.

The end product is a more realistic view of citizenship and citizens in democratic politics—a view which understands citizens in the contexts of the real-world constraints imposed by their own inherent limitations as collectors and processors of political information. In many ways, this revised view of the citizen is not only more realistic but also more political, organised around a view of interests and information that is located in the characteristics not only of individuals, but also of the groups and settings to which they belong.

REFERENCES

Aldrich, J. H. 1993. Rational choice and turnout. *American Journal of Political Science*. 37: 246-78.

Beck, P. A. 1991. Voters' intermediation environments in the 1988 presidential contest. *Public Opinion Quarterly*, 55: 371-94.

Berger, B. M. 1960. *Working-Class Suburb*. Berkeley: University of California Press.

Bobo, L 1983. Whites' opposition to busing: symbolic racism or realistic group conflict. *Journal of Personality and Social Psychology*, 45:1196-210.

Granovetter, M. 1973. The strength of weak ties. *American Journal of Sociology',* 78: 1360-80.

Grofman, B.; Handley, L; and Glazer, A. 1993. Modeling the link between race and electoral change using aggregate data. Mimeo., University of California, Irvine.

Hamill, R.; Lodge, M.; and Blake, F. 1985. The breadth, depth, and utility of class, partisan, and ideological schemata. *American Journal of Political Science,* 29:850-70.

Simon, H.A. 1957. *Models of Man.* New York: Wiley.

Sinderman, P.M. 1993. The new look in public opinion research. Pp 219-46 in *Political Science: The State of the Discipline II,* ed. A Finifter. Washington, D.C.: American Political Science Association.

Sprague, J., and Westefield, L.P. 1979. *Reasoning and Choice.* New York: Cambridge University Press.

Sprague, J., and Westerfield, L.P. 1979. An interpretive reconstruction of some aggregate models of contextual effects. Presented at the annual meeting of the Southern Political Science Association Gatilinburg, November 1-3.

Stimson, J.A. 1991. *Public Opinion in America: Moods Cycles and Swings.* Boulder, Colo: Westview Press.

Tingsten, H. 1963. *Political Behaviour: Studies in Election Statistics,* trans. V. Hammarling-Totowa, N.J.: Bedminster; originally published 1937.

Weber, M. 1966 On the concept of sociology and the meaning of social conduct. Pp. 29-58 in *Basic Concepts in Sociology,* trans. H.P. Secher. New York: Citadel Press; originally published 1925, ch. 1 of *Wirtschaft und Gesellschaft.*

7

Old and New Concepts

> "I find that a great part of the information I have was acquired by looking up something and finding something else on the way."
>
> —*Franklin P. Adams*

In the present chapter we will make an attempt to present a comparative picture of old and new concepts in political behaviour. The facts are supported by ample instances.

A historical review of political behaviour in the United States should really encompass at least three epochs, the new, the old and the very old. If one, therefore, bypasses the early work of Stuart Rice (1928), Samuel P. Hayes, Jr. (1932), or better known figures such as Merriam and Gosnell (1924), the era of the "Old" must be introduced with Lazarsfeld and Berelson. The Huckfeldt-Carmines chapter provides a good statement on their work, as well as that of our role model in political science, V.O. Key, Jr. The only major omission from their review of the literature are the contributions provided by Stein Rokkan, including his well-known collaboration with Lipset.

Rokkan, along with Lazarsfeld, saw politics and mass political behaviour as manifestations of social structure and social experience. Against that Old World backdrop, the introduction of a micro-analytic social psychological perspective was more dramatic than many retrospective accounts reveal.

It is remarkable that for many of us in the next generation, the world of political behaviour was introduced in 1952 with the first national election study carried out by the Political Behaviour Program of the University of Michigan's Survey Research Center. The 1952 study did not spring full-blown from imaginative minds (or deep pockets) at the University of Michigan. Under the leadership of Pendelton Herring, then President of the Social Science Research Council, the Council Committee on Political Behaviour had been formed in 1949 and was, in fact, the sponsor of the 1952 study.

In the same period the Ford Foundation created the Center for Advanced Study in the Behavioural Sciences in Palo Alto, symbolising the emergence of the behavioural emphasis in the social sciences. Political behaviour in general, and electoral behaviour in particular, owes much to the private foundations, including Rockefeller, Carnegie, Russell Sage and Markle.

These organisations provided a context of enthusiasm, as well as funding, throughout the decades of the 1950s and 1960s. The Ford Foundation, through the efforts of Foundation officers such as Peter de Janosi and Kalvin Silvert supported research activities and the development of institutional infrastructures associated with pioneering work in political behaviour at numerous sites in South America as well as Europe, The National Opinion Research Center at Chicago and the Institute for Social Research at Michigan were new institutional homes for behavioural research. Organized support for the behavioural approach to Political Science was centered in the SSRC, but the

American Political Science Association provided disciplinary legitimacy, in part through the leadership provided by Evron Kirkpatrick, Executive Director of the then recently established Washington office. As one example, Kirkpatrick was directly responsible for the recognition of Political Science by the National Science Foundation. Kirkpatrick and others in the APSA leadership also were involved in making the International Political Science Association a supporting mechanism for cross-national collaboration. IPSA recognized "work groups" that provided legitimising umbrellas covering like-minded research scholars whose research projects would often turn to UNESCO for institutional support.

It is useful to begin this essay with the many references to institutional support for political behaviour in order to make the point that there were many new, highly relevant, organisational initiatives outside the halls of the academy proper. In their newness, the leaders of the initiatives conveyed a shared sense of optimism and challenge that encouraged members of the political science research community to explore new work ways. It also, unhappily, permits one to contrast the "Old" with its many sources of funding support with the "New," in which NSF has, by default, come close to the role of sole source supplier in the United States. However, to my mind, the contrast is less well defined by the resulting levels of financial support than by the diversity of organisations outside of government and academe that were ready to help those who saw in the new methods of data collection and data analysis the means of doing innovative research on traditional intellectual problems of the disciplines.

Which is not to say there was no institutional resistance in the halcyon days of the 1950s and 1960s. For too long the norm across political science departments in the United States was for each department to have one political behaviourist in captivity—one, but usually no more. Even at Michigan, the late George Belknap—a co-author with Angus Campbell of the pioneer article on Party Identification (and a University of Chicago Ph.D. under Avery Leiserson, a member of the SSRC Political Behaviour Committee) was not accepted as a member of the department, and Samuel I. Eldersveld was the lone representative of the behavioural persuasion in the Michigan department until the late 1950s. Indeed, the era began with some likelihood that political behaviour would become political sociology as it was on the eastern side of the Atlantic. Illustratively, James C. Davies, one of the colleagues working on the 1952 study, joined the American Psychological Association because of a fear that political science would never accept the social psychological perspective being emphasised at Michigan.

Put more positively, political behaviour had its origins in the multidisciplinary world of post-World War II social science. For example, the leader of the quadrumvirate responsible for *The American Voter* (1960), Angus Campbell, was trained as an experimental psychologist at Stanford and was one of the pre-World War II initiators of social psychology as an academic discipline. The second in the alphabet of authors, Philip Converse, was an early product of the University of Michigan's post-World War II doctoral program in social psychology who brought a degree in sociology to his emerging specialisations (after a baccalaureate in English literature). As the third of the group, I was a mutant political scientist whose academic work as a doctoral student in social science at Syracuse University consisted of one course in international relations and three sequences of course work in the methodologies and research methods of anthropology, sociology and social psychology. Donald Stokes was the only one with professional training as a political scientist out of Princeton and Yale; and even he came to Michigan on a pre-doctoral fellowship to study mathematical statistics in an era in which the slide rule and McBee sort cards were only slowly giving way to Hollerith cards and analog computers.

It is remarkable that the 1950s Michigan was joined by Yale University and the University of North Carolina as pre-eminent centers for the study of political behaviour. In the case of UNC, the disciplinary environment was similar to Michigan in that sociology, anthropology and social psychology were *companion* disciplines to political science, and research scholars benefitted, from the UNC Institute for Social Research—a parallel to the Michigan ISR. The North Carolina focus in political behaviour was somewhat more sociological than at Michigan, and their signal contribution, among many noteworthy works, was the Prothro and Matthews study, *Negroes and the New Southern Politics* (1966).

The fieldwork was done by the Michigan Survey Research Center and the study design included four intensive community studies purposively selected from the primary sampling units that were the basis for their cross-sectional study of voting behaviour in the South.

The most celebrated of the community studies of political behaviour was directed by Robert Dahl at Yale (another member of the SSRC Political Behaviour Committee) and published as *Who Governs: Democracy and Power in an American City* (1961). It complemented other political behaviour research of the day as empirical work of a behavioural orientation clearly prompted by questions of primary concern to political science.

In 1962 the Michigan SRC carried out the fieldwork for a study of public attitudes toward and understanding of the United States Supreme Court. The principal investigators were Joseph Tanenhaus, Professor of Political Science at the University of Iowa, and Walter Murphy, Professor of Politics at Princeton. Their data collection reflected the excitement created in different corners of the discipline by the capacity to use the new methods and techniques of social science to create data tailored to the research needs of the research scholar.

The generic contrast, to be found in sociology as well as political science, lay in the many differences between data collected in the course of society's social bookkeeping for administrative or bureaucratic purposes (birth rates, divorce rates, election statistics) and data collected expressly for use in social research. It is true that *The American Voter,* as the successor to *The Voter Decides* (Campbell, Gurin and Miller 1954) with its early emphasis on predispositions (party, candidate, and issue orientations), made heavy use *of* attitudes and beliefs in attempting to understand individual level vote decisions. And the psychological nature of party identification apparently imprinted the emphasis on social psychology as the hallmark of the Michigan school.

It should be noted, however, that politically relevant relationships between the individual citizen and the social group—both primary and secondary—were major themes in the Michigan data collections of 1952 and 1956, well beyond the innovative measurement of party identification.

And, indeed, at least seven chapters in *The American Voter* were given over to "sociological" concerns. It is pertinent to note how many of the themes introduced by Huckfeldt and Carmines under the heading of political sociology's challenge were, by sterday's lights, in the same intellectual mode as *The American Voter.*

At least in part because Ted Newcomb of Bennington Study fame was a prominent part of our social and intellectual environment, we started planning for what has become the flagship of studies of political socialisation hard on the heels of the completion of *The American Voter.*

The initial planning and negotiating with the Danforth Foundation, the ultimate funding source for the first 1965 data collections under the direction of Kent Jennings, were prompted by our shared conviction that crucial values and beliefs of voters are first formed in pre-adult years, and the contributions of family, school and peers to that formation should be systematically studied. The idea that there was something essentially sociological and therefore "different" about our projected panel study of political socialisation and maturation did not occur to us.

The urgency of the need to expand the age range coverage of our subjects and the need to introduce diachronic variations in their experience into our research design seemed obvious and completely in the intellectual mode of *The American Voter.* In like manner the data skillfully analyzed in Finifter's study of politics and the workplace (1974) were collected by Miller and Stokes in 1961 as that year's Detroit Area Study. To be sure, the Detroit Area Study was a research vehicle maintained by the Department of Sociology at Michigan but, as with the Jennings socialisation study, being in Michigan made the workplace study seem a natural outgrowth of analyses.

Political Science *was* the intellectual and disciplinary home for the Miller-Stokes study of Representation in Congress. That study joined a growing list of innovative uses of new methodologies to investigate age-old questions of political behaviour. The Wahlke-Eulau study of state legislators, published as *The Legislative System* (1962), had begun in 1955 (again with the sponsorship of the SSRC Committee on Political Behaviour) and demonstrated the feasibility of carrying out systematic data collection from political elites.

This capacity was exercised again by Eulau a decade later as he and Prewitt published *Labyrinths of Democracy: Adaptations, Linkages, Representations, and Policies in Urban Politics* (1973). In 1974, near the end of the "Old" period, three closely interrelated studies were promoted by the Michigan Center for Political Studies.

With support from the National Science Foundation and Russell Sage, the 1974 elections were the center of attention for interrelated studies of (1) the voters (2) the campaigns for election to the U.S. House of Representatives as reported by a national sample of candidates and campaign managers in contested races and (3) the media presentation to the voters of those campaigns. Some of the research of Erbring and MacKuen reported by Huckfeldt and Carmines exploited the data from that 1974 effort. Studies of campaign strategies as planned by campaign managers, as reported by editors and political reporters, and as viewed by voters had been synchronised because of the obvious functional interdependence of the three sets of actors.

Incidentally, the three element design, this time centered in elections to the United States Senate, is currently being replicated by two of my Colleagues, Professors Kim Kahn and Patrick Kenney at Arizona State University. Both are Political Scientists and both are well trained in behavioural research approaches and methods that originated in a wide array of social science disciplines. The list could be extended, but the point is not so much to review the research program originating with the Michigan Center for Political Studies as to illustrate how many different studies were seen by their principal investigators as tightly interconnected parts of a substantive, coherent whole that only coincidentally embraced components that might be identified with different disciplines and were made possible by a thoroughly inter-disciplinary set of research methods and techniques.

Each study was shaped by principal investigators with somewhat different combinations of interests and skills and varied disciplinary training but with virtually no self-conscious interest in being "inter-disciplinary." The strengths of the studies depended on borrowing concepts, hypotheses and research methods and techniques from each of several academic disciplines and applying them as the internal logic of each component of an overall research design took shape.

It may be useful to sort out the various disciplinary contributions—or origins—of "New" research on political behaviour. Among the "Old" studies the interdisciplinary mix of insights and skills seemed thoroughly natural.

NEW ASPECTS

The Old and the New differ in at least three respects. In part because so many of the "Old" data collections were simple cross-section snapshots of a large and complex set of "variables derived from large and heterogeneous populations, methodological creativity was called upon to overcome limitations inherent in the data.

Inadequacies were particularly obvious in data intended

to represent a "process" such as involved in voters arriving at vote choices. This need for methodologies to overcome deficiencies in the data was complemented by an inventiveness that was soon its own spur, speeding new developments as courses on "research methods" proliferated and "political methodology" became the focus for professional organisational activity. For whatever reasons, analytic sophistication, or complexity, now seems to be of the essence in much newly published work. The propensity to begin data analysis with simple bivariate or trivariate inquiries has disappeared in order to hasten on to "model" a new idea with many-termed multi-variate equations.

Whether this, in general, is a mark of the superiority of the "New" over the Old is a matter for another set of chapters. It would appear, however, that being up-to-date in Method City is at least as important as testing a new substantive idea or theoretical insight. As a consequence, "New" research is less often inspired by the prospect of a new venture into heretofore unchartered domains of politics and government and more often a trek through essentially familiar terrain in a new analytic vehicle. The evolution of new analytic perspectives and techniques has, of course, been made possible largely through the agency of the computer, a second source of transformations from the "Old" to the "New."

As the data were collected for Almond and Verba's *Civic Culture,* Dahl's *Who Governs,* or *The American Voter,* data processing and analytic calculations were accomplished with the eighty-column Hollerith (IBM) card and mechanical card sorting devices—the counter sorter or the "101" with its complex wiring boards to produce more complex counting and sorting. The original data for the Elmira Study underlying Lazarsfeld and Berelson's seminal volume. *Voting*

(1959), are still carried in the ICPSR archives on multiply-punched cards—with two variables often encoded in a single column dividing the twelve rows between them.

Analyses for *The Voter Decides* were based on "analysis cards," in which a sub-set of variables pertinent to a single piece of analysis had been transferred from their original storage cards and brought together so they were physically located on the same analysis card. Although this cumbersome technology was a vast improvement over hand recording on tabulating paper, it placed a high premium on data management, and documentation tailored to fit each stage, and it placed severe limits on the complexity of analytic techniques that could be used.

The computer changed—and is still changing—all of that. All twenty-three studies in the American NES forty years series are now available, with complete detailed documentation, on a single compact disc that also carries front-end software to facilitate access to the data. The capacity of computer software for multivariate analyses will today accommodate data sets ranging across scores of variables for thousands of cases.

These storage, retrieval and processing capabilities have encouraged the proliferation of be methodological and substantive interests and have made possible research that could scarcely have been imagined forty years ago. The third crucial change that has occurred over the past thirty years has been in the social organisation of access to data. The first years of the behavioural revolution were marked by a veritable explosion of empirical studies based on data collected from large and politically significant populations.

In electoral behaviour, there were studies of national

electorates, and in legislative behaviour, studies of second chambers in national governments. However, by virtue of traditional academic culture, and in the absence of any alternative, exploitation of each new data collection in the 1950s was largely restricted to the principal investigators and their graduate students. In an effort to expand the numbers of scholars who could have access to the 1952 and 1956 Michigan election studies, the same SSRC Political Behaviour Committee so essential to the funding of those studies sponsored and underwrote two summer training seminars at the Michigan Survey Research Center in 1954 and 1958. Participants included such latent luminaries as Robert Lane and Heinz Eulau. Converse, Miller, and Stokes were the instructors and each summer was devoted to teaching about and learning about codebooks and crosstabs and computation of Chi squares.

The summers were exciting, new experiences in collegial learning and doing, and new experiences in the world of data processing. The 1954 experience inspired Eulau to return to Ann Arbor in 1955 and launch his work on politics and social class. The modal sequel to the seminars was less rewarding. Scholars returned to their departments with a new awareness of the absence of the infrastructure necessary to extend or continue the Michigan experience.

And this even in many of the best departments of political science. Out of an awareness of the difficulty experienced by most seminarians who wanted to continue their new work ways at home, the idea of the Inter-University Consortium for Political Research was born. The idea had two components. The first was to establish the cultural norm of sharing data. The traditional norm gave to the creator or generator of data a virtually proprietary right to control access to the data.

The new concept emphasised sharing data resources, particularly if they were initially created through public funding. The other principal component of the original idea of the Consortium was the goal of creating a new organisation to facilitate individual research efforts, but to be supported by departments of political science.

It would maintain data libraries (unfortunately improperly labelled "archives"), built on data contributed by principal investigators to be shared with colleagues. The organisation would also provide the training needed for access to the data and for facilitating data analysis.

It would provide the infrastructure needed for the exploitation of extensive data resources to be shared by individual research scholars otherwise separated from each other. Today ICPR has become ICPSR, and through the early leadership of people such as Jean Blondel, Stein Rokkan, Erwin Scheuch and Rudolf Wildenmann there is a thriving ECPR. Bergen, Cologne, Essex, and others have established data archives that complement the largest of the data collections maintained in Ann Arbor by the ICPSR. Most recently, yet another organisational innovation has appeared to promote the "Comparative Study of Electoral Systems." With the leadership of John Curtice from England, Soren Holmberg from Sweden, Hans-Dieter Klingemann from Germany, Steven Rosenstone from the United States and Jacques Thomassen from the Netherlands, plans are *underway* to make national election studies, around the world, vehicles for systematic cross-national comparative studies.

The focus is sharply on electoral behaviour, but the micro-analysis of individual behaviour in each country will be enhanced with data on the contexts provided by social and economic factors relevant to each country.

The ultimate consequences of the revolutions in methods, computer applications and human organisation cannot be anticipated in any detail. There will certainly be an extraordinary increase in the sheer volume of research. Technical standards will almost certainly go up on all fronts—data collection, data analysis and theoretical explanations of political behaviour in varied settings. However, given cultural and linguistic differences across communities of scholars, it is also likely that research technology will continue to outpace and overwhelm substantive discovery.

On the other hand, concerns such as those expressed in the previous chapter are not simply methodological concerns, and they are slowly being addressed, or redressed. The work of Huckfeldt and Sprague, among others, certainly speaks directly to the need for disaggregation and reaggregation at the level of individual experience. Among the "older" works that attended to similar concerns involving a quite different topic is the Verba-Nie volume on political participation.

In general, it is as easy to underestimate the very real concerns of "Old" behavioural researchers over questions of heterogeneity among their respondents as it is to underestimate the cost of doing something about it. At the same time, it may be that there is a real problem in overestimating the extent or the consequence of experientially based heterogeneity. At least in the domain of trying to explain an elector's vote choices, the search for evidence that voters coming from different circumstances use different paradigms in their decision-making has not been rewarding. Noting that virtually every summary measure of a relationship represents some "average" among voters, including many for whom the summary is just not appropriate, is well and good— but what to do? The "Old" did not do well in this domain, but not because the problems were not recognised.

Franz Pappi's concern is another version of the Dunleavy concern. The particular application to the multi-party election has not drawn enough attention in the United States largely because it is so seldom that American voters have a real opportunity for strategic voting in Presidential elections. It is possible that a repetition of 1992 would change all of that. In particular, it brings the consideration of coalition formation into the analytic calculus.

On this score I can only say, tell us more. Most American analysts do not cope well when the voter has more than two alternatives. A third candidate is either ignored, as were Wallace in 1968 and Anderson in 1980, or given separate treatment, as with Perot in 1992. The notion that some voters may have a calculus based on strategic voting is often enunciated but seldom examined. At the same time, we would note the possibility of utilising candidate "thermometer" data as an alternative to many examples of modeling rational choice theories.

The problem can at least be reduced if analyses seek to adopt the voter's perspective and are, therefore, limited to the apparent contest, voter-by-voter, between the two most favored candidates. In 1992, analyses eliminating less preferred candidates provided persuasive explanations of the Perot vote without invoking concepts of strategic voting (Miller and Shanks 1996).

In as much as each line of inquiry into mass electoral behaviour develops its own empirical generalisations united by their own logic, and progresses by the constant interplay of theory and evidence, it would take the unseen guiding hand of an Abigail Smith to produce *a* new empirical model of *the* democratic citizen. It seems to me that we are not in the process of developing a new model of *the* democratic citizen so much as we are learning about the conditions and circumstances under which varied and different categories of citizens respond politically in understandable and understandably different ways. Although much political philosophy and much elite political behaviour rests on one or another conception of the average or typical or modal member of the rank and file citizenry, much of the research on large populations, such as national electorates, documents the heterogeneity of responses to common stimuli. More generally, it seems to me that the challenge of democratic theory has, indeed, supplied "much of the agenda for political behaviour research during the past 50 years," but only in the broadest sense. It is true that the felt need to understand better the voting behaviour of an entire electorate is drawn from the conviction that elections are vital institutions in democratic politics. Much work on specific topics is on the agenda by virtue of institutional definitions of a problem.

It is also true that *after the fact* there is often speculation about the meaning which a newly verified generalisation has for this or that aspect of normative philosophy. However, it is also true that verification of empirical generalisations is seldom sought because of their potential implication for theories of democratic governance. Generalisations are usually re-examined because verification, or rejection, has implications for our theories about the causes of a given behaviour. What we have learned about mass electoral behaviour certainly has meaning for theories of democratic politics. But as yet we are often uncertain as to what the various meanings ultimately will be. It may be that greater self-conscious attention to the assumptions that underlie democratic theory *would* channel programs of research to meet various challenges posed by the theory. Thus far the meandering course of research into mass electoral behaviour has more often followed the decisions of scholars intent on better "understanding" some obvious feature of political topography than testing a normative construction.

REFERENCES

Almond, G., and Verba, S. 1963. *The Civic Culture.* Princeton, N.J.: Princeton University Press.

Campbell, A.; Converse, P.E.; Miller, W.E.; and Stokes, D.E. 1960. *The American Voter.* New York: Wiley.

Dahi, R.A. 1961. *Who Governs?* New Haven, Conn.: Yale University Press.

Eldersveld, S.J. 1964. *Political Parties.* Skokie, III.: Rand McNa'ley.

Eulau, H., and Prewitt, K. 1973. *Labyrinths of Democracy.* Indianapolis, Ind.: Bobbs- Merrill.

Finifter, A.W., 1974. The friendship group as a protective environment for political deviants. *American Political Science Review,* 8:607-25.

Hayes, S.P., Jr. 1932. Voter's attitudes towards men and issues. *Journal of Social Psychology,* 2: 164-82.

Prothro, J., and Matthews, R. 1966. *Negroes and the* New *Southern Politics.* Chapel Hill: University of North Carolina.

Rokkan, S., and Lipset, S.M., eds. 1967. *Party Systems and Voter Alignments.* New York: Free Press.

Tingsten, H. 1937. *Political Behaviour: Studies in Elections Statistics.* Stockholm: Knopf. London: P.S. King.

Verba, , S., and Nie, N.H. 1972. *Participation in America.* New York: Harper and Row.

8

International Relations

> "Security is the priceless product of freedom. Only the strong can be secure, and only in freedom can men produce those material resources which can secure them from want at home and against aggression abroad."
>
> —*B.E. Hutchinson*

International relations (IR) an important branch of study in the political science. Around this revolve the world order of the day in all respects.

Here in the present chapter we shall address all salient theories of international relations and foreign affairs.

There are two main approaches to the task of reviewing a discipline: by surveying its findings or by examining its foundations. Neither will be attempted here. The former approach is open only to those who are well-read across the entire discipline, which few can claim to be in the case of the multifarious discipline of international relations (IR).

Four contentious issues will be .reviewed: (1) the role of the state in present world politics; (2) the reason for doing research about matters such as this; (3) the significance of purpose and meaning in IR; and (4) whether theories of

IR are to be seen as tentative conjectures or as instruments of power.

These are issues of concern to many of us IR scholars but which we debate in a confusing way. One reason for the confusion, is the prevailing conception of the field of IR as an arena in which a small number of "schools" or "approaches" fight out their differences. If all the problems of a discipline are subsumed under an all-encompassing opposition between "realism" and one or two other "schools" or "approaches," they easily become obscured—as if by political parties during an election campaign.

In what follows we shall distinguish between differences over substance, —over values and over methods. Students of IR, like other social scientists, may differ: (1) over the substantive features of the subject matter they are investigating; (2) over the values that ought to be promoted by research; and (3) over the research methods that ought to be used.

To make these distinctions is not to suggest that substance, value and method are unrelated to each other; there is no nostalgia here for the illusions of value-free research and theory-free substance. The reason for making these distinctions is pragmatic rather than epistemological: the appropriate way of managing conflict between academics depends on the nature of their differences. Thus if the difference is over substance (if it concerns, say, the validity of deterrence theory, or the relative merits of interdependence and institutions for peace-building) further analysis is the obvious way of proceeding.

If on the other hand the difference is over value (if it concerns, say, whether deterrence is a Justifiable way of avoiding war, or whether Social Justice rather than the avoidance of war should be our focus) peaceful coexistence would seem to be the appropriate academic response; political disagreement between scholars cannot be resolved by academic analysis and should not be resolved by political dictate. Differences over method (whether for example deterrence theory is a hypothesis to be tested or an ideology to be deconstructed, or whether it is possible or impossible to gain future-oriented knowledge about peace-building) are the difficult ones, since an academic community needs to be both open-minded and principled on this score. A pre-condition for meaningful debate about matters such as these, at any rate, is that we be clear whether we are debating substance, value or method. This has not always been the case in the discipline of IR. In the growing literature about IR as an academic discipline, there is agreement that there has been a shift from "grand" to "middle-range" theory in the last quarter-century, with Waltz's *Theory of International Politics as* a lonely exception. The conventional wisdom of the discipline is that the pursuit of "grand" theory has proven a "chimera" (Hoffmann 1977: 52) and that the generalising aspirations of the 1960s "now seem untenable and even pretentious" (Olson and Onuf 1985: 13).

Another trend, it is often suggested, is the emergence of international political economy as a subfield on a par with the study of international peace and security and the conditions for international order.

It is pertinent to note that the most remarkable feature of the discipline's self-image, however, has been mentioned already: the image of a field characterised by fundamental cleavages giving rise to recurrent "debates" of central importance. The first debate, according to the standard view, was between the original "idealism" of the discipline and the challenge of "realism." What participants pretentiously called the "second grand debate" was conducted between advocates of a "scientific" approach and of a "traditional" approach.

Then, we are told, a "third debate" ensued. One party to it was "neo-realism": realism, it turned out, "was not dead; it had merely gone underground" (Banks 1984: 13). It is less clear who its adversary was: "globalists" (Maghroori and Ramberg 1982); "pluralists" and "structuralists" (Banks 1984: 15; Hollis and Smith 1990: 38-40); "globalists" and "neo-marxists" (Holsti 1985), "post-positivism" (Lapid 1989); the "transactional paradigm" and the "globalist paradigm" (Knutsen 1992: 235-6); "world society approaches" and "structural approaches" (Olson and Groom 1991); "interdependence" and "globalism" (Waever 1992: 19-21).

Remarkably, *Theory of International Politics* was a main object of the "third debate." Waltz's work is seen in the literature as a realist counter-attack against "bureaucratic politics," "interdependence" and other subational and transnational concerns (Waever 1992: 20; Brown 1993: 5). The counter-counter-attack has been intense. There is by now a large literature in which *Theory of International Politics is* criticised from all conceivable points of view. The social-scientific equivalent of political correctness has become to dissociate oneself from *Theory of International Politics.*

Criticisms range from substance to method to value. Neo-realism has been criticised for being wrong in its account of what it sets out to account for, for being based on untenable epistemology, for being politically conservative. It is intimated that these things naturally go together. Peculiarly, there seems to be agreement that "realist orthodoxy"—with its emphasis on the international system, nation-states and problems of peace and security—has maintained its hold on the discipline in spite of the massive criticisms leveled against it for years.

The debate over realist theory has helped to specify theoretical issues and propositions of great importance. It is joined, in this spirit, by David Sanders in his contribution to this volume. It has been less helpful in defining the field as one of opposing overarching "schools" which between them exhaust our menu for choice. The conventional image of IR has, in effect, become one of an oligopolistic competition between U.S.-led conglomerates offering packages which have to be accepted or rejected *in toto,* rather than one of a marketplace in which large numbers of independent producers from all corners of the world offer a diversity of products.

There is controversy, furthermore, about what each of the packages contains. The consumer's task has been made even more difficult by the tendency to advertise the packages with flashy concepts. The rest of this chapter, therefore, is written in the spirit of a consumer's guide. The object is to make it easier to see what the disagreements in the discipline are and are not about. It goes without saying that major issues such, as those raised here can be surveyed only in broad outline within the compass of this chapter.

Nation-State

One issue concerns the nation-state. No concept is more important for the discipline of international relations. The state, in the sense of nation-state, is a denning feature of "international." If the state did not exist, neither would IR. "Without the concept [of state] to fall back on, scholars would have to abandon the claim that there is something unique about the 'international' or 'interstate' realm" (Ferguson and Mansbach 1989: 2).

And yet mainstream IR research is commonly criticised for being "state-centric." It could be argued that the concept of nation-state is overly ambiguous, controversial, or normative (Ferguson and Mansbach 1989: 41-80)—too much so to define an academic discipline.

This, however, is rarely what critics of the discipline's "state-centrism" have in mind; they rarely question the meaningfulness of the notion of "international" relations. What they criticise is, rather, a particular assumption which they believe is dominant in the discipline—namely, that "nation-states or their decision makers are the most important actors for understanding international relations" (Vasquez 1983:18). One's view of the validity of this assumption has been one of the litmus tests in sorting scholars into contending camps.

State as Object of Support

When the significance of "non-state actors" such as international organisations and transnational popular movements is emphasised, this sometimes seems to mean that phenomena such as these *ought to* be considered legitimate international actors, alongside states and governments—that is, scene nun-state actors *ought* to be important.

"State-centrism," in this sense, is a defense of the nation-state against internationalist challenges. At the same time, when the significance of non-state actors like multinational corpora-lions (MNCs) is stressed, the point is sometimes apparently to emphasise that the activities of MNCs are cause for as much concern as are those of states and governments—that we should devote attention not only to the "direct" violence of states, but also to the "structural" violence exercised by multinationals.

And when the concept of national interest is rejected, this sometimes is on the ground that the interests with which we *ought* to identify are those of individuals or social classes or transnational groupings or maybe even systems of ideas, rather than those of states.

As such the controversy over "state-centrism" is in part one over political legitimacy and rightful concern. This matter is one of political values rather than of social-scientific analysis. Two of the foremost critics of the slate concept in IR theory actually urge us to regard this concept as a frankly normative one (Ferguson and Mansbach 1989: 87).

Evidently they are prepared to embrace the conclusion that the very definition of "international relations" as a field of study—and its inclusion in a handbook of political science—are political acts.

State as Object of Study

On a second interpretation, the issue is about what to seek to explain and understand. In this sense if no other, mainstream IR research is unquestionably "state-centric." To cite a programmatic statement reprinted in a widely-used text from a quarter-century ago, "the substantive core of international relations is the interaction of governments of sovereign states" (Platig 1969:16).

So it remains. If the discipline has an established research program, this is it. This emphasis may be criticised on the grounds that the actions and interactions of nation-states and governments are unimportant, that the "real groups or entities in politics" are classes or transnational coalitions (Vasquez 1983:214), and therefore that it is a waste of time to examine why states and governments act and interact the way they do.

Or, less radically, states and governments are increasingly constrained by interdependence and institutions, war is becoming increasingly dysfunctional, national security concerns are getting obsolete—in short, the "pillars of the Westphahlian temple" are "decaying" (Maghroori and Ramberg 1982: 16-17; Zacher 1992).

The issue of "state-centrism," thus interpreted, is whether developments such as these reduce our ability to explain and understand whatever it is that concerns us (peace and security, political economy) by focusing on state or government actions and interactions. This issue cannot but be empirical.

- First is the examination of the extent to which international outcomes can be explained and understood without taking nation-states and governments into account.
- Second is the enquiry into the way in which the influence, independence and identity of nation-states have in fact been affected by the growth in international interdependence and institution-building. Integration in Western Europe, it has been paradoxically argued, has been a condition for the strengthening of state power rather than a cause of its demise (Milward 1992).
- Third is the exploration of the extent to which the independence, influence and identity of one's own state have, in fact, ceased to be regarded as top-priority issues in politics.

Of those three lines of research, the third is especially important because of the crucial role played by the urge for national independence in mainstream theory. Authors do not always explain why they regard the state system as a constant.

Morgenthau (1985: 535), however, is an exception. World government is impossible, he argues, because of people's attitudes:

> [T]he overwhelming majority would put what they regard as the welfare of their own nation above everything else, the interests of a world state included.... [T]he peoples of the world are not prepared to . . . force the nation from its throne and put the political organisation of humanity on it. They are willing and able to sacrifice and die so that national governments may be kept standing.

As per this line of thought, "state-centrism" in research simply reflects the fact that national independence is regarded by *peoples* (not just by their governments) as a fundamental human need or value—an idea shaped and reinforced by political developments over centuries and proclaimed as a right in solemn, twentieth-century international declarations. Whether attitudes actually are now turning in new directions is, perhaps, the most basic issue raised by debates over "state-centrism."

State as Explanatory Factor

On a third interpretation, the accusation of "state-centrism" means that mainstream research errs in its assumption that the actions and interactions of states and governments can be fully explained at the state and inter-state levels. This criticism, importantly different from the last, is a distinctly peculiar one. Whereas the discipline of IR remains unquestionably state-centric in its choice of *explananda,* that is not true so far as its explanantes are concerned. Even the 1960s text cited earlier lists a large number of intra-state and non-state factors with which students of IR need to be concerned. True, Waltz's *Theory of International Politics is* limited to the level of the inter-state system. But this is in explicit opposition to trends in the discipline. It is strange that this unusual work has come to epitomise mainstream research. There, almost every conceivable level of analysis has been embraced. Standard collections in comparative foreign policy—such as East, Salmore and Hermann (1978) and Hermann, Kegley and Rosenau (1987)—are virtual inventories of the many-folded search in which the discipline has been engaged.

If anything, the variety exceeds that in other parts of political science, thanks to the inclusion of individual-level phenomena such as perception alongside situational variables such as crisis (both reflecting common notions of what distinguishes international from domestic politics). What can be said about this eclecticism is that we know little about the relative significance of factors at different levels.

To conclude, the issue of "state-centrism" is, thus, in part political and in part a non-issue. There remains the challenge of investigating how the state and attitudes toward the state are affected by the new international relations that are emerging. Scholars have long pointed out that politics is becoming transnational and that nation-states are becoming penetrated, but there is more to be done.

Post-Cold War Europe, with its paradoxical combination of revived nationalism and advancing internationalism, has much to offer empirically minded scholars on this score. The European Union in particular is emerging as a major object of study for IR scholars with an interest in the foundations of their field.

Differences about the purpose of IR research, implicit in the "debates," could usefully be made explicit. The proper focus and method of research depends on the reason for conducting it.

An orientation useful for one purpose may be unsuitable for another. Three purposes of IR research are outlined in the present section, not to typologise authors but to focus attention on the way in which orientation is contingent on purpose. The problem that the end of the Cold War poses for the discipline will be used as illustration. Few IR scholars anticipated the changes that took place in world politics in the second half of the 1980s.

It is difficult to quarrel with Gaddis's (1992: 53) conclusion that "none of the three general approaches to theory that have evolved since 1945"—the behavioural, the structural and the evolutionary, in Gaddis's view—"came anywhere close to anticipating how the Cold War would end."

Indeed, IR scholarship from the mid-1950s to the mid-1980s may be characterised as the accumulation of explanations of the Cold War's persistence. Propositions ranged from international anarchy with its attending security dilemmas, to the built-in propensity of arms races to escalate, to the machinations of military-industrial interests, to the propensity of men and women to reject discrepant information.

The sum was a powerful theory of international non-change. There was little basis in this rich literature to expect the East-West confrontation to end—and to do so peacefully and in a short time. Hence the "end-of-the-Cold-War problem."

A distinction is first made between positive and negative research. In the terminology adopted here, the purpose in the former case is to add positively to existing knowledge; and in the latter case, it is to examine the limitations of what others take to be knowledge. Positive research is further subdivided into research motivated by extra- and intra-academic concerns, respectively. The purpose in the former case is to produce social effects; the purpose in the latter case is to improve our comprehension of ourselves and our existence.

A similar distinction has not been made with regard to negative research for reasons that will be explained below. Terminology is a problem here, since obvious labels may have unintended overtones. What we will call type-I research is similar to what some might call "problem-solving" or maybe "positivism." Type III includes, among other things, what is known as "post-positivism" and "critical theory." It has seemed best to avoid labels such as these. The three types of purpose are not mutually exclusive in the sense that a scholar must choose between them. On the contrary, it, has been commonly taken for granted that intra-academic comprehension and extra-academic applicability go hand in hand, and that negative criticism is a condition for positive comprehension. we hope to show, however, that the tension between them is increasingly obvious in the field of IR and hence that research orientations are not equally suitable regardless of purpose.

A Type-I Research

Type-I objectives would seem to have dominated the scholarly study of international relations. Those preferring to call themselves "peace researchers" have been particularly explicit (or pretentious) on this score. Johan Galtung, for one, has compared peace research with medical science and has argued that the object is to do away with the quack-doctoring of international relations (Galtung 1964: 4; 1967: 13-20). David Singer has maintained that continued acquiescence with pre-scientific analysis qualifies as "the ultimate in war crimes" (Singer 1986:59).

Such Enlightenment zeal has been common in IR, whether the object of study has been decision making, deterrence, crisis management, peace-making or international order. Alexander George, an exceptionally respected political scientist, follows Galtung in drawing a parallel between IR research and the medical profession (George 1993:17-18). Type-I objectives have not been associated with a particular methodology. So-called "Quantitative International Politics" (QIP) was launched under its banner a generation ago, and statistical data analysis as well as mathematical modeling have become standard procedure in type-1 research about peace and war (e.g. Russett 1972; Hoole and Zinnes 1976).

At the same time, when QIP was criticised for invalid abstraction, this came not least from scholars with extra-scientific concerns, and that in part was what the "second debate" was about. Type-1 research can thus take "humanistic" as well as "scientific" forms. What is inherent in a type-I orientation is something else: the need to be concerned with the future—to anticipate future developments to which we may have to adapt, to assess the outcomes of courses of action that we may choose to pursue, or at least to contribute to the intelligent consideration of such matters. Few seem to have believed in the feasibility of strict prediction. But future-oriented knowledge in a looser sense has long been sought by IR scholars using a variety of methods. The end of the Cold War is problematic from this perspective. It will not do to argue that there has been no ambition to predict particular events.

We must be able to anticipate particular events (at least major events like the end of the Cold War) with reasonable certainty in order for our knowledge to be policy relevant. Nor will it do to demonstrate that existing theory did in fact imply that the Cold War would come to some sort of end at some future point in time. For policy-makers and citizens looking ahead in 1983 or 1984, at the peak of what was termed the "new" Cold War, crucial issues were not just whether but when and how the Cold War would come to an end. Sooner-or-later theory is not good enough for type-I purposes. There is no getting away from the fact that the difficulty of anticipating the end of the Cold War on the basis of IR theory is cause for concern in a type-I perspective. Different conclusions may be drawn from this insight.

(a) One is that, in spite of this spectacular failure, it remains sensible to take the findings of IR scholars into account in policy-making, but we should refrain from claims to the effect that we can provide strong, research-based advice on international affairs. What needs to be modified is our way of participating in public debate—our extra-academic rhetoric, so to speak (see George (1993) for the elaboration of a similar view).

(b) A second possibility is to make distinctions between more and less predictable international relations. History, according to this thought, is a better guide to the future in some respects than in others. Scholars are beginning to distinguish between the North and the South on this score. Matters are hanging, they argue, but only among the developed countries;

traditional patterns are likely to continue, but only in the developing world (Holsti 1991; Jervis 1992).

(c) A third possibility is to conclude that a type-I orientation remains appropriate only as a long-term goal. Presently existing IR theory is too weak to be of more than marginal use for policy-making. Matters will become different in the long term, but type-II is a more appropriate orientation for the time being.

(d) There is a fourth possibility: to conclude that type-I research has proven impossible in principle because of the inherent unpredictability of international relations. The end of the Cold War may be taken as confirmation of the fact that the hope of solving international problems with the help of IR research is illusory.

This is an important debate for today's IR scholars, but only insofar as they assume that the purpose of their efforts is of type I. The matter is different on other assumptions, as will now be argued.

Type-II Research

What is problematic from the type-I point of view is an exciting challenge from a type-II perspective. Some of the theory from which the end of the Cold War could not have been predicted had a respectable conceptual and empirical basis. Obviously, the better a theory, the more exciting discrepant evidence. The issue raised in this perspective is not whether we should stop doing what we have been doing but how to improve our theory in the light of new experience. One example must suffice. It has been common for scholars pondering the end of the Cold War to emphasise the need to take political beliefs and values as well as domestic-political structures and processes into consideration, in addition to (or in place of) the factors traditionally emphasised in IR theory.

Even though the IR tradition is eclectic on this score, theory has been dominated by structures of various kinds, ranging from the international system to states to bureaucracies to cognitions. Neither the substantive content of foreign policy ideas nor the domestic politics by which competing ideas lead on to foreign policy actions have attracted commensurate attention—an American trait, according to Hoffmann (1977: 58).

The end-of-the-Cold-War experience emphasises the need to bring politics back in, so to speak—politics in the dual sense of political ideas and domestic political process. This will complicate theorising. There is a dilemma between parsimony and comprehensiveness (Allan 1992).

The trade-off is a long-standing bone of contention in type-II research. But there should be room for both simplifiers and complexifiers among those seeking comprehension for its own sake. The matter is more intriguing so far as type-I research is concerned. Scholars should recognise, it has been argued, that "too strict a pursuit of the scientific criterion of parsimony in their efforts to theorise is inappropriate for developing useful policy-relevant theory and knowledge" (George 1993: 140).

It is difficult, however, to see how policy could be made and citizens' opinions formed except on the basis of models singling out the main features of a situation or a problem.

Whereas it may be possible to take more-or-less everything into account in an academic effort to explain the past, this may not be a realistic objective for policy-makers and citizens who are pondering the future. The obvious solution to the end-of-the-Cold-War problem in type-II research—to include political ideas and domestic political processes in models of international politics—thus maybe problematic within a type-I orientation. Politics in the sense of ideas and dynamic processes would seem to be inherently less predictable than structures; if these are the kind of variables that must be taken into account in a valid theory of international relations, this is a serious problem in a type-I perspective.

Conversely, it may be a source of inspiration in a type-II perspective, since most of us find it more rewarding to plunge into the substance of the play and the performance of the actors than into the structure of the theatre.

Type-III Research

Emancipation from the constraints implied in what is taken by others to be knowledge is the essence of type-Ill research. Its focus is on conceptions of necessities and impossibilities. To demonstrate that the necessary may be avoided and that the impossible may be actualised is what type-III research aims to do. The distinction between the extra- and the intra-academic is difficult to maintain in the case of negative research.

Logically, a difference can be made between extra-academic emancipation and intra-academic skepticism similar to the one between affirmative and skeptical postmodernism (Rosenau 1992). It is controversial, however, whether radically negative research can be a means to extra-academic ends; it has been argued that "by refusing any task more positive than that of undermining existing theory, this approach] effectively leaves the world as it is".

Since it does not matter for the purposes of this chapter

whether the reason for conducting negative research is extra- or intra-academic, it has seemed unnecessary to join the debate about the political implications of postmodernism by attempting to distinguish between the two. What distinguishes both from positive research is that effective criticism suffices for goal-attainment and that is the important point in the present context. Academic wrecking operations may be limited to specific propositions, . based on traditional epistemology and intended to show that what is widely accepted is ill-supported in fact, thus clearing the way for research with a positive purpose. This is research on the border between types I or II and type III. It is something else that justifies the retention of type III as a separate category, to be distinguished from types I and II. What is counted as knowledge in research of types I and II, some IR scholars argue, are "arbitrary cultural constructs."

This is the thesis of scholars who "resist knowing in [the modernist] sense." Their emphasis is on "ambiguity, uncertainty and the ceaseless questioning of identity"; their objective is "to interrogate limits, to explore how they are imposed, to demonstrate their arbitrariness and to think *other-wise*" (Ashley and Walker 1990: 262-4). Their task is to "destabilise the assumptions [IR theorists] . . . take for granted and then to show how other ways of thinking might be opened up" (Walker 1992: 23).

This, of course, is the application to IR of widespread views about the arbitrariness and oppressiveness of knowledge claims. Now, what has made the end of the Cold War an issue among students of IR is the tension between theory and evidence. If one rejects the very idea that the validity of theory is contingent on its agreement with data, as some IR scholars do explicitly and others implicitly (for example. Walker 1992: 19), the appropriate attitude toward the datum of the end of the Cold War is one of indifference. What is from other points of view a piece of discrepant evidence, and hence a reason either for concern or for excitement, is irrelevant if "truth is something we can—and must—do without in our thinking" (Brown 1992:204). If data-based theory is an illusion, the occurrence of a datum is a non-event.

Three professional roles of IR scholars have now been outlined: the constructive citizen; the detached analyst; and the systematic skeptic. One's assessment of the discipline hinges on one's role-conception. The "debates" have proceeded as if all students of IR had the same purpose, or as if their purposes were compatible. Neither presumption is valid. Some type-III research assumes that a type-I or II orientation is based on illusions. Similarly, the search for future-oriented knowledge inherent in type-I research may lead to results that are superficial from the point of view of type-II analysis, while the more profound comprehension sought in a type-II perspective may do little to solve the problems central to type-I research. Paradoxically, the most controversial of the roles is the one which IR scholars have traditionally adopted, the role of expert citizen.

It is from this point of view that the performance of the discipline—as exemplified by the end-of-the-Cold-War problem—is a disappointment. The choice, however, is not "between detailed, high-confidence prescriptions for action and nothing at all," as Alexander George puts it (1993: 17). One of the larger challenges that lie ahead is precisely to go beyond George's pioneering efforts in considering the methodological requirements of type-I research and to consider how they differ from those of research of type II. At any rate, rational debate within the discipline would benefit if rolè-conceptions were made explicit. Today's encounters between type-I professors and type-III graduate students would be more rewarding, or at least less confusing, if it were clear that the meaningfulness of "positivist" research and the relevance of Foucault depend on what we set out to perform.

Mentalism—the view that phenomena are explicable only in terms of creative and interpretative minds—was challenging structuralism in the study of international relations by the first half of the 1990s. Purpose and meaning were emphasised, just as in other parts of political science (see Giandomenico Majone chap. 26 below). The "subjective" was stressed rather than the "objective."

The implications of this challenge—the current variation on a perennial theme—will be considered in the present section with regard to the analysis of foreign policy and of international institutions.

Foreign Policy

There is nothing new in an interest in the subjective side of international relations. It is a myth that mainstream IR theory has conceived of states as soulless creatures responding "automatically" or "mechanically" to external stimuli. Even in a work like *Theory of International Politics,* Waltz explains why structure determines behaviour in terms of mental processes (rational calculation and socialisation). What is hypothesised in such reasoning is not that men and women are machines but rather (a) that they act rationally to further their objectives, on the basis of their definition of the situation, and *(V)* that their definition of the situation accords with reality, as assessed by outside observers, to an extent sufficient to give structural theory some degree of explanatory power.

This is the logic of systemic theory such as Waltz's as well as of many other works in which structures, whether international or domestic, are presumed to determine state action and inter-state interaction. It is also the logic of deterrence theory, arms race theory from Richardson (1960) on, and other theories of escalatory and de-escalatory processes. Mental phenomena, furthermore, have loomed large in studies of foreign policy decision-making and bargaining. In particular, much has been published about perceptions and cognitive processes.

The psychological approach to international relations is well-established. Why, then, the feeling that the subjective side has been improperly left out? One reason is dissatisfaction with the explanatory power of non-ideational theory. It is said that structural features such as Waltz's explain little unless actors' perceptions of meaning are taken into account (Wendt 1992) and that much in foreign policy cannot be explained except by reference to ideas (Goldstein and Keohane 1993).

The end of the Cold War has been taken as evidence that ideas must be taken into account in IR analysis, as we have seen. Notably, the shift in emphasis from structure to ideas in fact may reflect a wish to substitute "understanding" for "explanation" in the study of IR. "Explanation" is generally presumed to deal with causes, and causes are generally presumed to be "external" to the actor whose behaviour is to be explained. "Understanding," in contrast, is taken to deal with meaning, and meaning can only be understood from "within."

According to Hollis and Smith, there are "two plausible stories to tell, one from the outside about the human part of the natural world and the other from inside a separate social realm. One seeks to explain, the other to understand... [and] combining the two stories is not as easy as it at first seems" (Hollis and Smith 1990:6-7). Many, however, recommend a combination. Views vary as to whether foreign policy actions are in fact properly "understood" if exogenous variables remain unaccounted for: some seem satisfied with an interpretation couched in terms of the preferences and perceptions of actors, whereas others insist upon the further step of asking why preferences and perceptions are as they are.

Views also vary as to whether every link in the chain between cause and effect must be investigated in order for an "explanation" to be convincing: no cliche is more familiar to international relationists than the assertion that the black boxes of decision-making must be opened up in order to make proper explanation possible.

Thus, one of the divisions in the discipline, often confounded with other differences, concerns what constitutes a satisfactory analysis of action and especially whether and how to mix the "external" and the "internal" in the analysis of foreign policy. By the mid-1990s the trend was to emphasise the "inside" and de-emphasise the "outside." A second reason to urge more attention be paid to purpose in the analysis of international relations may be the way in which the substance of politics has been marginalised. Mainstream analysis examines whether foreign policies are "adaptive" (Rosenau 1970) and why states "realign" (Holsti 1982), rather than the substantive contents of the adaptations and the realignments. Many of us have attempted to find out what makes governments "co-operate" or "defect," rather than to examine what governments do in fact do when they co-operate and defect. The explananda of mainstream theory, furthermore, have been structures (international, organisational, cognitive) and processes, rather than purposes.

The purposes of foreign policy, to the extent that they have been mentioned at all, have been assumed rather than investigated ('power," "security," etc.). Against this background, Holsti's 1991 work—analysing the substantive motives states have had for waging war and the prevailing attitudes toward war in various epochs—constitutes one noteworthy effort among several to bring more of substantive policy analysis into the theoretical analysis of foreign policy. More may be at stake, though. To argue that we should take into account actors' substantive purposes and their own interpretations of reality is different from denying that any external reality exists independently of the perceptions of actors.

Now, however, the discipline of IR is witnessing the appearance of mentalism in that literal sense, according to which all there is to study is how actors believe things are or say things are. According to this view, actors' environments exist only in their beliefs or in their texts. The constraints to which they are submitted are neither structural nor material, but merely perceptual or textual. Issues such as these have been discernible in recent "debates" and are becoming increasingly topical, especially in a type-II perspective.

International Relations as Institutions

It is pertinent to note that institutions may be seen as generalised purposes and meanings. International relations may be seen as institutionalised, in the sense that "much behaviour is recognised by participants as reflecting established rules, norms and conventions" (Keohane 1989: 1).

Thus an emphasis on purpose and meaning in analysing action, and a focus on institutions in analysing systems, are two sides of the same coin. In both cases, there is a stress on the subjective, on seeing things "from within." When the "new institutionalism" was launched in political science its aims were, among other things: (1) to emphasise the autonomous role of politics in society; (2) to focus on "the ways in which political life is organised around the development of meaning through symbols, rituals and ceremonies" rather than on decision-making and the allocation of resources; and (3) to see political actors as responding to obligations and duties rather than to calculated self-interest (March and Olsen 1984: 735).

Neither the first nor the second point seems to have impressed students of IR, but the third point has been all the more important. As regards the autonomy of politics at the international level, the tone was historically set by Morgenthau, who conceived of politics in terms of the concept of interest defined in terms of power."

This concept, he wrote, sets politics as an autonomous sphere of action and understanding apart from other spheres, such as economics..., ethics, aesthetics, or religion." It alone makes a theory of politics possible, "for without it we could not distinguish between political and non-political facts" (Morgenthau 1985: 5).

When institutionalism made a breakthrough in IR in the mid-1980s, however, it appealed to those critical of what was conceived of as realist orthodoxy. To join Morgenthau in emphasising the autonomy of politics would have been an anathema.

Apart from Morgenthau and maybe Waltz, students of IR appear to have been unconcerned with the distinction between the political and the non-political, as is evident from their inclination to include a variety of economic, psychological and other "non-political" variables in their research. As regards the second point, students of IR have certainly been aware of the role of "symbols, rituals and ceremonies" in inter-state relations, ranging from the formalities of diplomatic negotiation to the power demonstrations of tacit bargaining.

They appear, however, to have been prone to interpret these phenomena in instrumental terms, as methods that actors use to further their objectives (to make others accept their demands as legitimate, to signal commitments and intentions, etc.). The increasing interest in purpose and meaning does not seem to include an increased concern with the non-instrumental side of politics. The remaining point concerns obligations and duties rather than calculated self-interest as the propellant of political action. Even if it has been difficult to determine what precisely the "debates" have been about, the role of self-interest has often been suggested as the crux of the matter.

"Liberal institutionalism" (Keohane 1989) is maybe the most recent incarnation of the rejection of the notion that "interest defined in terms of power" is the essence of international politics. Institutionalism may be attractive to students of IR in a fourth way, as well. One advantage of institutions is that they can change. According to non-realists, static necessity rules in the harsh world of realism; institutionalism, in contrast, assumes that action is determined by man-made institutions, not bylaws of nature. What is more, institutions transform interests (Wendt 1992).

Institution-building has been a standard ingredient of peace proposals since the Middle Ages, and present-day institutionalism promises to show that this is a realistic rather than an idealistic notion. In part, the renewed interest in institutions has taken the form of the study of international regimes, construed as "implicit or explicit principles, norms, rules and decision-making procedures around which actors' expectations converge in a given area of international relations" (Krasner 1983:186).

Regimes differ from institutions in general by being "more specialised arrangements that pertain to well-defined activities, resources, or geographical areas" (Young 1989:13). A large literature exists about regime formation and regime change, which is one dimension of the phenomenon of "governance without government" (Rosenau and Czempiel 1992) that has interested many students of IR. The challenge of the institutional approach is well-known.

Keohane suggests that we distinguish between institution as a "general pattern or categorisation of activity" and as a "particular human-constructed arrangement, formally or informally organised" (Keohane 1988: 383). Sovereign statehood is an instance of the former, the United Nations of the latter. Compliance is more problematic in the latter case than in the former: problematic though it may be whether particular institutions can be counted or to determine action, few students of IR would deny that the institution of sovereign statehood has an impact on international politics. Indeed, the necessities presumed to obtain in realist theory about anarchic politics may be seen as institutions, in the sense of general patterns that have evolved over long periods (Wendt 1992).

Whatever the issue between realists and others, it is not whether patterns such as these are important. When it comes to the sources of compliance, we may distinguish between a "rationalistic" and a "reflective" approach. In the former, institutions are assumed to affect actors' calculation of cost (Keohane 1988: 166). The logic is identical with that of structural theory: institutions are features of actors' environments that affect what is rational and hence what will likely be.

The distinguishing feature of the reflective approach is the assumption that preferences and perceptions are not fixed but are affected by institutions. The assumption of fixed preferences and perceptions, it is argued, prevents us from understanding "how interests change as a result of changes in belief systems," thus obscuring rather than illuminating "the sources of states' policy preferences" (Keohane 1988: 390-1).

Logically, this too is analogous with some forms of structuralism: features of the environment (in this case, institutions) are 'presumed to affect actors' preferences and perceptions, and hence their conceptions of rationality, and hence their actions. Institutions and structures are indistinguishable from this point of view. Or, better, institutions are social structures in the sense of patterns that exist regardless of single actors and actions. Where do we go from here? What is an institutionalist research program like? One possibility is to set out to gain generalised knowledge about the factors determining the impact of various kinds of institutions on actors' preferences and perceptions under varying circumstances; this in effect has been suggested by Wendt (1992) and embarked upon by Young (1979).

Another possibility is to emphasise the indeterminate nature of "changes taking place in consciousness" (Keohane 1988:391) and to focus on ex post investigation of the impact of institutions on perceptions and preferences in single cases. The former should appeal to type-1 researchers, who would see that the more we know about the conditions for compliance, the more useful data about institutions are for future-oriented purposes.

The latter should be attractive from the point of view of type-II research, for whom the institutionalist perspective promises to enrich our understanding of what may be called the role of political culture in IR. A particular challenge is to explore the interaction between political cultures at the international, national and subnational levels.

If compliance is problematic mainly as regards particular institutions, general institutions are problematic as regards change. Whereas particular institutions maybe changed by agreement among those concerned, general institutions are largely contingent on the practices of individual actors, and compliance means that they tend to remain as before.

Institutionalists argue that non-institutionalists are incapable of accounting for change, but they face problems of their own in this regard. The common-sense solution is to assume that actions and rules are interdependent. Action is affected but not determined by rules; it strengthens or weakens rules, depending upon compliance. This thought, elaborated by Dessler (1989) in relation to the agent-structure debate in the form of what he calls a "transformational model," is in truth not much different from the old notion that international law is both an influence on and a function of state practices. This notion in turn may be seen as an instance of the view that action results from previous action and affects the conditions for future action—in other words, feedback and learning.

What may be new in recent scholarship of a

constructivist orientation is a focus on the role of interaction in "constructing" identities and interests (Wendt 1994), a notion that has often been left implicit in IR analysis. So far as single institutions are concerned, the issue is obviously the degree to which rules influence action and the degree to which action influences rules.

An institution may be strong in the sense of being a powerful influence on actors and in the sense of being invulnerable to discrepant action. Some institutions may be both influential and invulnerable (the institution of state sovereignty, perhaps); others may be influential but vulnerable (a newly established international regime, perhaps) or invulnerable but non-influential (the UN Charter prohibitions of the use of force, perhaps); still others may be weak on both accounts. The realist position translated into these terms is that some institutions (state sovereignty, the rules of "power politics") are so strong in terms of both influence and invulnerability that it is "realistic" to treat them as facts of international life. Radical internationalism would seem to imply that the institutions of state sovereignty and "power politics" are indeed dangerously influential but at the same time vulnerable to change by discrepant action.

Moderate internationalism implies that even if the institutions of state sovereignty and "power politics" are both influential and invulnerable, other institutions can be set up as counterweights that will grow influential and invulnerable over time (Goldmann 1994). The strength of international institutions, in the dual sense of influence and invulnerability, deserves to be a major focus of research.

What this means depends on whether one's purpose is of type I or type II. In the latter case, the task is to examine the interplay of rules and actions in sufficient detail to provide explanation and understanding. Carlsnaes, who has outlined a program for such research, says that the effort will be "painstaking" but that it will "undoubtedly give a 'truer' and more 'realistic' picture of the complex, dynamic and determinative empirical mechanisms and processes preceding and underlying a given foreign policy decision"; this, he suggests, indicates in a nutshell "both the costs and the benefits of incorporating the agency-structure issue into foreign policy analysis" (Carlsnaes 1992:266).

Viewed from a perspective of type I, the need is more simply to investigate the predictive utility of such information about institutions as can be acquired with a lesser effort: the rules of international regimes, the substantive contents of foreign policy doctrines, the conditions for institutional change by deliberate action, and such like. This, however, brings us back to the question of how to analyze action. Regardless of whether we think that satisfactory analysis makes it necessary to examine the actor's perceptions and preferences in each individual instance, or whether we rest content with postulating them, an analysis in terms of institutions will require us to operate at two levels of subjectivity: the shared subjectivity of institutions; and the individual subjectivity of actors.

What brings about action is assumed to be the actor's subjective preferences together with his subjective perception of the subjective perceptions and preferences of others—all of this being observable in a fashion that is at least quasi-objective. I suspect that this paradoxical position is widely held in the discipline of IR, a fact overshadowed by our propensity to engage in polarising "debates."

When Stanley Hoffmann edited a text called *Contemporary Theory in International Relations* three and a half decades ago, he made a distinction between "theory as a set of answers" and "theory as a set of questions." By the former he meant "a set of explanatory hypotheses which purport to reveal the rules of the game of international politics." By the latter he meant "efforts to devise a right way of studying the phenomena of world affairs" by focusing on "the most important variables, even though no attempt is made at the outset to present any laws governing the behaviour of those variables"; the claim is merely "to put into the hands of the researchers an adequate tool for their studies" (Hoffmann 1960: 29). To make some such distinction between claims that theorists make or between functions that theories perform has recently become even more important.

IR academics seem to disagree over what sort of thing a theory is. What is to some a set of conjectures a la Popper (that is, assumptions that are accepted provisionally, pending efforts at refutation) is to others a discourse oppressively compeling us to adopt a particular mode of thought. Similarly, what is to some an ideal type with which empirical observations may be compared for the purpose of identifying interesting deviations is to others a truth-claim. Only by postulating some such difference over what theory is can we comprehend the intensity of the attacks on the mainstream by "dissidents in exile" (Ashley and Walker 1990).

Notably debate about *Theory of International Politics* is indicative of such a difference. Waltz's work, on one interpretation, is a contribution to an ongoing search for an understanding of what goes on in world politics. Those taking Waltz's account of some features of international politics as their point of departure will find that it has limitations, such as the difficulty of pinpointing the explanatory power claimed for it. They will also find it easy to point to empirical evidence that is difficult to reconcile with it. If conjectures and refutations are the name of the game, however, bold conjectures such as Waltz's are what is needed. Without them, there would be little worth refuting. While some critics of *Theory of International Politics* have rested content with indicating explanatory variables that have been left out of Waltz's conception of systemic theory, others have gone further. Waltz has thus been criticised for having written a book intent on explaining persistent patterns in the present international system rather than one about something else, namely, the history of this system (Ruggie 1986; Cox 1986). Even more indicative of what is at stake is Ashley's (1986: 258) assertion that what emerges from Waltz's book is an "ideology that anticipates, legitimises and orients a totalitarian project of global proportions: the rationalisation of global politics."

Ashley (1986: 255) pointedly prefaces his criticism with d quotation from Bourdieu claiming that "the specifically symbolic power to impose the principles of the construction of reality . . . is a major dimension of political power." The vehemence of the attacks on *Theory of International Politics suggests* that it has been seen more widely as the exertion of discursive power rather than as a provisional statement to be exposed to efforts at refutation. The discussion about the use of game theory in IR analyis provides another indication of a cleavage over what theory is and is not. Critics have gone beyond posing the question of whether there is sufficient similarity between international relations and standard games such as the Prisoners' Dilemma in order for a theory of the latter to improve our understanding of the former. Game-theoretical analysis is also said to address the wrong problem, since it is concerned with the implications of given preferences and perceptions without asking how preferences and perceptions are formed (Jervis 1988: 322-9).

More fundamentally, to "model human actions as individually oriented, instrumentally rational actions" is a form of micro-economic imperialism" whose "ideological character" should be highlighted rather than obscured; the use of game theory, it has been argued, implies that conflict "should" be regarded as driven by interests and not by passion; people do not accept the model of "perspicacious, self-interested decision-makers" as representing "how they should act in all circumstances" (Hurwitz 1989:115-16). Feminist critiques of IR theory, which Ann Tickner considers in her contribution to this book (below: chap. 18), may be a third indication of disagreement over what theory is.

The claim is not merely that mainstream theory is limited in its ability to explain what it sets out to explain because of its being gendered. The claim is also that mainstream theory actively prescribes male-oriented concerns. Again the view is of theory as oppressingly normative rather than conjectural and analytic. Walker (1992: 5-6) is clear about what a normative view of theory entails. IR theories, he asserts, are interesting mainly as "expressions of the limits of the contemporary political imagination."

Attempts to "think otherwise about political possibilities are constrained by categories and assumptions that contemporary political analysis is encouraged to take for granted." IR theory may be read as "a constitutive practice whose effects can be traced in the remotest interstices of everyday life." Maybe it should not simply be assumed that, say, the use of game theory by some academics has such profound implications.

Granted, however, that established theory is normative in the sense of defining the central puzzles and legitimate concerns of a discipline and that this is not devoid of political implications, there is a dilemma here, since many if not most IR scholars take it for granted that "theory as a sei of questions" is indispensable in research. The dilemma is obvious; that is not the issue.

The issue is whether we should set out to refute theories by empirical observation and conceptual reflection or by examining whether their implications accord with our preferences—whether, to put it bluntly, our proper professional role is that of a truth-seeker or an ideology-producer. This is one of the matters that the debate in the discipline is about.

Often it is seen that students of IR disagree about what ought to be their main concern (peace and security, political economy, the situation of women, etc.). They disagree over whether to favor the integration, internationalisation and transnationalisation of states and politics or the maintenance of national independence and identity.

They differ, furthermore, as to whether their proper role is that of an activist, an analyst, or a critic—and, it seems, over the legitimate role of political persuasion in social-scientific writing. Students of IR are thus like other academics, disagreeing over matters that are political rather than academic.

These challenges, rather than divisions over value and substance, make international relations today a fragmented discipline. They also differ over matters of substance, most fundamentally about the states system as a political institution (its impact on action, its vulnerability to change) as well as over the relative significance of various factors at various levels in accounting for foreign policy, including in particular the autonomous role of ideas. Differences over substance invigorate research, but only if there is agreement on the fundamentals of method.

If there has been an appreciable consensus on these matters in the discipline, it is being challenged on three fronts: (a) what a proper analysis of action is like; *(b)* whether knowledge is an "arbitrary cultural construct" or whether there can be objective standards; and *(c)* whether theory is a constructive guide for research or an oppressive constraint on thinking.

REFERENCES

Ashley, R.K. 1986. The poverty of neo-realism. In Keohane 1986: 255-300.

Buzan, B.; Jones, C.; and Little, R. 1993. *The Logic of Anarchy.* New York: Columbia University Press.

Gaddis, J.L 1992. International relations theory and the end of the Cold War. *International Security,* 17:5-58.

Galtung, J. 1967. *Fredsforskning.* Stockholm: Prisma.

Groom, A.J.R., and light, M., eds. 1994. *Contemporary International Relations.* London: Pinter.

Lapid, Y. 1989. The third debate: on the prospects of international theory in a post-positivist era. *International Studies Quarterly,* 33: 235-61.

Nardin, T., and Mapel, D.R., eds. 1992. *Traditions of International Ethics.* Cambridge: Cambridge University Press.

Walker, R.B.J. 1992. *Inside/Outside.* Cambridge: Cambridge University Press.

Waltz, K.N. 1975. Theory of international relations. Vol. viii, pp. 1-85 in *Handbook of Political Science, ed.* F. I. Greenstein and N. W. Polsby. Reading, Mass.: Addison-Wesley.

Bibliography

Aldrich, J. H. 1993. Rational choice and turnout. *American Journal of Political Science.* 37: 246-78.

Ashley, R.K. 1986. The poverty of neo-realism. In Keohane 1986: 255-300.

Baldwin, D. 1985. *Economic Statecraft.* Princeton, N.J.: Princeton University Press.

Banks, M., ed. 1984. *Conflict in World Society.* Brighton: Wheatsheaf Books.

Beck, P. A. 1991. Voters' intermediation environments in the 1988 presidential contest. *Public Opinion Quarterly,* 55: 371-94.

Berger, B. M. 1960. *Working-Class Suburb.* Berkeley: University of California Press.

Bobo, L 1983. Whites' opposition to busing: symbolic racism or realistic group conflict. *Journal of Personality and Social Psychology,* 45:1196-210.

Brown, C. 1992. *International Relations Theory.* London: Harvester Wheatsheaf.

Brown, R. 1993. Introduction: toward a new synthesis of international relations. Pp. 1-20 in *From Cold War to Collapse,* ed. M. Bowker and R. Brown. Cambridge: Cambridge University Press.

Burt, R.S. 1987. Social contagion and innovation: cohesion versus structural equivalence. *American Journal of Sociology,* 92:1287-335.

Buzan, B.; Jones, C.; and Little, R. 1993. *The Logic of Anarchy.* New York: Columbia University Press.

Carlsnaes, W., 1992. The agency-structure problem in foreign policy analysis. *International Studies Quarterly,* 36: 245-70

Carmines, E G., and kuklinski, J. H. 1990. Incentives, opportunities, and the logic of public opinion in American political representation. Pp. 240-68 in *Information and Democratic Process,* ed- J. A. Ferejohn and I. H. Kuklinski. Urbana: University of Illinois Press.

Downs, A. 1957. *An Economic Theory of Democracy.* New York: Harper and Row.

Eulau, H. 1963. *The Behavioural Persuasion in Politics.* New York: Random House.

Ferejohn, J.A.. and kuklinski, J.H., eds. 1990. *Information and Democratic Processes.* Urbana: University of Illinois Press.

Fiorina, M.P. 1981. *Retrospective Voting in American National Elections.* New Haven, Conn.: Yale University Press.

Gaddis, J.L 1992. International relations theory and the end of the Cold War. *International Security,* 17:5-58.

George, J. 1989. International relations and the search for thinking space: another view of the third debate. *International Studies Quarterly,* 33:269-79.

Giles, M.W., and evans, A. 1985. External threat, perceived threat, and group identity. Social Science *Quarterly,* 66: 50-66.

Glaser, J. M. 1994. Back to the black belt: racial environment and white racial attitudes in the South. *Journal of Politics,* 56: 22-4 1.

Goldstein, J., and Keohane, R.O., eds. 1993. *Ideas and Foreign Policy.* Ithaca, N.Y.: Cornell University Press.

Granovetter, M. 1973. The strength of weak ties. *American Journal of Sociology',* 78: 1360-80.

Lapid, Y. 1989. The third debate: on the prospects of international theory in a post-positivist era. *International Studies Quarterly,* 33: 235-61.

Maghroori, R., and ramberg, B., eds. 1982. *Globalism Versus Realism.* Boulder, Colo.: Westview Press.

Otson. M. 1965. *The Logic of Collective Action.* Cambridge, Mass.: Harvard University Press.

Platig, R. 1969. International Relations as a Field of Inquiry. Pp. 6-19 in *International Politics and Foreign Policy, ed.* J.N. Rosenau. 2nd edn. New York: Free Press.

Popkin S. L. 1991. *The Reasoning Voter: Communication and Persuasion in Presidential Campaigns.* Chicago: University of Chicago Press.

Przeworksi, A. 1974. Contextual models of political behaviour. *Political Methodology,* 1: 27-61.

Ruggie, J.G. 1986. Continuity and transformation in the world polity: toward a realist synthesis. In Keohane 1986:131-57.

Singer, J.D. 1986. Research, policy, and the correlates of war. Pp. 44-59 in *Studies of War and Peace, ed.* O. Osterud. Oslo: Norwegian University Press.

Vasquez, J. A. 1983. *The Power of Power Politics.* London: Frances Pinter.

Wendt, A. 1992. Anarchy is what states make of it: the social constructicn of power politics. *International Organisation,* 46:391-425.

Index

●●●